Presenting Keynote:

The Insider's Guide to Creating Great Presentations

Presenting Keynote:™
The Insider's Guide to Creating Great Presentations

ERIK HOLSINGER

SAN FRANCISCO | LONDON

SYBEX®

Associate Publisher: DAN BRODNITZ
Acquisitions Editor: BONNIE BILLS
Developmental Editor: PETE GAUGHAN
Technical Editor: JOHN RIZZO
Production Editors: KELLY WINQUIST AND LESLIE LIGHT
Copyeditor: KIM WIMPSETT
Proofreaders: EMILY HSUAN, ERIK LACK, LAURIE O'CONNELL, NANCY RIDDIOUGH, MONIQUE VAN DEN BERG
Compositor: HAPPENSTANCE TYPE-O-RAMA
Technical Illustrator: CARYL GORSKA
Icon Illustrator: TINA HEALEY ILLUSTRATIONS
CD Coordinator: DAN MUMMERT
CD Technician: KEVIN LY
Indexer: TED LAUX
Interior Designer: CARYL GORSKA
Cover Designer and Illustrator: SARA STREIFEL, INGALLS + ASSOCIATES

Dear Reader,

Thank you for choosing *Presenting Keynote*. This book is part of a new wave of Sybex Mac and graphics books, all written by outstanding authors—artists and professional teachers who really know their stuff, and have a clear vision of the audience they're writing for.

At Sybex, we're committed to producing a full-line of quality books on a variety of Mac-related topics. With each title, we're working hard to set a new standard for the industry. From the paper we print on, to the designers we work with, to the visual examples our authors provide, our goal is to bring you the best books available.

I hope you see all that reflected in these pages. I'd be very interested in hearing your feedback on how we're doing. To let us know what you think about this, or any other Sybex book, please visit us at www.sybex.com. Once there, go to the product page, click Submit a Review, and fill out the questionnaire. Your input is greatly appreciated.

Best regards,

Dan Brodnitz
Associate Publisher
Sybex Inc.

Dedication

To Anne O'Rourke, the keeper of my heart and my home.

About the Author

Erik Holsinger is a journalist, writer, editor, and producer with extensive media production experience. He has written more than 100 articles for publications such as *CNET, MacWEEK, PC World, AV Video, Film and Video,* and *Digital Magic* and has been an editor at *Publish, New Media,* and *MacWEEK.* He is the author of three previous books: *The MacWEEK Guide to Desktop Video, How Music and Computers Work,* and *How Multimedia Works.* He is also one of the founders of DigitalMediaNet.com, a Contributing Editor with *AV/Video Multimedia Producer* magazine, and a Contributing Writer with *Film and Video* magazine.

Holsinger also has a diverse production background. For over 14 years he has created a variety of video and interactive productions for numerous clients, including Adobe Systems, Kaplan Learning, and Disney. He has produced everything from consumer CD-ROM titles to streaming media websites to interactive theme park rides. Finally, as a musician and a composer, his musical scores have appeared nationally on PBS and in award-winning independent films.

Currently Holsinger is the CEO/Executive Producer at Media Alchemy, a Seattle-based entertainment company specializing in original video, print, and interactive productions.

Acknowledgments

No matter what the medium—film, television, or theater—no creative work happens in a vacuum. This is also true when writing; many skilled folks toil behind the scenes to take an author's concept and turn it into a finished book. ■ My thanks to Dan Brodnitz at Sybex, who helped get the project green-lighted with the powers that be. Dan and I worked on my first book together, so it's great to collaborate on another project. ■ Bonnie Bills, Sybex's acquisition editor, was also a champion of my book from the start and a great help in focusing the book's direction. ■ During the actual production of the book, a crack team at Sybex worked feverishly to get it to print. Maureen Forys and Kate Kaminiski, the book's compositors, produced and arranged the page layout and many of the graphics. Kelly Winquist and Leslie Light, the production editors, made sure that files made it through the system on a timely basis. ■ My thanks and apologies to Kim Wimpsett, who had to endure my late-night Grammar of the Damned yet always managed to make me sound intelligible. ■ I was lucky to get John Rizzo on board as the technical editor. I've known John for many years, and he's one of the best Macintosh technical experts on the planet. An author himself, he also plays a mean bass guitar. ■ Last, but never least on the editorial side, my thanks and praise go to Pete Gaughan, my development editor and the true hero of this book. I know without a doubt that Pete's incredible patience, good humor, and excellent editorial eye were the only things that kept this book on track. ■ Many thanks to the professionals who added their expertise and art throughout this book: Marie C. Morzenti, C. David Pinà, Mikkel Aaland, Gene Zelazny, Jeff Beckstrom, John Rizzo, Steven Katz, Jesse Busby, Paul G. Hewlitt, and Donna James (of the Seattle Mayor's Office of Film). ■ Like all Mac applications, Keynote is not an island when it comes to interacting with other hardware and software. I was also able to test many of Keynotes capabilities thanks to Epson, Apple, Microsoft, and Keyspan, all of whom loaned me software and hardware during the making of this book. ■ Finally, thanks to my family and friends who didn't see a lot of me for several months. Especially to my good friends David Lawrence, Robert Luhn, Llysa Holland, Andrew Litzky, and Karen Wickre: Thanks for many laughs, much support, and friendly shelter. As always, thanks to my wonderful five-year-old sons, Spencer and Kyle, who provided me with follies and reminded me often while I was writing that playing in a park with your kids is still one of the best things in the world.

CONTENTS AT A GLANCE

Foreword ■ **xiv**

Introduction ■ **xv**

PART I ■ **GETTING STARTED** **1**

Chapter 1 ■ A Quick Keynote Tour **3**

Chapter 2 ■ Working with Keynote **23**

Chapter 3 ■ Putting It All Together: Building a Presentation **51**

PART II ■ **KEYNOTE PRESENTATIONS FOR THE REAL WORLD** **67**

Chapter 4 ■ Sales Presentation: Chart and Table Finesse **69**

Chapter 5 ■ Class Lesson: Learning with Pizzazz **81**

Chapter 6 ■ Artist Portfolio: The Portable Image Gallery **97**

Chapter 7 ■ Video Storyboard: Building Slide Actions **113**

Chapter 8 ■ Do-It-Yourself Documentary: Adding Audio and Video Elements **131**

PART III ■ **KEYNOTE MEETS WORLD** **153**

Chapter 9 ■ Keynote in the Networked World **155**

Chapter 10 ■ Keynote on the Road: Peripherals and Projectors **171**

Chapter 11 ■ Slide, Print, and Video Output **193**

PART IV ■ **APPENDIXES** **209**

Appendix A ■ Keyboard and Mouse Shortcuts **211**

Appendix B ■ The Keynote Graphics Inventory **217**

Appendix C ■ Additional Resources **223**

Index ■ **240**

Contents

Foreword   xiv

Introduction   xv

PART I ▪ GETTING STARTED   **1**

Chapter 1 ▪ A Quick Keynote Tour   **3**

Getting a Keynote Road Map   4

Using the Slide Organizer   5

Using the Slide Canvas   6

Using the Toolbar   8

Chapter 2 ▪ Working with Keynote   **23**

What Is a Theme?   24

Exploring the 12 Themes of Keynote   25

Using Multiple Themes in One Show   33

Working with Text   35

Working with Graphics   43

Chapter 3 ▪ Putting It All Together: Building a Presentation   **51**

Organizing Your Project   52

Picking a Theme   53

Adding Text   55

Creating a Chart   62

Setting Slide Transitions   65

Show Time!   66

Attach Sticky Notes to add interest

PART II ■ **KEYNOTE PRESENTATIONS FOR THE REAL WORLD**   **67**

Chapter 4 ■ **Sales Presentation: Chart and Table Finesse**   **69**

Building a Seattle Locations Sales Extravaganza   70

Working with Charts   73

Modifying a Chart with the Chart Inspector   75

Chapter 5 ■ **Class Lesson: Learning with Pizzazz**   **81**

Roughing Out the Lesson   82

Adding Details and Notes   86

Adding Graphics   88

Using Transitions   92

Chapter 6 ■ **Artist Portfolio: The Portable Image Gallery**   **97**

Importing Files   98

Converting Unsupported Files   101

Editing Graphics   104

Building a Portfolio   105

Preparing Your Portfolio for Delivery   109

Chapter 7 ■ **Video Storyboard: Building Slide Actions**   **113**

Getting the Story Behind Storyboards   114

Creating a Demon Encounter   114

Building with Builds   116

Chapter 8 ■ **Do-It-Yourself Documentary: Adding Audio and Video Elements**   **131**

Introducing Theater Simple   132

Prepping the Project   133

Setting Up Fancy Transitions   141

Adding Video   145

Adding Audio Using iMovie   147

Exporting Your Show   148

PART III ▪ KEYNOTE MEETS WORLD   **153**

Chapter 9 ▪ Keynote in the Networked World   **155**

Comparing PowerPoint and Keynote   156

Exporting to PowerPoint   159

Importing from PowerPoint   163

For IT Managers: Where Keynote Puts Files   168

**Chapter 10 ▪ Keynote on the Road:
Peripherals and Projectors**   **171**

Understanding the Perils of the Road   172

Using OS X Presentation Peripherals   173

Examining Projectors   174

Using Apple Laptops with Keynote   182

Setting Up a Keynote Presentation System   185

Chapter 11 ▪ Slide, Print, and Video Output   **193**

Transferring Keynote Presentations
to 35mm Slides   194

Improving Print Output   199

Converting Keynote to Video   201

PART IV ▪ APPENDIXES   **209**

Appendix A ▪ Keyboard and Mouse Shortcuts   **211**

Appendix B ▪ The Keynote Graphics Inventory   **217**

Appendix C ▪ Additional Resources   **223**

Index   240

Foreword

At Apple Computer, we designed Keynote to be a truly unique approach to presentation software. Keynote is a next-generation Mac OS X tool that allows *anyone* to create beautiful presentations that look like they were produced by a professional design team. Our goal was to make sure that you spend less time designing and more time on your ideas.

Erik Holsinger's *Presenting Keynote: The Insider's Guide to Creating Great Presentations* is a unique book in that it both shows you everything Keynote can do and gives you important information about what it takes to make great presentations. Business presenters will especially appreciate the chapter on using projectors and working with AV companies.

Inside you'll find dozens of tips and tricks to help you get the most out of Keynote. Erik Holsinger has drawn on his experience as a producer and a presenter to provide real-world tutorials that guide you through creating presentations from start to finish. These tutorials cover a wide range of topics, from developing charts for sales presentations to manipulating graphics for video storyboards. These are great examples of the many ways that you can use Keynote in business, art, and education.

At Apple we are always striving to create tools that people can use to get the most out of their life. *Presenting Keynote* adheres to this principle, by helping you explore the full potential of Keynote and your presentations.

—Alan Eyzaguirre
Senior Product Manager, Apple Computer

Introduction

So, just what is Keynote? The short answer is that Keynote is a new kind of presentation software. But the better answer is that Keynote is one of those rare and amazing feats in software development—a custom-built program that became an application anyone could buy.

Before it even had a name, Keynote was a custom presentation tool developed by Apple Computer for one client—namely the company's CEO, Steve Jobs. Jobs needed a powerful tool that could handle complex graphics and yet still be easy enough that his staff could pull together his major presentations at Macworld keynote speeches—hence the name.

Personally, I can't think of a higher-pressure performance. These keynote addresses are viewed not just by the thousands in the auditorium, but they are also carefully scrutinized by investors and analysts—whose recommendations can directly affect Apple's stock price. For more than a year, Jobs used the beta version of Keynote as his main presentation tool, which says a lot about the power of the program.

After a year of extensive "beta testing" by Jobs and others, Keynote was finally released in January 2003. When Jobs presented the program, everyone in the audience—myself included—was floored. Here, after years of dealing with the limitations of PC-based programs, we had a new presentation tool for MacOS X that takes full advantage of the Mac's great graphics and design capabilities.

How You Can Use Keynote

Because of its ability to create incredible transitions and handle complex graphics, Keynote is more than just a presentation tool. The following sections present a few ideas of how you can use Keynote. These are just a few suggestions, which (by pure coincidence) tie into actual projects that you will work on in later chapters.

Keynote in Business

Okay, this is an obvious one—imagine, being able to use a presentation program in a business context! For many people, this is an everyday task—just breakout PowerPoint, try to put in as much information as you can, and hope for the best.

Keynote's simple interface and incredible graphics capabilities put it well ahead of the competition. Now you can add great transition effects, blend a wide variety of graphics, and even add video and audio clips to spice up your show. Keynote's ability to use 32-bit graphics—in other words, graphics with alpha channels—is a major advantage for smoothly blending images. You can add a company logo to a slide and change the background—without having to also change the background behind the logo.

Besides better graphics capabilities, Keynote gives you a major advantage over other presentation programs—you can set up and customize a complex slide show quickly. Instead of breaking out in a cold sweat and wondering if you should start revising your resume, in most cases with Keynote you can confidently build up or revise a great-looking presentation the night before your meeting.

Keynote in Education

To explain why I believe Keynote is one of the best academic presentation tools available, I need to give you a bit of background from my college days. At San Francisco State University (SFSU), I still remember that one of the best college courses I ever took was a class on conceptual physics, based on a textbook by Paul G. Hewitt.

I had a chance to interview Hewitt for the SFSU broadcasting department. I found that Hewitt is a true academic maverick: a former boxer, uranium prospector, and sign painter who didn't start college until he was 28. Instead of using mathematics to try to teach physics, in his book on conceptual physics, Hewitt used a unique approach that translated the main concepts of physics to common English.

What made Hewitt's course so enjoyable were the constant demonstrations of physics principals. For example, in my course at SFSU, instructor Ron Hipschman used a toy submarine, some soap, and a giant beaker to demonstrate the principles of surface tension—all while the soundtrack to *Voyage to the Bottom of the Sea* played in the background on a boom box. This type of education is not only incredibly creative and effective but also brings out the joy of learning in students.

By combining graphics, sounds, and video, you can use Keynote to quickly create curriculum tailored to your students and course needs. Imagine setting up a concept in Keynote using text and image slides and then showing a slide with a video clip that demonstrates that principle to your class. Like Hewitt's physics examples, with Keynote you can add a sense of wonder to otherwise bland or overly complex course topics. To give you an idea of how this can work, you'll create a classroom lesson from scratch in Chapter 5, "Class Lesson: Learning with Pizzazz."

Keynote in Art

Keynote's ability to show still images makes it ideal for a variety of artistic projects. For photographers and still artists, you can use Keynote to create portable portfolios, implementing all the great transitions to move the viewer through a sampling of your artwork.

Another fantastic area for Keynote in the arts is in video production. As a video producer for many years, I'm painfully aware of how the decisions you make in preproduction have to be accurate because of the monstrous costs of video and film production. One of the primary tools that producers and directors use to help take the guesswork out of production is a storyboard, which shows shot-by-shot illustrations of how the film or video will flow together.

A typical storyboard uses still images to show how one shot flows into another in a film or video production. You can use Keynote not only to show still images but also to provide transitions from scene to scene.

With Keynote, you can move beyond the traditional storyboard into actually showing movement, simulating dissolves from scene to another, and even trying out different locations for each scene. You'll tackle creating a video storyboard from scratch in Chapter 7, "Video Storyboard: Building Slide Actions."

Who Should Read This Book

This is typically the part where the author tells you that their book is for every reader in every occupation and at every age ("...cures arthritis and grows hair! Step riiiiight up!"). Because I don't buy that when I read it, I don't expect you to either.

Here are the facts: *Presenting Keynote* is aimed at three groups of people: those who want to know more about Keynote, those who want to make better presentations, and those who need both.

If you've already bought the program, then you know that Keynote's manual is rather slim on details and tutorials. This book will not only fill in the blanks that the manual omitted, but it also has five different tutorials that will help you put the power of Keynote to use.

However, it's not enough to just know what keys to push to make a great presentation. That's why I've also included a section in most chapters called *Tips from the Pros*. These include tips from professional designers, photographers, presenters, and many others who share their expertise on everything from typography to storyboarding.

How This Book Is Organized

To make it easy to use, *Presenting Keynote* is broken up into three main sections. There are three chapters in Part I, "Getting Started":

Chapter 1, "**A Quick Keynote Tour**," is your initial introduction to the features and interface of Keynote.

Chapter 2, "**Working with Keynote**," delves deeper with information on using themes (Keynote's custom backgrounds) and using graphics.

Chapter 3, "**Putting It All Together: Building a Presentation**," is where you get to test your newly found Keynote savvy with a tutorial project that you build from start to finish.

In Part II, "Keynote Presentations for the Real World," you look at and build actual applications for Keynote. Each chapter walks you through constructing a real presentation, each with a different purpose or design. In the process, you'll get hands-on experience with all the various tools and elements of excellent presentations:

Chapter 4, "**Sales Presentation: Chart and Table Finesse**," is where you build a sales presentation from scratch. You'll also focus on creating custom charts and tables inside of Keynote.

Chapter 5, "**Class Lesson: Learning with Pizzazz**," is the education example where you'll build a slide show to back up an educational lecture.

Chapter 6, "**Artist Portfolio: The Portable Image Gallery**," is for artists; you'll create an electronic portfolio that you can use to show potential clients.

Chapter 7, "Video Storyboard: Building Slide Actions," goes Hollywood by showing how you can use Keynote to create moving storyboards for film and television.

Chapter 8, "Do-It-Yourself Documentary: Adding Audio and Video Elements," enables you to create a promotional video project using graphics, video, audio, Keynote, and iMovie.

Finally, Part III, "Keynote Meets World," provides information that you'll need when showing your Keynote presentations in the big, wide world:

Chapter 9, "Keynote in the Networked World," deals with Microsoft PowerPoint (Keynote's evil twin) and shows how to import files from and export files to PowerPoint. There is also some good information in this chapter on working with networks and PC-based files.

Chapter 10, "Keynote on the Road: Peripherals and Projectors," is all about presentation hardware, including remote mice and projectors. There is even great information on working with audio/visual companies.

Chapter 11, "Slide, Print, and Video Output," looks at ways you can output your Keynote shows to 35-millimeter slides, high-quality print, and even videotape.

In the three appendixes at the back of the book, you'll find a complete list of keyboard and mouse shortcuts, a full catalog of Keynote's graphics library, and additional online resources for presentation information and technology.

 Finally, I've managed to stuff the CD-ROM full of tutorial files, demonstration movies, and demo programs to add to your Keynote experience. For example, you'll find a few custom themes that you can add into Keynote for use on your presentations, as well as demo versions of great software from Adobe and others.

How to Contact the Author

I've worked hard to make the book easy to read and fun to use. However, if you are stuck or have additional questions not answered by the book, feel free to contact me via e-mail at presentingkeynote@yahoo.com. Due to the sheer volume of e-mail that I get everyday, I can't guarantee a prompt response, but I will do my best to help resolve any questions or concerns you might have about the book.

PART I

Getting Started

This part of the book is for anyone who has a low patience threshold—you've got the program and now you want to work with it. No problem—in this part, you'll take a quick tour of Keynote's capabilities, do a few exercises to warm up, and then immediately launch into your first project.

Chapter 1 **A Quick Keynote Tour**

Chapter 2 **Working with Keynote**

Chapter 3 **Putting It All Together: Building a Presentation**

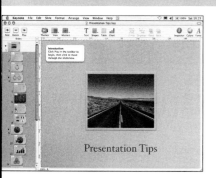

A Quick Keynote Tour

It's a job that's never started that takes the longest to finish. —*J.R.R. Tolkien (1892–1973)*

I've never been a big believer in manuals—my approach to learning software is to dive in and play around until I get stuck, until the program breaks, or until I have to get to other work.

Still, it's always a good idea to get a road map to show where things are located in a program. In this chapter, you'll look at the basic parts of Keynote and see how you can organize your workspace and your presentations. The good news is that Apple Computer built Keynote, and Apple has the market cornered on great user interfaces. Once you get used to it, you'll find Keynote's interface to be elegant and yet easy to use.

Ultimately, Keynote's ability to show still images, play audio, and even play videos makes it a handy tool.

However, if you want to dive right in, skip ahead to Chapter 3, "Putting It All Together: Building a Presentation," where you'll build a presentation from start to finish. If you decide to skip ahead but get stuck, just refer to this chapter or Chapter 2, "Working with Keynote," to find the information you need to move forward.

Getting a Keynote road map

Using the Slide Organizer, the Slide Canvas, and the toolbar

Customizing the toolbar

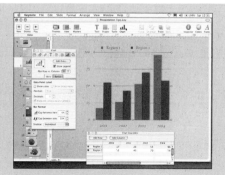

Getting a Keynote Road Map

When you first double-click the Keynote icon, the program opens and then gives you a choice of *themes*. Themes are complete "looks" for your Keynote projects that Apple designed to help you quickly make good-looking presentations.

However, don't worry about this for now—you'll go over themes in depth in Chapter 2. For now, just click the Close Document button in the bottom-left side of the Themes window, which will close the Themes window and leave you with just the Keynote menu bar.

To get a better understanding of Keynote's interface, you'll use Presentation Tips, the sample presentation that Apple built, to show off the various capabilities of Keynote.

To open the Keynote sample presentation, select File → Open Samples. A window will open showing a single sample document called *Presentation Tips*; double-click this file.

A status bar will appear showing that Keynote is loading in the Presentation Tips show.

Once Keynote has loaded the Presentation Tips show, your screen will display a window with an image of a road with text below it saying *Presentation Tips*.

Welcome aboard—this is the main operating space of Keynote; every tool you use will simply be an add-on to this main window.

Although there are lots of icons bristling everywhere, there are actually only three main elements to the main Keynote interface: the Slide Organizer, the Slide Canvas, and the toolbar (see Figure 1.1).

Figure 1.1

The Keynote interface has three main parts: the Slide Organizer, the Slide Canvas, and the toolbar.

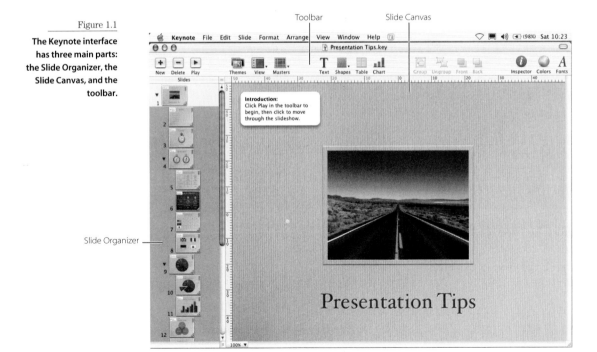

Using the Slide Organizer

On the left side of the screen is the Slide Organizer, a series of thumbnail pictures of each of the slides in the Presentation Tips project (see Figure 1.2). This is where you can view your slides at a glance, and also where you will organize the order of your slides, and even where you group slides together while building your show. Notice that some of the thumbnails don't quite line up. Within the Slide Organizer, you can organize your slides in a hierarchical order so that you can group slides together as needed.

As with the main MacOS X interface, the Slide Organizer has a "disclosure triangle," which is that small triangle shape you see above the fourth slide. By clicking this triangle, you can hide all the individual segments that are indented to the right of that particular slide—in this case, slides 5–8.

This was a critical feature when Apple was developing Keynote for Steve Jobs, because his Macworld presentations often had hundreds of slides to present.

Within the Slide Organizer, you can organize your presentation by "indenting," which provides an organization system that is similar to the standard MacOS X hierarchy. In the case of Keynote's Slide Organizer, the slide farthest to the left is the highest in the hierarchy, and all slides indented under it to the right are a part of its group.

To indent a slide, simply drag one slide under another to the right, or select the slide and press the Tab key. This will move the slide to the right, grouping it under the slide above it (see Figure 1.3). Holding down the Shift key and then pressing the Tab key will move the slide back to the left, effectively "un-indenting" it.

Indenting allows you to group slides by concept, section, or however you want to organize your presentation. For example, if you have different sections of your show (for example, a new products section and then a sales report), you could group all of your slides into two groups. All of the sales and new product slides could be indented under the first slide of their respective sections. This allows you to hide one group while working on the other, which can tremendously cut down on clutter (see Figure 1.4). Another big benefit is that you can indent as many levels as you want within Keynote. You can see this in Figure 1.4: The slides in the Slide Organizer jump from slide 4 to slide 12.

Figure 1.2

The Slide Organizer lets you organize your slides in a hierarchical format. Here, slides 5–8 are indented under slide 4.

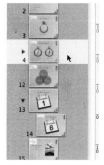

Figure 1.3

You can drag and drop slides in the Slide Organizer to indent them; this creates an organizational hierarchy.

Figure 1.4

Once grouped, you can hide entire sections of a slide show; to show the hidden sections, just click on the triangle next to the slide.

Using the Slide Canvas

The largest section in Keynote is the Slide Canvas, where you'll design and lay out all the elements for each slide. You can add pictures, text, Flash animations, even QuickTime movies to the Slide Canvas by just dragging these elements from the Desktop or file folder onto the Slide Canvas, as shown in Figure 1.5.

You can also cut and paste pictures into your Keynote presentation from other Keynote presentations or from any Mac application. In Figure 1.6, I've selected and copied an image of a walking man from within Adobe Photoshop. After that, I click over to the Keynote presentation, and either select Edit → Paste or press ⌘+V to paste the image into the slide (see Figure 1.7).

Figure 1.5

You can drag graphics directly onto the Slide Canvas from the Finder, or you can cut and paste from other applications.

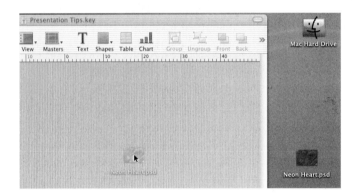

Figure 1.6

Copying an image in another application

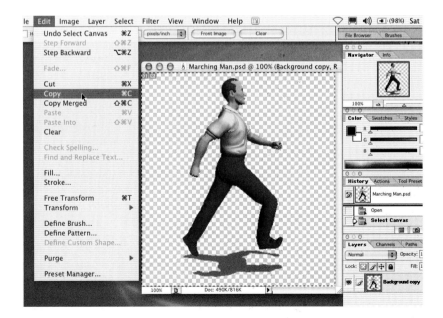

Figure 1.7

Pasting an image into Keynote

Notice how the background of the walking man image is completely transparent, which makes it blend nicely into the slide. This is because the walking man uses an alpha channel to suppress its background. For more on using alpha channel graphics, see Chapter 3, "Putting It All Together: Building a Presentation."

Although you can click and drag objects around on the Slide Canvas, often you'll find it more accurate and efficient to just use keyboard shortcuts instead of your mouse. Table 1.1 describes some of my favorite keyboard shortcuts for working with objects on the Slide Canvas. (Appendix A provides a more complete reference to all the shortcuts in Keynote.)

ACTION	SHORTCUT
Cycle through objects	Tab
Cycle backward through objects	Shift+Tab
Move object one pixel	Arrow keys
Move object 10 pixels	Shift+arrow keys
Constrain object movement	Shift+drag
Rotate object	⌘+drag handle
Rotate object 45°	⌘+Shift+drag handle
Move to next slide	Page Down
Move to previous slide	Page Up
Move to first slide	Home
Move to last slide	End

Table 1.1

Slide Canvas Keyboard Shortcuts

Using the Toolbar

The third and final piece to the Keynote interface is the toolbar, that collection of icons that rests above the Slide Canvas. This is where you'll find all the tools you need to customize your slides. Figure 1.8 gives you a quick look at the standard toolbar set of 17 tool icons.

The default toolbar divides the icons into different groups depending upon usage. To make things easier, I've divided them up into four areas—global controls, creation tools, object controls, and object palettes. The Keynote manual doesn't list the tools this way, but it's a good way to help remember what the tools are because I've grouped them according to how you'll use them.

Figure 1.8

The Keynote toolbar

Global Controls

The global controls are tools you'll generally use only a few times during the course of creating your show. These tools will make changes that will either change the Keynote interface or change the look of all the slides.

For example, clicking Themes will bring up a thumbnail display of all 12 of Keynote's built-in themes. Click one of those themes, and every slide in your presentation will change to match the new theme. Again, these are not controls you will be working with all the time. Chances are that once you initially set the theme for your slide show, you probably won't play around with this again.

New Slide and Delete Slide

These are as straightforward as they sound. The New Slide button (the one with the plus sign) will add a blank slide after the current slide, and the button with the minus sign will delete the current slide and move you ahead to the next slide in the series.

Also, when you add a new slide using the New Slide button, the new slide will have the same characteristics as the slide you were on when you click the button. To see this in action, click the first slide (in the Presentation Tips show, this is the intro slide with the picture of the highway).

Now click the New Slide button. Keynote will add a new blank slide after the first slide that not only shows the same style but also the same horizontal Photo master slide type (see Figure 1.9). Duplicating both the theme and the slide master type is handy, especially when creating slides with multiple themes.

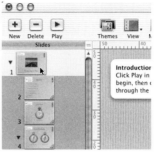 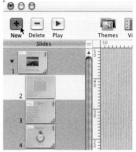

The Delete Slide button says what it means and means what it says; click on your slide, hit delete, and it's gone. You can also add a slide by just pressing **Return** or **Enter**, which will add a new slide at the same level as the last selected slide.

Figure 1.9

Clicking New Slide creates a slide of the same type as the one you highlighted before clicking the button.

Play

Clicking Play will start the slide show from whichever slide you've selected. You can also play the slide show by pressing ⌘+Option+P on the keyboard.

Themes

As mentioned earlier, themes are customized looks for every type of slide style that you might use in a presentation, such as pictures with text and bulleted lists.

Clicking the Theme button displays all 12 of Keynote's themes (see Figure 1.10). To select a new theme, all you do is just double-click it; Keynote will automatically change all the slides in your presentation to match the new theme.

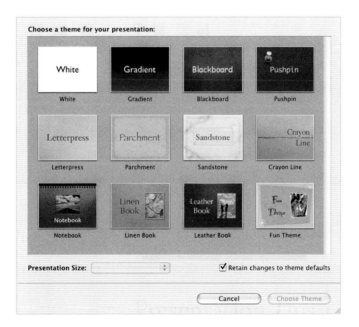

Figure 1.10

Clicking Theme allows you to select one of 12 built-in themes.

If you make changes to master slides and want to hang onto those changes—yet still try a new theme—make sure you click the Retain Changes to Theme Defaults box.

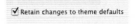

> The Presentation Tips slide show uses Keynote's Letterpress theme, an elegant look that makes each text and graphic element look like it was pressed onto a paper background.

Views

The Views tool tells Keynote what to display, both in the Slide Navigator and the Slide Canvas. The Views tool has several options to choose from:

Organizer This is the default view setting, where you see small thumbnails for each of your slides.

Outline If you need to read all the text on your slides, then you can turn the thumbnails into text by just selecting Outline (see Figure 1.11). You can also indent slides in the Outline view; instead of thumbnail images, you just indent text. When you indent text, you actually are creating a hierarchy within your presentation. This hierarchy can be between slides so that many slides can be grouped under one slide, or it can be bullet points within one slide.

Slide Only Is your desktop a little crowded for space? Selecting Slide Only will hide the Slide Navigator pane, which will give you more room for the Slide Canvas (see Figure 1.12).

Show Notes For every slide, you can also type in a complete set of notes to remind you of key points during your presentation. During a show, the audience will not see this—but you can refer to it at any time by selecting Show Notes from the View menu, as illustrated in Figure 1.13.

Show Master Slides This is a quick toggle that hides or shows the master slide thumbnails in the Slide Navigator (see Figure 1.14).

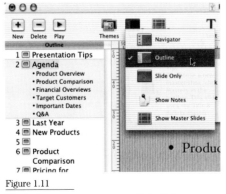

Figure 1.11

The Outline view concentrates on the text of your slides, not their look.

Figure 1.12

Slide Only saves you space by hiding the Slide Navigator pane.

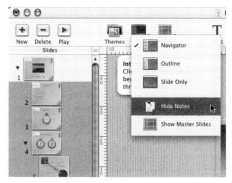

Figure 1.13

The Notes view is for you and you alone.

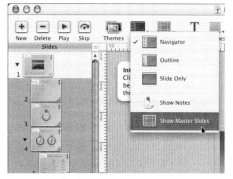

Figure 1.14

Show Master Slides view to see the basic layout of your slides.

Masters

This button refers to the master slides used in your presentation. Similar to every other presentation program, Keynote uses formatted templates—which it calls *masters*—to keep each slide stylistically consistent. These are different from themes, in that master slides are a specific type of slide, while themes contain all the formatting for an entire set of slide types. Figure 1.15 shows a selection of master slide types.

Creation Tools

These are tools you'll use frequently in Keynote to create and align objects.

Text

This is the way you add text into Keynote; just click the Text button and a small text box that says *Text* appears smack in middle of the Slide Canvas. An interesting thing about the Text button is that it automatically defaults to the typeface specified by the theme you use. In the case of the Presentation Tips show, the text style is a "stamped" Hoefler typeface.

Notice that there is both a Text button and a Fonts button on the toolbar, which serve different functions. Text merely adds text to the Slide Canvas, and the Font palette allows you to change the typeface, size, and style of the text.

Figure 1.15

Keynote uses masters to provide consistent formatting for your slides.

Shapes

Although Keynote doesn't have a wide range of drawing tools compared to PowerPoint, it does have a few within the program to cover most situations. You can resize, reposition, colorize, and adjust the transparency of any shapes from this menu.

To add a shape to your show, just click the Shapes pull-down menu and select a shape. Naturally, because you can resize each of the shapes, you can also get ovals out of the Circle shape and rectangles out of the Square shape.

Notice again that when you select a shape, the shape automatically takes on the attributes of the theme you use, just like the when you add text. In this example, the shape takes on the look of paper to keep with the Letterpress theme.

Table

Clicking the Table tool does two things, as shown in Figure 1.16: It inserts a table onto the Slide Canvas and also brings up the Table tab within the Inspector palette. The Inspector palette is the most important set of tools that you'll consistently work with in Keynote, but you'll learn about it in depth in just a minute. Just know that all the controls for formatting and adjusting the table you create when clicking on the Table toolbar icon happen in the Table tab of the Inspector palette.

Figure 1.16

The Table tool inserts a table and presents you with controls to manipulate it.

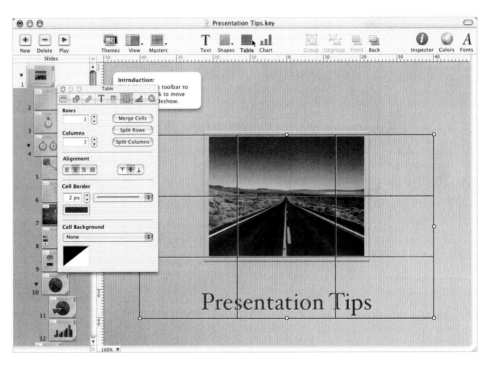

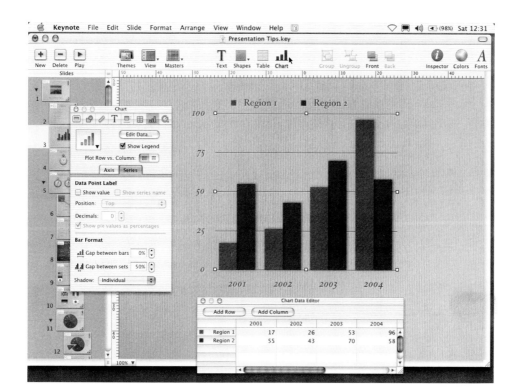

Figure 1.17

The Chart tool inserts a chart and presents you with controls to manipulate it.

Chart

Like the Table tool, the Chart button adds a default chart to the top layer of the Slide Canvas (see Figure 1.17). It also opens two other dialog boxes: the Chart tab on the Inspector palette (did I mention you will be using this palette a lot?) and the Chart Data Editor. The Chart tab is where you format the chart, and the Chart Data Editor is a simple spreadsheet program where you'll enter the text and numerical data to create the chart.

Again, with a nod to the Letterpress theme, Keynote creates colored paper segments to complement the look of your show.

Object Controls

The next four icons—Group, Ungroup, Front, and Back—control the layering and merging of objects. These are especially handy when you have several elements placed on the Slide Canvas.

Figure 1.18

The Group icon lets you link together multiple objects, which makes it easier to reposition them all at once.

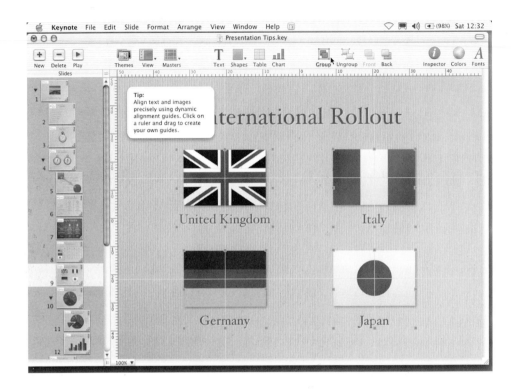

Group and Ungroup

Group and Ungroup simply let you link objects together. When you group a series of objects, such as the ones in Figure 1.18, they are then linked so that if you move one, you'll move them all. When you need to move or edit just one object, hit Ungroup to get at the individual elements. You can select multiple items by Shift+clicking each item, then clicking the Group button.

Front and Back

The Front and Back tools are easy to understand if you think of the Slide Canvas as the surface of a table or desk over which you are standing. When you place items on top of each other on the table, the item on top is the most visible, and the item on the bottom is not visible.

Keynote uses the same principle, only instead of top and bottom, Keynote defines the layer position of an object as "front" and "back." An object in the back position is in the background, and an object in front is in the foreground.

To see how this works, click the photo of the desert road in the opening slide of the Presentation Tips show (see Figure 1.19). Notice how white boxes or "handles" appear in the corners and in the middle of each side of the graphic. Even though the graphic appears only in the middle section, in fact it is much larger. As part of the Letterpress theme, this horizontal Photo master page uses a frame through which a graphic can show. This frame is called an *alpha channel*, which you can add to graphics to define which part of the image is transparent.

Figure 1.19

Clicking an object brings up control handles for it.

Now, click the Front button on the toolbar. The highway picture now covers the background, which—although nice—completely covers the background's picture frame. With the highway picture still selected (which you can tell by the six white corner handles), return the picture to its original look by clicking Back in the toolbar. The picture is instantly sent behind the background plate, which reveals the highway picture through the background image's frame opening.

Object Palettes

Now you've come to the heavy-hitter tools, which you will either have open or have on hand to work with constantly as you create your presentation. These are not individual tools but are floating palettes that provide many different ways of customizing your presentation.

The Inspector Palette

As mentioned previously, the Inspector palette is the most used and important palette in Keynote (see Figure 1.20). Inside the Inspector you'll find not one, but eight different sections (called *tabs*) that control everything from table formatting to transitions to QuickTime movie performance. This is where you'll add drop shadows, determine when objects appear on your slide, and decide dozens of other important style issues. The Inspector palette is something you will work with constantly throughout the book as you build different types of presentations.

Figure 1.20

The Inspector palette holds controls in eight tabbed categories, such as the Slide Inspector tab shown here.

The Colors Palette

The Colors palette is where you—believe it or not—pick the colors of the text and shape objects in your slide show (see Figure 1.21). A great feature of the Colors palette is that it not only offers you the standard Apple color wheel or color "picker," but also offers four other ways (color sliders, spectrum, swatches, and crayon) of selecting colors.

The Fonts Palette

Finally, at the far right of the toolbar is the button to access the Fonts palette, which is the standard font dialog box used in nearly every MacOS X application (see Figure 1.22).

The Fonts palette is actually quite impressive in the level of type control and type information it provides. The Fonts palette groups each typeface four ways:

Figure 1.21

Pick colors using the control type you prefer: Apple color picker, sliders, swatches, and so forth.

- By type collection or category (such as serif, sans serif, or even your favorite fonts)

- Family (the font group)

- Typeface (the particular style)

- Size

If you dig a bit deeper in the Fonts palette by clicking the Extras pop-up menu located at the bottom, you also get a Character palette, which shows you an amazing amount of information (see Figure 1.23). The Character palette can show all the Roman characters for each font, as well as all the Japanese, Traditional Chinese, and Simplified Chinese characters in the fonts on your system. Need to find a specific style of arrow? No worries—simply select an arrow from any typeface, and then (with the arrow still selected) select different fonts in the Font pull-down menu inside the Character palette.

Figure 1.22

The Fonts palette organizes your faces and styles in several ways.

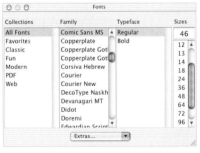

Customizing the Toolbar

One of the best features of the Keynote interface is that you can customize it to the way you like to work. Although the toolbar contains some default icons, you can add or subtract tools to suit your working style.

Besides, you'll find that once you've customized your toolbar the way you like it, you'll probably only need to customize the toolbar for specific projects. For example, if your presentation uses a lot charts—as the project does in Chapter 4, "Sales Presentation: Chart and Table Finesse"—it's a good idea to add the Chart Data Editor icon to the toolbar. So let's customize the Keynote toolbar—to get started, you need to select View → Customize Toolbar.

Adding and Removing Toolbar Icons

When the Customize Toolbar dialog box opens, it's tool-icon heaven, with all the icons you normally see when you first start up Keynote, as well as another 16 icons.

Most of these tools you won't really need to work with, but some are handy—especially when working with large amounts of slides. Adding or subtracting icons within Keynote is quite easy:

> **To add one of these new tool icons to the toolbar**, just drag the icon from the Customize Toolbar window onto the toolbar, as shown in Figure 1.24. Your new tool will then appear where you placed it on the toolbar. This is exactly the same way you add files or applications to the Finder toolbar in MacOS X.

> **To remove any icon**, while the Customize Toolbar window is open, simply click the offending icon and drag it off the toolbar, where it will disappear with a satisfying "poof" animation.

> **To restore the original default toolbar**, just drag the Default Toolbar Group icon from the Customize Toolbar window to the toolbar (see Figure 1.25). Presto changeo—your toolbar will return to the standard 17 icons.

Next, you'll enter into the area of custom tools that you can add using the Customize Toolbar feature. You won't use these tools all the time, but they can be helpful when dealing with specific types of presentations. Or you could just include them in the toolbar because it fits your working style.

Skip

This is a useful tool if you have to make last-minute revisions to a presentation and need to skip a section. Let's say you are presenting a new line of food products, only you find out at the last minute that 80 percent of your audience members are Militant Vegetarian Knife Throwers, who probably won't respond well to your section on traditional meat products.

No problem—just add the Skip tool to your toolbar. Select the offending meat product slides and click Skip, and Keynote will skip those slides when you click Play. The slides that you've "skipped" show up as a horizontal bar in the Slide Organizer; just click the bar, click the Skip button again, and your slides reappear. The great thing about this is that you didn't delete the slides from your original presentation, so you don't have to go back and re-create them from scratch.

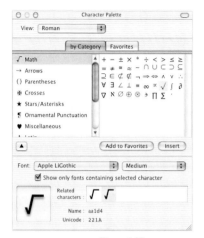

Figure 1.23

The Character palette can help you find interesting characters among the many MacOS X typefaces on your system.

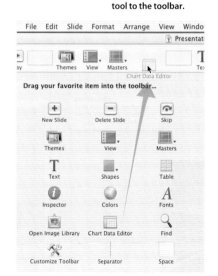

Figure 1.24

Dragging an icon to the toolbar adds the tool to the toolbar.

Figure 1.25

Toolbar getting cluttered with too many icons? Drag the Default Toolbar Group icon to the toolbar.

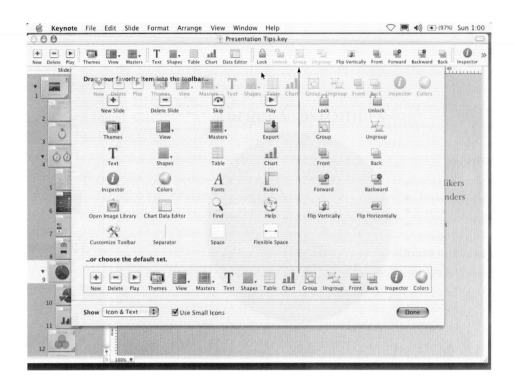

Let's see how this would work on the Presentation Tips presentation. Use the Skip tool to skip the second slide in the Presentation Tips slide show, which tends to detract from the blinding truth and ultimate pathos presented later within the show (come on, let's give a little praise for the person who gave up their nights and weekends to add this example into the program).

First, open the Customize Toolbar window and then add the Skip tool by dragging it onto the toolbar. You can drag it anywhere, but I usually add it next to the Play button because it affects the playback of the slides. Click Done to close the Customize Toolbar dialog box.

Now click the second slide in the Slide Organizer, which will bring up the agenda for the slide show in an all-text slide. Like I said, it is not exactly a jolt to the system, so let's skip this slide. With the slide still selected, click the Skip button in the toolbar.

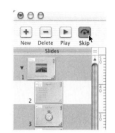

The slide is now hidden, showing up in the Slide Organizer as a horizontal line. The original third slide, which showed a stopwatch, is now the second slide of the presentation (for those fans of the British TV show *The Prisoner,* this is especially appropriate, as you are removing the agenda and presenting the "New Number 2").

If you click the first slide and then click the Play button, the show will play from the opening slide to the Last Year stopwatch slide. To show the slide again in the presentation, just click the horizontal bar between slide 1 and slide 2 and hit Skip again—the slide returns, the preceding slides are renumbered, and the original agenda slide returns as an icon for the second slide in the Slide Organizer.

Lock and Unlock

The Lock and Unlock tools are useful when you have many different objects on one slide. When these tools are on the toolbar, you can prevent an object from being moved or modified by "locking" it.

This makes the object impossible to select until you "unlock" it, which you do just by clicking the Unlock icon on the toolbar. Locking and unlocking is also a good way of getting background items out of the way so you don't accidentally select them when working with nearby text or graphics.

> You can also lock and unlock an object using keyboard commands. To lock an object, just click that object and press ⌘+**L**. To unlock the object, click it again and then press ⌘+**Option+L**.

Export

If you are only exporting files from an existing Keynote presentation, then adding this tool to the toolbar makes sense. Otherwise, just ignore this and select Export from the File pull-down menu when you need it.

Forward and Backward

These tools add some subtlety to the Front and Back buttons by moving objects forward or backward one layer at a time. Again, if you have many objects on your slides, which would add more than two layers to the Slide Canvas, then it's a good idea to add these to the toolbar.

Open Image Library

If you add many images to your presentations, then adding this icon to the toolbar will add years to your life. This is also the one of the main ways to import graphics into Keynote, which the next chapter covers.

The Image Library folder resides in the Library folder on the main hard drive that contains your MacOS. Specifically, it's at /Library/application support/keynote/image library.

Chart Data Editor

The Chart Data Editor normally opens when you first add in a chart. However, if you find that later you need to rework all of the data on a chart, then adding the Chart Data Editor icon to the toolbar is a handy way of quickly bringing up the Chart Data Editor as needed. You can also bring up the Chart Data Editor by pressing ⌘+Shift+D.

Find

Lose something? A phrase, a sales figure, a mention of a VIP somewhere in the midst of 300 slides? To find your missing item, you pull down the Find Panel option from the Edit pull-down menu, or you just press ⌘+F. If you'd like even faster access, then by all means add the Find icon to the toolbar, which will instantly open the Find dialog box.

Help

We can all use a bit of help sometime. However, avoid placing the Help icon on the toolbar for two reasons. First, you can access the Help menu by pulling down the Help menu or by pressing ⌘+?.

Second, although the Keynote Help is okay, it is far from detailed, and it can take some time to open. So Help is good—but not on the toolbar.

Flip Vertically and Flip Horizontally

Adding Flip Vertically and Flip Horizontally to your toolbar is only necessary if you are working with a lot of photos or other graphics that you need to reorient for whatever reason. You can also avoid adding these to your toolbar by simply pulling down the Arrange pull-down menu and selecting Flip Vertically or Flip Horizontally.

Customize Toolbar

Clicking the Customize Toolbar button will bring up the Customize Toolbar dialog box. However, this is one of the few icons that you shouldn't bother to add to the toolbar, because it's a bit of a waste of space. Not only can you access the Customize Toolbar selection from the View pull-down menu, but you can also get at Customize Toolbar by right-clicking on the toolbar.

Separator, Space, and Flexible Space

The Separator, Space, and Flexible Space options are not tools so much as ways of cleaning up and organizing your toolbar. They are also about as handy as a second belly button— clearly the Apple Interface design team had too much caffeine one day and succumbed to "Gotta-add-another-feature-itis." Using the spacer icons is a bit like using a 26-blade Swiss Army knife to open a letter—true, you have lots of tool options, but it's not a task on which you are going to spend a lot of time. Still, these toolbar icons are there, so I'll mention them this once and never bring them up again (I promise!).

To see the spacer tools in action, open the Customize Toolbar menu item, again either by selecting it in the View pull-down menu or by right-clicking the toolbar (see Figure 1.26).

Notice how there are now three "boxes" in the toolbar, with one each after the Masters, Chart, and Back buttons. These boxes are Flexible Space placeholders—literally empty spaces that separate icons. The Flexible Space icons adjust in width so that if you remove a tool, then the Flexible Space expands to fill in the extra space on the toolbar.

The Separator and Space placeholders work the same way, only in a fixed width. The Space placeholder is the width of one icon, and the Separator placeholders provide only about half that space.

Cleaning Up the Toolbar

Finally, you can clean up your toolbar by limiting what is displayed. At the bottom of the Customize Toolbar dialog window is a small pop-up menu named Show, which gives you three choices: Text & Icon, Icon Only, and Text Only.

The default setting is Text & Icon, so you can see the icon for the tool as well as the name of the tool. If you are building your presentation on a smaller iBook or on the 12′ PowerBook, you can add some precious screen real estate by selecting Text Only.

For the graphically minded, you can select Icon Only, ridding yourself of the scourge of text, which again buys you a bit more real estate. If you like the icon view but still need more room, click the Small Fonts box next to the Show pull-down menu. This will further reduce the size of the icons in the toolbar, again to provide you more toolbar and Slide Canvas space.

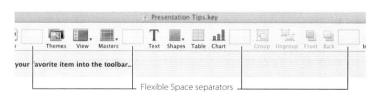

Figure 1.26

You can add spacers to the toolbar.

IN PRAISE OF TWO-BUTTON MICE

Even though most Macs come with a single-button mouse, I urge you, most passionately, to open your mind, heart, and wallet and buy a new mouse with two buttons. Gasp! A non-Macintosh ideal—nay, even a PC-based suggestion—in a MacOS X book? Mercy!

Okay, with a quick genuflect before the idol of all things Mac, let me state that—as strange as it may seem—there really are other computers in the world than Macs. And, some-times, the plodding world of PC tradition and non-innovation comes up with a good idea. In

this case, it's the two-button mouse. Kensington's Optical Elite mouse is just one example of a two-button mouse that works well under MacOS X.

Dozens of programs on the Mac take advantage of two-button mice with a horde of features that you can access simply by right-clicking. Keynote especially takes advantage of this; just right-click any object or section within Keynote, and you'll instantly get a window that provides a variety of tools you would normally have to access via a pop-up menu. To find out all you are missing, refer to Appendix A, which lists what you can access in Keynote using a right-click. Incidentally, you can also access hidden menus from your single-button mice by holding the Control key when you click.

CHAPTER 2

Working with Keynote

The task I am trying to achieve above all is to make you see. —*D.W. Griffith (1875–1948),*
pioneer American film director, in a 1913 interview

Now that you've taken a whirl through the Keynote interface, it's time to take a closer look at
three critical areas in Keynote: themes, text, and graphics. In this chapter, you'll really dive into
the different aspects of each area, as well as get professional tips on the way to use backgrounds
and type to create great presentations.

Again, if you think you are ready to move on, skip ahead to Chapter 3, "Putting It All
Together: Building a Presentation," where you'll build a presentation from scratch.

What is a theme?

Looking at Keynote's 12 themes

Working with text

Working with graphics

Tips from the Pros: Marie Morzenti on Presentation Design Basics

Tips from the Pros: David Piná on Typography

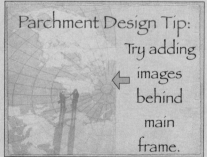

What Is a Theme?

Apple-designed themes are a way to solve a long-standing presentation problem: design chaos. This is a painful affliction for both presenter and audience; it's where every slide is different in design—from background graphics to typeface position and color. This is so distracting that even if the speaker is compelling, the audience is left with a sense that the presentation just didn't come together.

Fortunately, the 12 themes in Keynote provide a solution to this problem. Each theme was designed to have a variety of slide types yet share a common design. Once you've selected a theme, you simply pick the type of slide (photo, bulleted list, and so on) that fits with your contents.

To give you an idea of how this works, boot up Keynote and again open the sample presentation by selecting File → Open Samples and then clicking Presentation Tips.

With a few exceptions (namely slides 6 and 17–19), all of the Presentation Tips slide show uses the Letterpress theme. Each of the slides has the same brown background, and each of graphic elements (charts, tables, and so on) has a cutout paper-look that is consistent with the background.

So let's take a tour of the different themes. With the Presentation Tips show loaded into Keynote, change the theme for that show by just selecting Themes from the toolbar and then double-clicking on that theme. Because it is a global command, when you change themes you'll affect every slide in your show. This is great when you don't want to change the information or slide order but are truly tired with the overall look of your show.

VIEWING MASTER SLIDES

Notice the double bar to the right of the word *Slides* in the Slide Navigator? This is actually the hiding spot for the master slides. To view the slides, pull down on this line, and you'll see thumbnails of all the master slides in the theme you are using.

This allows you to access and edit the master pages, which is especially important when you are modifying or creating a theme. To hide the master pages, just pull down the View menu and select Hide Master Pages.

Exploring the 12 Themes of Keynote

As you look at each description of a theme, click that theme to see how it handles different types of slides, such as the chart on slide 9 and the table on slide 5.

White

Background	White
Typeface	Gill Sans (sans serif)
Best Medium	Print
Best Use	Use this theme as the base for a new theme

White as snow, white as a whiteboard, this is the Great Blank, baby. No graphics, no designs, nada.

In the midst of all this design splendor, why use the White theme? Just think of the white background as paper, and it makes sense. With a white background, you are not burning ink trying to print a solid black or colored background, so this theme is ideal if you plan to print your presentation. Also, if you want to build your own design from scratch, then this is the theme to use because you won't spend any time deleting elements as you build your own designs.

You should keep two things in mind when using the White theme in its pure form: First, you should probably avoid using this theme if you plan on showing your presentation in a dark room because this contrast (dark letters on a white screen) can be hard on your audience. However, if you are showing your presentation in a place that has a lot of ambient light, then this might be just the right amount of contrast to ensure that people can see your text.

In this theme, use drop shadows liberally on your text to make your text pop out from the screen. A drop shadow is a shadow that appears to be underneath text or an object. Because even colored text on a white background can seem two dimensional, adding a drop shadow can really improve readability. Chapter 3, "Putting It All Together: Building a Presentation," and Chapter 4, "Sales Presentation: Chart and Table Finesse," cover adding a drop shadow.

Gradient

Background	Dark gradient
Typeface	Gil Sans (sans serif)
Best Medium	Projected
Best Use	Business presentations

The Gradient theme is typical of what you'll see in 90 percent of all slide show presentations (see Figure 2.1). The background is a gradient that starts with black at the top and fades to a dark gray at the bottom. All of the original text is white, which helps highlight the text against the dark background.

As mentioned, all of the text is white, which helps highlight the text against the dark background. However, all-white text on a black background can lead to slide monotony. To fix this, add some color to your text for emphasis. For example, a title such as "The Seattle Sales Solution" could be all white except for the word *Seattle*. However, avoid "rainbow-itis," where you have so many colors on the screen that you emphasize nothing.

Blackboard

Background	Blackboard
Typeface	Comic Sans MS (sans serif)
Best Medium	Projected
Best Use	Educational or training presentations

A blackboard background (complete with smudged chalk marks), white handwritten type, and brightly colored chart and table elements are the highlights of this theme. In this theme, images appear to be held in place with tape, as shown in Figure 2.2.

While an obvious theme for classroom presentations, Blackboard is also a great theme for presenting difficult concepts in a presentation. The academic feel of the show—especially in a serious corporate setting—can open up your audience to new ideas. On the other hand, it could remind people of some traumatic educational crisis in their lives and make you about as effective as a screen door on a submarine. In other words, use this theme with a bit of discretion.

Here again, using a drop shadow on the text can really help pop the text out from the background. Another design you might try is to make the distance between the text and its shadow further for large titles and closer for smaller text. Again, Chapters 3 and 4 cover how to create drop shadows.

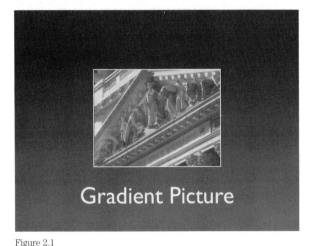

Figure 2.1

The Gradient theme

Figure 2.2

Tape "holds" your pictures in the Blackboard theme.

Pushpin

Background	Dark corkboard
Typeface	Monaco (sans serif)
Best Medium	Projected
Best Use	Casual business presentation

Using a corkboard image as a background, the Pushpin theme also uses custom images of (gasp!) pushpins for bullets (see Figure 2.3).

This theme also uses brightly colored and slightly transparent elements for the charts and tables, which show up nicely against the background texture. Overall, I found this to be a classy theme. One design tip you might want to use is to extend the "office corkboard" design by adding typical things you'd find on a corkboard for emphasis and visual interest, as shown in Figure 2.4.

Letterpress

Background	Light brown textured paper
Typeface	Hoefler Text (serif)
Best Medium	Projected or printed
Best Use	Corporate annual or status report presentations

By now, you should be comfortable with this theme, as this is what the Presentation Tips slide show uses. This is a classy theme, which uses a custom image of pressed paper on all the text, chart, and table elements (see Figure 2.5).

Figure 2.3

Pins "hold" your pictures in the Pushpin theme.

Figure 2.4

Adding other elements to the Pushpin theme

Because of its brown background, this theme is not easy to see when the ambient light in the room is too bright. To make it clearer, use 100-percent black text and italics to emphasize points (see Figure 2.6). To *really* emphasize points, use both 100-percent black and italics at the same time.

Parchment

Background	Light brown paper on stone
Typeface	Papyrus (serif)
Best Medium	Both print and projected
Best Use	Sales presentations, especially when selling image or creative projects

This is my favorite theme; it has an old Egyptian design that is both simple and elegant (see Figure 2.7). The custom background image has a piece of light-colored parchment paper placed on top of a darker stone background.

All of the colors of the chart elements are muted, which helps accentuate them against the background. The background also adds a nice "frame within a frame," which brings even more focus to charts and other graphic elements that are placed toward the center of the slide. A nice design touch that you can use is to add a slightly transparent graphic to the background, which adds even more texture to the frame (see Figure 2.8).

This is Letterpress

Letterpress Design Tip:

Use 100 Percent Black and *italics* to emphasize *important* points.

Figure 2.5

The Letterpress theme

Figure 2.6

Using 100-percent black and italics can help add emphasis to Letterpress presentations.

Sandstone

Background	Light yellow, aged stone
Typeface	Hoefler Text (serif)
Best Medium	Print
Best Use	Business, especially when the subject matter is dry or dull

Sandstone is similar to the Parchment theme; however, in my opinion, it is not as successful (see Figure 2.9). The aged stone background is nice, but it requires a lot of contrast in both text and graphics to stand out from the background. Overall, this is a better theme for print or sending presentations in Portable Document Format (PDF). This is another theme that can benefit from drop shadows, especially when you add charts.

Crayon Line

Background	Light brown paper
Typeface	Times (serif)
Best Medium	Both print and projected
Best Use	Sales and image presentations

Crayon Line is a hip theme, while still fun and slightly whimsical (see Figure 2.10). The crayon line is generally used to separate titles from the background. The paper background makes a good contrast for bright colors, so this theme works well in either printed or projected mediums.

Figure 2.7

The Parchment theme

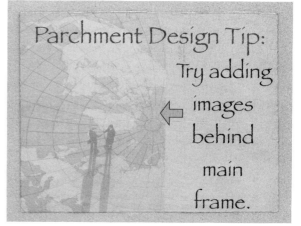

Figure 2.8

Adding a slightly transparent graphic to the Parchment theme

One thing to watch out for in with this theme is the type size. Because the Crayon Line theme uses a serif font for its bullet points, using small font sizes makes it hard for the audience to read. For more on serif versus san serif fonts, see C. David Piná's typography tips later in this chapter (the "Tips from the Pros: C. David Piná on Choosing Typography" sidebar).

Notebook

Background	White paper with notebook spiral image
Typeface	Stone Sans Semi ITC TT (titles) and Bradley Handscript ITC TT (body and bullet points)
Best Medium	Print
Best Use	Educational, travel, business party presentations

Notebook has an interesting look, with all of the titles attached to a spiral notebook. The other interesting thing is that this is the first themes mentioned that uses more than one typeface. Stone San Semi is used for the headlines, and Bradley Handscript is used for the body and bullet points (see Figure 2.11).

Notebook is a good idea to start your presentation in Notebook, rather than converting a different presentation to the Notebook theme. Notice how nearly all the slides in the Presentation Tips presentation need to have the text realigned, which wasn't the case when switching over to the other themes. This is because of the spiral notebook image, which necessitates the text starting lower in the screen.

Figure 2.9

The Sandstone theme

Figure 2.10

The Crayon Line theme

Finally, I would also change the font used for the body and bullet points because I find the Bradley Handscript to be nearly unreadable.

Linen Book

Background	White page in green book frame
Typeface	Optima
Best Medium	Print
Best Use	Album or nostalgic presentations

Linen Book, as with the other book themes, has a different book-like cover page, with a solid paper background for all the following slides (see Figure 2.12). The background is effective, with only part of the slide canvas taken up with the background's folded page image.

Linen Book also uses the Optima typeface, which is easily read—but not as good when projected, especially at smaller type sizes. This is my only complaint with the Linen Book theme—the type size used for the bullet points and supporting lines is too small when projected. To enhance the "notebook" look, be sure to add graphics throughout your presentation.

Figure 2.11

The Notebook theme

Figure 2.12

The Linen Book theme

Leather Book

Background	Plain white page
Typeface	Optima
Best Medium	Print
Best Use	Nostalgia, remembrance presentations

Leather is simple yet effective (Figure 2.13). The opening leather book cover is good for print output, especially when you use the Horizontal Photo slide master. Any picture nicely stands out in the embedded picture frame, and the white text on cover is elegant.

Although Leather Book uses the same Optima font as the Linen Book theme, Leather Book has a subtle difference by adding a slight blue color to the titles instead of the black used in the body and bullet text.

Fun

Background	Art Deco Orange frame on a light yellow background with white ornaments
Typeface	Party LET (serif)
Best Medium	Print
Best Use	Party announcements and surprise personal resignations

The Apple design team got playful with this theme design, which although colorful is extremely hard to read. If you do some work changing the barely legible Party LET typestyle used throughout the Fun theme, then it could work. However, if you don't plan on doing some fairly major editing on this theme, then you might want to move on to a different theme. For example, changing the font to Marker Felt makes this theme much more workable (see Figure 2.14).

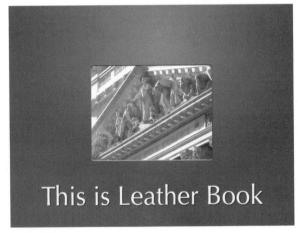

Figure 2.13

The Leather Book theme

Figure 2.14

The Fun theme, with the Marker Felt font replacing the default font

So there you have it, the 12 built-in themes in Keynote. In the next section, you'll start working with text and the many tools in Keynote that you can use to format that text.

For more about creating your own themes, see Chapter 8, "Do-It-Yourself Documentary: Adding Audio and Video Elements."

Using Multiple Themes in One Show

Notice in the Presentation Tips slide show that there are several different themes in the show besides the Letterpress theme (check out slides 6, 17, 18, and 19). The only way to add a slide with a different theme is to open a new show with the different theme, copy the master slide that you want to use, copy it to your old show's master slides, and then apply that new master slide in your old show.

Let's add a Pushpin theme slide to the Presentation Tips slide show. If you haven't done it already, open up the Presentation Tips slide show. Now with the Presentation Tips slide show still open, start a new Keynote presentation.

When the new presentation opens, the first thing Keynote will ask you is what theme you want to use. Double-click the Pushpin theme, which Keynote will load. Now you'd think that you'd just be able to make your slide, copy it, and then just paste it into your presentation. Not so fast—life is just not that simple. Instead of copying, you need to click and drag your slide from the Pushpin theme to the Presentation Tips show. However, if you don't want to add a slide but want to add a new themed master slide, just drag a master slide from the Pushpin theme to the Presentation Tips show.

Just to make things interesting, use a Horizontal Photo master slide. To select this, pull down the master slide section in the Slide Navigator. Now just click and drag the thumbnail for the Horizontal Photo master over to the master slides section in the Presentation Tips Slide Organizer.

To use this, select Views → Hide Master Slides and then scroll up and click the thumbnail for slide 1 in the Slide Navigator, which shows the photo of the road and the Presentation Tips title. Now, here's the fun part; change the theme of this slide by clicking Masters in the Toolbar and selecting the Pushpin Horizontal Photo master slide in the pull-down list. Presto, the first slide has now been changed to a Pushpin master; it even kept the same image and text. Very cool, no?

**TIPS FROM THE PROS: MARIE C. MORZENTI
ON PRESENTATION DESIGN BASICS**

Marie C. Morzenti is the key trainer at the Information Resources and Technologies department at the University of St. Thomas in St. Paul, Minnesota. Marie has trained many students and teachers to use a variety of applications, including Microsoft PowerPoint. Here are some tips based on some of her training material. These are some great basic ground rules to keep in mind when building your presentation:

Keep the design simple. Adding too many elements or making a presentation too design intensive can distract from the points you are trying to make. Let your message be the main focus, which is easier to do when you keep a basic design.

Don't use graphics as filler. Never use graphics to "fill space"—every graphic element, even elements used in the master slide, should have a clear purpose. Use graphics to make a point that can't be made as well without the illustration.

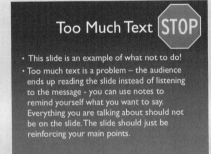

Establish your main and supporting points. For each new concept in your presentation, use a slide for emphasis. Also, be sure to add supporting points for each concept, either on the main slide or on a separate slide.

Use contrasting colors. Contrasting colors can help bring out graphic elements and text elements in your show. When colors are too similar, they can make text and graphics difficult to read or understand.

Working with Text

Now that you know how to apply a theme to your presentation, you'll need to add text to get across your message. The good news is that Keynote has amazing flexibility when it comes to formatting and presenting text within the Slide Canvas.

Now for some bad news: Getting text into the program is somewhat limited. You won't be able to import a Word or text document straight into Keynote.

There are basically only three ways to get text into Keynote:

- Type the text yourself.
- Cut, drag, or copy and paste text from a word processor program such as Microsoft Word or a text editor such as Apple's SimpleText.
- Import a PowerPoint presentation that contains text.

Of all the methods you could use, it's best to just type the text from within Keynote. Of course, if you are just converting a pre-existing PowerPoint presentation, then you can save yourself some time. However, pasting or dragging and dropping from another application means you first have to write up the presentation there, and then you have the added work of pasting each section into Keynote.

Besides, you can use the master slides within each theme to properly format and position the text for each slide. Let's start a new presentation and use the master slides to provide a formatted template for the text:

1. Select File → New or press ⌘+N to create a new file.
2. When the Themes window comes up, select the Gradient theme, and click the Choose Theme button.

USING PDF TEXT

You can also import textual content by bringing in a PDF file into Keynote. Because you can print to a PDF file in MacOS X, this means that nearly any program that can print out text could create PDF files for use in Keynote. The problem is that Keynote will treat the PDF as though it were a graphic, so you won't be able to edit the text or apply any effects from the Text section of the Inspector palette.

3. The Slide Canvas now shows the Gradient Title and Subtitle slide; if you click either the top title or bottom subtitle, your cursor automatically enters your text in the correct font and position.

4. Type **The Big Title** into the top title box and then type **It's just that easy to add text.** into the bottom subtitle box.

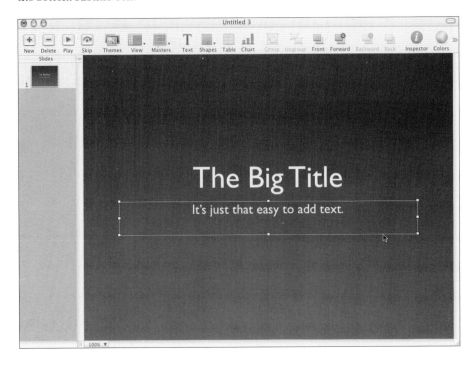

Now let's change the master slide to feature both titles and bullet points:

1. With the Gradient theme still open, click the Masters icon in the toolbar and select the second option, Title & Bullets.

2. Notice how the subtitle line "It's just that easy to add text" now becomes one of the bullet point lines.

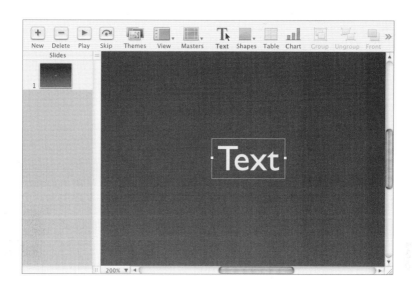

Figure 2.15

To add text to Keynote, just click the Text icon in the toolbar.

3. Double-click at the end of the "It's just that easy to add text" line. A text cursor appears behind the line. Press Return to add another line of text. A bullet point appears below the first line so that any text you type will be indented behind the bullet point.

To add text that does not appear within the preset text boxes of a master slide, click the Text icon in the toolbar. This will add a text box with the word *Text* to the center of the Slide Canvas (see Figure 2.15). Like the text boxes that appeared when you changed master slides, clicking the text box will insert a text cursor so you can type in whatever you want.

Okay, now you know how to get text into the program; how do you format it to get it just the way you want it? Enter the text "dynamic duo": the Text palette and Font palette.

Using the Text Inspector

The Text palette, or *Text Inspector*, is part of the Inspector palette; to open it, click the Inspector icon in the toolbar or press ⌘+Shift+I (see Figure 2.16). Then inside the Inspector palette, click the Text tab. The Text Inspector provides control over the color, positioning, and list formatting used in the text.

If you want to change only part of the text using the Text Inspector, select that part of the text before making any adjustments. Conversely, to change all the text in a text box, just make sure that only the text box—and not any individual text—is selected.

Figure 2.16

The Text Inspector

Text color

Horizontal alignment

Vertical alignment

Bullet type

Bullet color

Bullet character or image

TIPS FROM THE PROS: C. DAVID PINÁ
ON CHOOSING TYPOGRAPHY

To give you a better understanding of how to approach type when creating your Keynote masterpiece, I interviewed C. David Piná, an award-winning designer and producer based in Burbank, California. David has been on the front lines of graphic design for decades and has produced graphics for broadcast television, the Web, and print design for more than 100 television shows. The following are some tips that you should keep in mind when deciding which fonts and faces to include in your presentations:

Use serif fonts for elegant designs. The serif font has a built-in connotation of being old and elegant. Piná finds that serif fonts really look great on paper, so they are good fonts to use when you plan on printing your slide shows. However, be careful, because smaller-sized serif typefaces can be somewhat unreadable on screen or in print. Piná's favorite serif font is Times Roman—for him, it is the perfect model of a letter.

Use san serif fonts for clarity. San serif fonts are bolder and easier to read, particularly at smaller point sizes. San serif fonts can range from narrow (such as Futura Condensed) to quite wide (such as Arial Black). Piná's favorite san serif fonts are Franklin Gothic and Gil Sans.

Avoid mixing typefaces. Generally, you never want to mix more than three typefaces per page or screen. More than this turns your design from an effective slide to a ransom note. Still, remember that these are good general rules, but you can also break these rules when you think it is necessary. One year for the Tony Awards, Piná came up with a design that used a different typeface for every letter, which included both serif and san serif typefaces. This provided the diverse look the producer wanted, even though it broke the standard rule for mixing fonts.

San Serif Font Examples
- **Arial Black**
- **Gil Sans**
- Optima
- Stone Sans Semi
- **Tahoma**

If you do mix typefaces, try using a serif headline with san serif bullet points. If you need to mix typefaces, then a good plan is to use serif typefaces as the headline typeface and use a san serif typeface for the smaller bullet points. Serif fonts—especially the more ornate ones—can be unreadable when reduced in size, whereas san serif fonts look just fine in smaller point sizes.

Color & Alignment

The first controls in the Text Inspector are pretty straightforward; they're typical of what you'll find in other graphic and productivity applications. To use these controls, you need to first select the text you want to change.

You can also set the color of the text here. Once you click the Color box, which is the first icon on the left, the Color palette appears. Interestingly enough, you can't change the color of the text by directly clicking the Color icon in the toolbar.

The next two sets of icons on the top of the toolbar are for horizontal and vertical alignment. The middle collection of icons provides the standard left, middle, right, and justified alignments that you'll find in most word processing programs. The far-right icons are for vertical alignment, which in order are top, middle, and bottom.

Spacing

The Character control in desktop publishing or other graphics programs is called the *kerning*, where you control the space between letters. You can add more space between letters by moving the slider to the right and increasing the Character space value.

The Line control is what most other programs call the *leading*, where you can adjust the distance between individual lines. Again, to increase the distance between lines, just move the slider to the right to increase the value.

Finally, the Bullet slider in the spacing section moves bullet images closer or farther apart vertically.

Bullets & Numbering

This last section at the bottom of the Text Inspector is where you can customize how bullets and numbers appear in your presentation.

At the top of this section is a pop-up menu where you select whether you want a bullet category or numbers. As with much of Keynote, there is a lot of control buried in the Inspector palette. You have an incredibly wide range of options when it comes to bullets. The "Working with Graphics" section covers this more in depth, but for now, the following provides an overview on the three different bullet categories:

Text bullets This is where you type in any letter or symbol that you'd like Keynote to use as a bullet.

USING RULERS AND TABS

Although each theme will automatically reposition itself as you add text, there are times when you might want to adjust the amount of indentation or distance between the bullet and the text. To do this, adjust the tabs that are shown on the ruler. To see the ruler, select View → Show Rulers or press ⌘+R.

When you click in a text area that has bullets, the ruler will show you the tabs being used. Keynote uses four different types of tab stops: Left Tab, Center Tab, Right Tab, and Decimal Tab.

Moving a tab is easy; just click and drag the appropriate tab to where you want it. Changing the tab type is not as straightforward. To do this, Control+click the tab that you would like to change. A small dialog box showing the four tab icons will appear. Select one from the menu or Control+click the tab again to change it to the next tab type.

Keep in mind that, when you do any custom adjustments on your text layout, the text you change will be out of sync with any other slides that simply use the default parameters set by the theme.

Custom image This is where you can add your own pictures or artwork for bullets. Select Custom Image from the Bullets & Numbering pull-down menu, and then select the artwork you want to use. Keynote will automatically place the image as a bullet.

Image bullet This is the same as a custom image, but it draws upon Keynote's built-in images.

If you select Number from the pop-up menu in the Bullets & Numbering section, all of the bullet points are converted to a series of numbers. Once you select Numbers, another pull-down menu appears and shows the Numbers options. Here you have a few basic numerical or alphabet style types to choose from: Arabic, Roman, Small Roman, Alphabet (Capitalized), and Alphabet (Not Capitalized).

Using the Fonts Palette

As mentioned in the first chapter, Keynote uses the same standard Fonts palette that comes with MacOS X. However, there are a few things to remember that are particular to the Keynote Fonts palette (see Figure 2.17). First, there is the Extras pull-down menu at the bottom of the palette.

You can also open the Fonts palette by pressing ⌘+**T.**

The Extras pull-down menu includes the following options:

Add to Favorites This helps you keep all your favorite font types as part of the Favorites folder. Just select a typeface from the list in the Fonts palette and then select Add to Favorites from the Extras pull-down menu. The typeface, style, and size you selected is now part of the Favorites section of the Font menu. This is a great time saver, particularly when you have to use specific fonts and size for different presentations.

Edit Collections This feature lets you select which typefaces make up a particular collection. For example, you could add different fonts to the Fun collection that better suited your shows.

Edit Size This is a great hidden feature, which allows you to set how you adjust the size of fonts in the Fonts palette. Here you can use a fixed size, a size slider, or both (see Figure 2.18). To go for the gusto, pick the option where you can show both controls; this can give you a lot of flexibility when you are designing your show.

Show Preview This option is a good one to turn on because it will display the name of the font at the top of the Font panel window using that same font. If things get too cluttered for you, you can also hide the preview by selecting Hide Preview from the Extras menu.

Figure 2.17

The Fonts palette

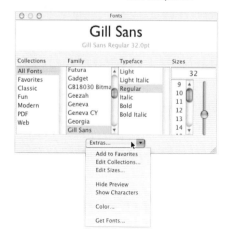

TIPS FROM THE PROS: C. DAVID PINÁ ON USING TYPE

The following are some tips from C. David Piná for how best to use type in your presentations:

Don't use more than 10 lines per screen. Too much text on a screen is disastrous—it clutters the screen and makes the audience work too hard to figure out what is really important. A good rule of thumb is to use no more than 10 lines per screen and even less when possible.

Use type to emphasize or de-emphasize "baggage" words. Any word on a presentation screen can become a design element, and some words—such as *fear* or *love*—come with baggage. Some words are more important than others, so use type to emphasize or de-emphasize these words when necessary.

Avoid "shouting" with type. From a typographic standpoint, it's important to use the proper weight for each part of your message. Think of the weight of the letter as the importance.

If you look at the boldness of an Arial Black, any word you type with that typestyle will become more important—or should. However, you can ruin a design by using Arial Black on all words, which gives the same importance to every design element—which completely ruins the effect.

Imagine someone with an important message yelling each word—because they think it is an important message. The yelling actually negates the value of the message because it numbs the audience.

So, when you begin your design, start with everything at a medium weight (both in size and style—say, use a normal or "Roman style" to start). This gives you room to increase or decrease importance to letters in the design.

Use color and drop shadows to emphasize text. Even when you have a set color scheme, don't be afraid to add an additional color to emphasize points or drop shadows to distinguish the text from the background. For example, in a black-and-white page, you can nicely emphasize letters by putting them in a different color such as red or yellow.

Don't be afraid to use opposite colors. Although some people say to stay away from using colors that are opposites on the color wheel (such as purple and yellow or red and green), the fact is that you see these colors together in nature. Nature is not afraid of playing with the opposites, so you shouldn't be afraid to do so as well.

However, be aware that you convey maximum action when using color opposites. Obviously, you'll need moderate this to not make the design louder than the message; remember, you can yell with colors as well.

Use type size for dramatic effects. Although type needs to be large enough to be readable, sometimes you can use smaller or larger type to create drama in your designs. For example, take a full white screen and put a small black "help" in the middle of the screen, and suddenly the word has much more emotional impact than it did before.

Show Characters As discussed in Chapter 1, "A Quick Keynote Tour," this is where you can select a wide variety of different specialty letters and characters. This is also a great feature to use when you need some special text characters for text bullets.

Color This opens Keynote's Color palette to adjust the color of a selected section of text.

Get Fonts Once you select this from the Extras pull-down menu, your web browser launches and you are directed to a site where Apple will sell you extra fonts for use in your programs.

Working with Graphics

Of all presentation programs, Keynote has the most flexibility in the type of graphics that you can bring into the program and the ways to import them. But there are few ways of creating graphics from within the program. Keynote only has basic drawing tools for drawing simple shapes such as circles, squares, and arrows.

The Shapes pull-down menu behaves much like the Text menu; just select a shape and Keynote places it smack in the middle of the screen. Each shape you select will initially have the same color as specified by the theme you are using. You can change the look and orientation of your shape using the Graphic section of the Inspector palette.

Figure 2.18

Add more control to the Font menu by using both fixed values and a slider control to adjust font sizes.

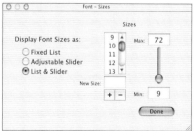

Let's add and modify a shape to see how this works. Follow these steps to make one and then read on to the next section to change it:

1. Create a new Keynote presentation by selecting New from the File pull-down menu or by pressing ⌘+N. This time, pick the Pushpin theme and then click Choose Theme.

2. To give you some room to work with, you should work with a blank slide. You can either delete the two text boxes on the screen by clicking each and pressing the Backspace key. Or, simply select Blank from the Master Slide pull-down menu on the toolbar.

3. Once you have a blank Pushpin background to play with, create a Square shape by selecting the square icon from the Shapes pull-down menu.

4. Now that you've got your square, make sure that it is still selected. You will know that it is selected by the white "handle" squares that appear at its corners. If not, select the square by clicking it.

Using the Graphic Inspector

Once the shape is on the screen, you can use your mouse to position, rotate, and resize your shape as needed. Now let's change the appearance of the shape using the Graphic Inspector.

To open this Inspector, click the Inspector palette icon in the toolbar. After it opens, click the Graphic Inspector icon, which is the second one from the left. Now click your square.

The Graphic Inspector has four areas that pretty much apply to any graphic that you bring in: Fill, Stroke, Shadow, and Opacity (see Figure 2.19).

Fill

A Keynote object can have one of four different fills: Color, Gradient, Image, and None.

Color is a solid hue applied to the shape that you can change using the Color box under the pull-down menu.

Gradient blends the color of the object between two different hues. Once you've selected gradient, you can also do the following:

- Set the colors in the blend.
- Change the angle of the blend, so you can have the gradient go from corner to corner, side to side, and so on.

Image is the default setting for shapes in Keynote because this is what is preset in all the themes. Here you can pick what image is used, as well as define how the graphic will fit into the space. Figure 2.20 illustrates the possibilities.

Figure 2.19

The Graphic Inspector

- **Scale to Fit** makes the image larger or smaller to fit inside the size of the shape. If your picture has a different shape, then part of your image could get cut off when you place it inside the shape.

- **Scale to Fill** makes the object fill the total space of the shape, either by increasing or decreasing the area.

- **Stretch** makes sure that your entire image is shown in the shape. Unfortunately, this usually means that Keynote has to distort the image to be seen, particularly if the shape has a different aspect ratio or size than the image you are using.

- **Original Size** means that no matter how you resize your shape, the original size of the image will not change.

- **Tile** uses copies of the image to fill in any open spaces inside the shape. If you have a small image, this can be a good way to add texture to it.

ROTATING WITH THE MOUSE

Besides clicking and dragging a graphic shape into position, you can also rotate that shape by holding down the Command key while using the mouse. As you move your mouse near a handle, the cursor changes from a straight in-and-out arrow to a curved arrow.

Click and drag on any handle on the object, and the object will rotate the direction that you move—and even show you what degree of rotation you've added to the object.

If you really want to get fancy, you can limit the rotation of your file by 45° by just holding down the Command and Shift keys while rotating the mouse. Now when you rotate a shape it will only move in 45° angles.

Figure 2.20

The methods of fitting images into a shape

Scale to Fit   Scale to Fill

Stretch   Original Size   Tile

Stroke

Stroke adds a line around any object. Here you'll be able change the width, style, and color of that line. The only drawback is that the stroke feature doesn't add a line around alpha channels—just around the image box. Upcoming chapters discuss alpha channels, but for the meantime just know that an alpha channel is what allows images that come into Keynote to have a transparent background. Not being able to stroke the alpha channel spoils the illusion of a free-floating object.

Shadow

Shadow means drop shadow, which is a great tool for adding depth and perspective to text and objects.

Plain   Drop Shadow

You can set the following options:

Color is usually set to black. You can also change the color of the shadow for special effect.

Angle controls where the shadow "falls." For example, a 307° angle means the shadow falls down and to the right.

Offset controls how far from the image the shadow is placed; the higher the offset, the farther away the object appears to be from the background.

Blur softens the shadow by smoothing the shadow's edge. The more blur you have, the more natural the shadow appears. Generally, you would always benefit from a bit of blur in the shadows, unless the object was so small (such as small text) that having blur would make it difficult to read.

Opacity sets how transparent the shadow is. Again, it's a good idea to leave the shadow somewhat transparent; few shadows in nature are totally opaque!

Opacity

At the bottom of the Graphic Inspector is the master Opacity setting for the object, which also applies to text and graphics. Here you can create some nice effects by making background elements mostly transparent. This is called *screening*, which is an effective way to create interesting backgrounds.

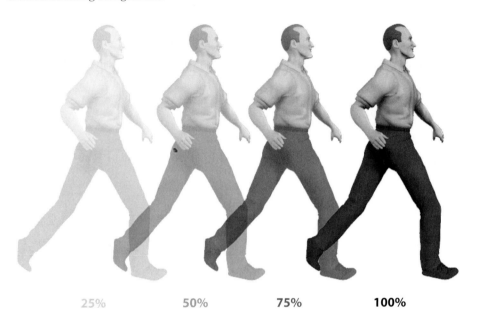

| 25% | 50% | 75% | 100% |

Using Images as Bullets

Many of the themes also contain custom images to use for custom bullets. You can use the bullets that Apple thought were appropriate for each theme or add your own. To add custom bullets to your show, follow these steps:

1. Click a text box that contains bullets.

2. Click the Text Inspector tab in the Inspector palette.

3. On the bottom of the Text Inspector is a thumbnail of the bullet currently being used. To select a different bullet, use the scroll bar in the thumbnail window to reveal the other custom bullet choices that Apple has provided for your shows. Notice that a few of the bullets, such as the Pushpin and the Pearls, actually seem to rest on top of the background, providing a nice bit of 3D perspective on the slide.

FORMAT	DESCRIPTION		Table 2.1
PICT	The standard Macintosh graphic format		**Keynote Graphic File**
GIF	A low-resolution Internet graphic format		**Formats**
TIFF	A standard high-resolution file format often used in print		
JPEG	One of the most ubiquitous web graphics formats		
PDF	Adobe's Portable Document Format, which can contain text as well as graphics		
MOV	QuickTime format		

As mentioned in Chapter 1 you can also create your own bullets (like the one in Figure 2.21) and import them into Keynote using the Custom Image selection in the Bullets & Numbering pull-down menu. Keynote will bring an image in and scale it to a "bullet" size.

Importing Other Graphics

There are three ways to get a graphic file into Keynote:

- Drag the file from the desktop or iPhoto to the Keynote Slide Canvas.
- Cut and paste a graphic from a different application.
- Import the graphic.

Strangely enough, Keynote doesn't have an official "Import" command. Instead, Keynote has an Open Image Library selection on the File menu. When you first select this, Keynote will go to the art collection (which include pictures, object, symbols and borders, and so on) that Apple provides with Keynote.

To see other files, just click the file navigator icon in the Image Library window. Then you can search your hard disk for any files you would like to add.

The variety of graphics file types you can use in a show is also a place where Keynote shines; Table 2.1 lists these types.

QuickTime is actually a major feature in Keynote because it brings not only movies and sound to Keynote but also access to any graphic that can be put into a QuickTime wrapper. QuickTime is like a media suitcase; you can stuff a wide variety of media into QuickTime—from video to photos to audio. For example, Windows graphics are often in BMP format. By just bringing these graphics into a file conversion program such as Cleaner 6 from Discreet or DeBabelizer from Equilibrium Technologies, you can convert this file from a BMP file to any format that Keynote can read—including QuickTime.

In the next chapter, you'll work on bringing in and modifying graphics while you put together a presentation from scratch. Now that you've successfully advanced through two chapters of Keynote basics, the next chapter will give you a chance to flex your Keynote muscles.

Figure 2.21

Creating a custom bullet using the Custom Image selection

Putting It All Together: Building a Presentation

Even if you're on the right track, you'll get run over if you just sit there.—Will Rogers

It's time to put some of those basic skills you learned in the first two chapters to work. Or, if you're allergic to introductory chapters, you've skipped to this chapter to find out how to make Keynote work. In either case, welcome—this is where the fun starts.

In this chapter, you'll build a simple presentation from scratch. Even though you'll add quite a few elements to this show, it shouldn't take too long to put this together—probably no longer than 20 minutes from start to finish. To make it fast, this chapter only gives basic information on the tools used to pull the presentation together; these tools were either covered in depth in the previous two chapters or will be covered later in the book.

Organizing your presentations

Choosing a theme

Adding text and graphics

Creating charts and tables

Setting slide transitions

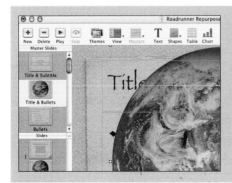

Organizing Your Project

The first thing when creating any presentation is to organize your thoughts—what do you need to say? Not that this is common with many presentations…I distinctly remember one convention when the speaker opened his PowerPoint presentation at the slide sorter level and revealed more than 95 slides. The entire auditorium groaned in despair—there is nothing worse than wading through dozens of slides, most of which probably don't add anything to the presentation.

Presentations are all about condensed information that enhances—but doesn't replace—the speaker. You want the presentation to reinforce each point you bring up while you elaborate on it.

So, with a nod to Warner Bros. cartoons, you are going to make a quick presentation to the board of directors of the Acme Corporation on repurposing all current anti-Roadrunner products to other commercial uses (hey, a new economy demands new thinking!). The presentation needs to be brief, especially because one of the board members has a tendency to fall asleep and snore when any person talks for more than five minutes.

Although creating this presentation might seem a bit silly, keep in mind that you will use just about every tool you might run across when making basic presentations.

Figure 3.1

Start your project off by picking a theme. For this presentation, choose the Parchment theme.

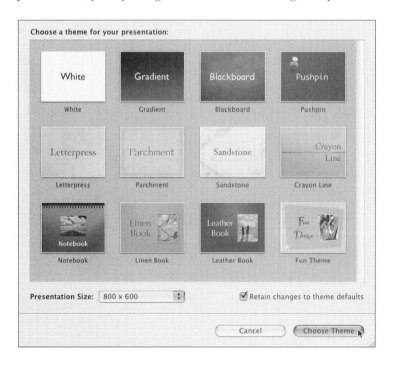

In this presentation, you need to show the following:

- A title slide that encompasses what you're doing

- A bulleted list of the benefits of repurposing

- A chart showing potential market share

- A table that shows how fast products can get to market

- A summary slide of the main points you'll hit (or in this case, you'll crash through)

You'll also need to add the infamous Acme logo to each of the slides, as well as a few other graphics to help boost interest. The board meeting starts in 10 minutes—it's best to get started....

Picking a Theme

First, you need to create a new file and pick a theme. For the purposes of this presentation, pick the Parchment theme. Start Keynote, which automatically shows you the Themes Page dialog box. Click Parchment and then click the Choose Theme button in the lower-right corner of the Choose a Theme for Your Presentation dialog box (as shown in Figure 3.1).

Second, you know that you need at least five slides, so now click the New button in the toolbar four more times. This will add four more slides to your show, for a total of five.

WITH PRESENTATION, LESS REALLY IS MORE

If you are ever faced with trying to condense massive amounts of information into a presentation, check out Peter Norvig's hilarious PowerPoint version of Abraham Lincoln's Gettysburg Address (www.norvig.com/Gettysburg). Norvig, who is the director of search quality at Google, took the entire address and reduced it to six slides.

"How many of us have been frustrated at seeing too many presentations where PowerPoint or other visual aids obscure rather than enhance the point?" notes Norvig on his website. "After one too many bad presentations, I decided to see if I could *do* something about it."

Although Norvig's version of the Gettysburg Address is primarily a parody on slide presentations, it also shows how you can condense any amount of writing to its basic points.

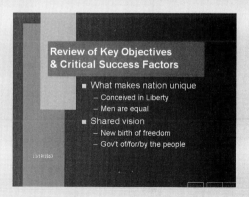

Once you've added these slides to the Slide Organizer, save this file as Roadrunner Repurpose. Now let's set the type of slides you want these to be—from bulleted lists to horizontal photo title cards. This is something you can set or change at any time when you make a presentation in Keynote. For this example, you'll do this using the Masters button on the toolbar.

Another nice thing about setting the type of slide using the Masters feature is that once you've set the type, no matter what theme you use, the slide type will stay the same.

The first slide is the title slide, so it should have a graphic or photo to add some interest. Let's change this to a title with a horizontal photo.

Just click the first slide and then click the Masters icon in the toolbar. This shows the masters list with a series of thumbnail icons of the different slide types. Move your mouse down to Photo – Horizontal, and select it (as shown in Figure 3.2). Your first slide now has the Photo – Horizontal master template, which you'll add a graphic to in a minute.

Now click the second slide. This still shows the Title & Bullets master slide, so leave this as is.

For your third slide on potential market share, let's do a quick pie chart (when you need to obscure the statistics, a pie chart can be your best friend). Clear out the bulleted area by applying the Title – Top master. Again, just click the Master button in the toolbar and select Title – Top, as shown in Figure 3.3.

Your fourth slide displays a table showing when products will be available, so like the third slide, change it from a title with bullet points to a Title – Top master. You don't have to do this ahead of time, but it makes things a bit easier as you work.

Finally, the last slide is still a Title & Bullets master, which is perfect for your summary slide—leave this alone for now. Now it's time to add the text.

Figure 3.2

The Photo – Horizontal master slide

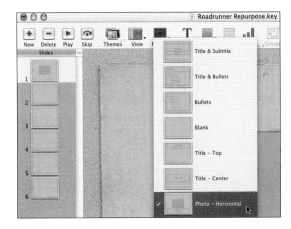

Adding Text

One of the great things about Keynote is how easy it is to add different elements to your presentation. Text is especially easy; you can type directly onto the screen by double-clicking the text box that says *Double click to edit* when you start a new theme, you can use the Text icon in the toolbar, or you can edit text using the Outline view. When you are first roughing together your show, typing up your project using the Outline view is the best way to go. By using the Outline view, you can concentrate on what you want to say in your presentation, as opposed to concentrating on how it looks.

To start editing the text of your slides in the Outline view, click the Views icon on the toolbar and then select Outline, as shown in Figure 3.4. This changes the thumbnails of the slides into smaller thumbnails with text boxes. Because you've already set up the type of slide used in this example, you can enter the text directly in each slide via the Slide Organizer.

With the Slide Organizer in Outline view, click the first slide and type **Roadrunner Products**.

In the Slide Canvas, this text is now the title of the first slide. Let's do this with the next slide, which has a title and several bullet points.

Click the second slide in the Slide Organizer and type **Why Repurpose?** As Figure 3.5 shows, you've now labeled your second slide. Now it's time to edit the bullet points.

Figure 3.3

Select Title – Top as the master slide for your chart and table slides.

Figure 3.5

Add in the titles and bullets by just typing in the Outline view of the Slide Organizer.

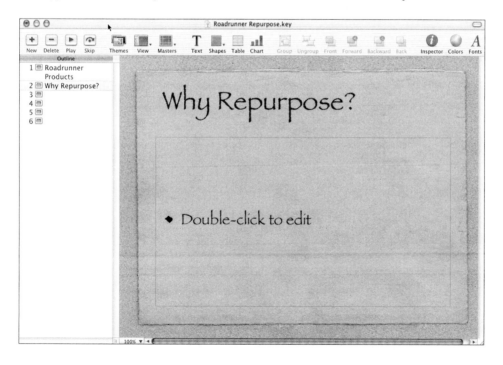

Figure 3.4

The Outline view is a good place to add and organize the text in your presentation.

After you've typed in **Repurposing Benefits**, hit the Enter or Return key. Keynote automatically adds a new slide after your Repurposing Benefits slide. But wait—you don't want a new slide; you were looking to add a bullet point.

To make this a bullet point, press the Tab key. Keynote will change the new slide into a bullet point inside your Why Repurpose slide (see Figure 3.6).

Now type **Coyote Market Dwindling**. This is now a bullet point, complete with the proper font (thanks to the great theme you picked at the beginning of the project).

Now hit Enter or Return again and type the following bullet points for this slide (remember to hit Enter or Return after each bullet point):

- Roadrunners can't be stopped
- Desert Conservationist complaints
- $5 billion spent on Anti-Roadrunner product development

If you make a mistake and accidentally create a new slide instead of a bullet point, click and drag that slide under the Why Repurpose slide, and Keynote will automatically add it to the bulleted list. To move a bullet point up or down in the list, click and drag that text to the spot you want in the list. Keynote will automatically move your bullet point to its new position.

Figure 3.6

Pressing the Tab key indents each new point under the title slide as a bullet point.

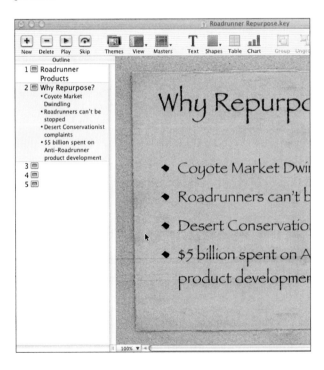

Now enter the titles for the next three slides:

Potential Market Share

Production Schedule

Summary

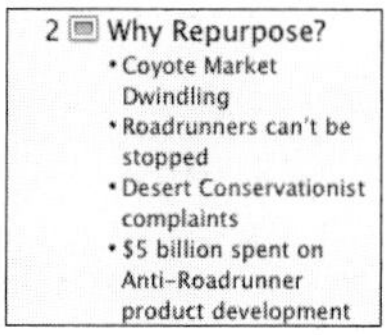

On the last Summary slide, add in the following bullet points, either by clicking the bullet points in the Slide Canvas where it says *Double click to edit* or by adding it through the Outline view of the Slide Organizer:

- Roadrunners unstoppable, Coyote market declining
- Help offset $5 billion R&D costs
- Senior citizen gardeners and hazelnut farmers = Huge untapped market
- Can ship in two quarters

Figure 3.7

Text ahoy!

Using Alignment Guides

Another great feature with Keynote is the ability to set up alignment guides so you can be sure that text and graphics are consistently aligned from slide to slide, as well as proportionally spaced from top to bottom. Let's add another line of text to the first title slide to show how this works, as well as format a little bit of text.

Click the first slide, the Roadrunner Products slide. Now click the Text icon in the toolbar, which will drop a text box in the center of the slide, as shown in Figure 3.7.

To edit the text, double-click the word *Text*, and enter **Repurposing For The Future**. Now you've got a subtitle, but it is in the middle of the screen. Let's move the *Roadrunner Products* line to the top of the screen and move the *Repurposing For The Future* line to the bottom of the page.

Click and drag the Roadrunner Products line to the top of the screen. Notice as you are doing this that a yellow line appears in the middle of the screen, which disappears as you move the line farther to the right or left. This is the center alignment guide that was developed as part of this theme. You can set up your own alignment guides, either when you set up your own themes or as you are working with new master slides. Move this line above the center picture placeholder, using the center alignment guide to put the title in the center of the screen (see Figure 3.8).

Now click and drag the *Repurposing For The Future* text below the picture frame. When you move the text lower, you'll get two alignment guides to help you out—on both the horizontal and vertical axes. Center this text by moving the line so that both the yellow horizontal and vertical alignment guides display.

Figure 3.8

Align text using Keynote's alignment guides.

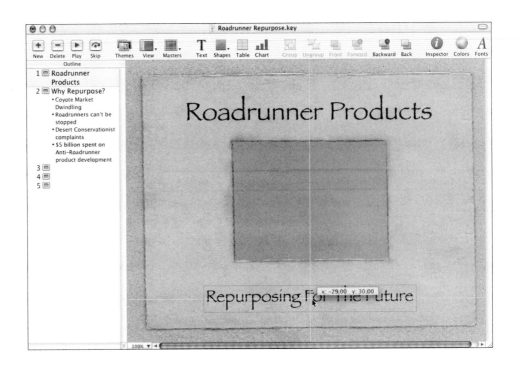

Adding Image Library Graphics

Now let's add some graphics from the 100 images and symbols that ship with Keynote. To get at these images, simply select File → Open Image Library.

This opens the folder of the five Image Library files: Chart Colors, Flags, Objects, Pictures, and Symbols & Borders. All of these files are actually Keynote presentations, where instead of slides each presentation is simply a collection of images.

For a full list and images of all the graphics in the Image Library, see Appendix B.

With the Image Library folder open, double-click Objects.key. This opens the 31 images of objects with alpha channels.

Alpha channels are an additional layer in graphics that provide 256 levels of transparency. The alpha channel is what allows you to add an image into Keynote and not show the image's original background.

Let's create the Acme company logo, which is a globe with the letter *A* stamped on it (clearly this company needs a logo redesign). To do this, first scroll down the list of slides until you come to a picture of the earth on slide 19. Click that slide and then select the earth image by clicking it, as in Figure 3.9. Now copy that image onto the Mac clipboard by selecting Edit → Copy or by pressing ⌘+C.

Now go back to the Roadrunner Repurpose presentation by selecting it under the Window menu. Now that you are back, you'll create the Acme logo by pasting and resizing the earth image with a text letter *A* over the top. However, this will be more than a bit tedious to do for each slide—can you imagine what would happen if you had to do this for 30 slides?

Fortunately, there is an easier way; instead of creating a separate logo on each slide, you'll just add a singe logo onto a master slide. To do this, open the master slide thumbnails by selecting Views → Show Master Slides in the toolbar. The master slides are now visible in the Slide Organizer.

Click the second master slide from the top, which is Title & Bullets (as shown in Figure 3.10).

With the Title & Bullets slide selected, paste the image of the earth onto the Slide Canvas. Notice that the earth image not only fills up the screen on your Title & Bullets slide, but also on the second and last slides in the presentation (see Figure 3.11).

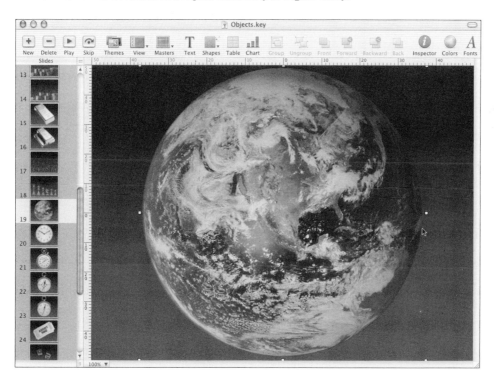

Figure 3.9

Click on the earth image to select it.

Ah, the joy of master slides—add anything to one master slide, and every slide that uses that template also changes. This is where you make global changes to Keynote and also where you create your own themes.

For more information on creating your own themes, see Chapter 8, "Do-It-Yourself Documentary: Adding Audio and Video Elements."

Now let's warp the earth image into a quick logo:

1. Select the earth image.

2. Scale it down to a small earth that would fit on one corner of the slide. Do this by clicking once on the earth image and then grabbing a handle with a mouse, dragging in toward the image.

3. Now move the earth image to the lower-right side of the slide.

4. With the earth image selected, click the Inspector icon in the toolbar. This opens the Graphic Inspector.

5. Make the earth image transparent by adjusting the Opacity control on the bottom of the Graphic Inspector (see Figure 3.12). You can change the opacity by dragging the control bar to the left or by simply entering a lower percentage than 100 in the Opacity percentage box. To get a nice "screened" look, adjust the opacity to about 36 percent.

Figure 3.11

By adding a graphic to a master slide, you add it to every slide in your show that uses that master slide. Here, you can spread the world to several slides with just one click and drag.

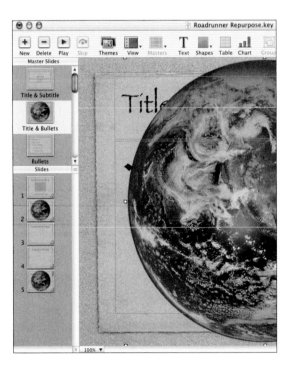

6. Now add the Acme *A*. To do so, click the Text icon on the toolbar. A text box appears in the middle of the slide.

7. Double-click the text box, and enter a capital **A**.

8. Next, click the Fonts icon in the toolbar. The Parchment theme automatically sets the typeface used by the text to Papyrus, which is just not going to work with this Acme logo.

9. With the *A* logo still selected, choose Gil Sans from the Font menu, set the style to Bold, and set the font size to 96, which should be large enough to cover most of the globe.

10. Now click the Inspector icon in the toolbar, and—with the letter *A* still selected—click the Text icon in the Inspector palette. This opens the Text Inspector, which is where you make formatting changes to the text.

Figure 3.12

Adjust your object's transparency using the Opacity slider.

The difference between the Text Inspector and the Font window is pretty basic. In the Font window, you can pick what typeface, style, and size you want to use. In the Text Inspector, you can choose the color, alignment, spacing, and style of bullet points.

11. Click the color box below the Color & Alignment title, and set the color from dark brown to white.

12. Drag the letter *A* to the center of the earth image. If your letter *A* appears behind the earth image, click the Front icon on the toolbar, which moves it in front of the earth image.

Now click the Graphic tab in the Inspector palette. To get the *A* to stand out against the world image, you'll add a drop shadow. With the *A* still selected, click the Shadow radio box. Your letter *A* now has a nice drop shadow to separate it from the earth image.

You'll need to add this logo into the Title – Top master slide. To make this a bit easier, you'll group the earth image and the letter *A* together. To do this, select both by clicking the letter *A* and then holding the Shift key down and clicking the earth image.

Now group these two images together by selecting the menu command Arrange → Group. Now you can move both objects as one. In this case, you need to copy it over the other slide master. Copy the grouped world and A object.

Now click the Title – Top master slide in the Slide Organizer and paste the combined graphic. Keynote will automatically remember where the image came from, so when you paste it, the graphic will go back to the same spot from which you copied it.

Finally, let's add a graphic to the opening page. Go back to the Image Library folder and double-click `Pictures.key`. When the Pictures show opens, click the third slide showing the open road. Click and copy the picture of the open road.

Now go back to the Roadrunner Repurpose show and paste the road image onto the first slide. The first slide that uses the Title master slide is now completely covered by the road image, but you can easily fix this. With the picture still selected, click the Back icon in the toolbar. The picture is nicely placed behind the background, with the image only showing through the horizontal picture frame, as shown in Figure 3.13. You can adjust how the picture is framed by clicking and then dragging the image within the frame. To get the image to look like the figure, you'll need to resize the image.

Creating a Chart

To show market share, you'll create a pie chart with some dubious numbers to impress the members of the board. Click the third slide in your really big show, which should be labeled *Potential Market Share*.

Now add a chart to this slide by clicking the Chart icon in the toolbar. By default, Keynote adds in a bar chart, which nicely complements the Parchment theme (see Figure 3.14). Keynote also automatically opens the Chart Inspector in the Inspector palette, as well as the Chart Data Editor, a simple spreadsheet program where you enter the data for your chart.

Change the bar to a pie chart by clicking the Chart thumbnail in the Chart Inspector and then selecting Pie from the bottom of the menu (see Figure 3.15).

Entering Chart Info

Now let's add the pertinent figures to the pie chart. First, you'll change the categories. You'll make all the changes in the Chart Data Editor. Double-click the first cell in the top-left corner of the Chart Data Editor, labeled *1999*.

With the *1999* selected, type **Golfers**. The pie chart will update that market segment so the section reads *Golfers* instead of *1999*.

Figure 3.13

The title slide with the image added.

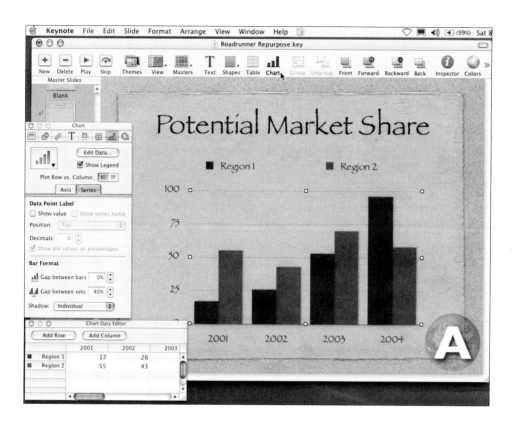

Figure 3.14

Your new bar chart, courtesy of Keynote

Second, you should add a number to show the correct percentage. Instead of 91, enter 10 in the cell below Golfers.

Now change the other categories as follows:

Coyotes	Seniors	Publishers
3	61	26

To remove the other pie segments (such as 2004), select them in the Chart Data Editor and press the Backspace key. When finished, your pie chart should look like Figure 3.16.

Changing Pie Slice Color

This is good, but it would be nice to emphasize the Seniors market size, as well as show how sales to Coyotes have severely dropped off.

Let's start with the Coyote drop-off, which is the 3% segment on the chart. Click the 3% pie "slice" so that you see two handles on the back and one in the front. You might have to click the slice twice to select the individual pie slice and not the entire chart. Now click the Graphics icon in the Inspector palette.

Figure 3.15

Cooking up a pie

Let's change the color of this particular slice by selecting Color Fill from the Fill Type menu in the Graphic Inspector. Instead of an image, the 3% pie slice is now a solid color. Change the color to bright red by double-clicking the color box and then clicking on red.

Exploding a Pie Wedge

To really get your audience's attention, let's move the Seniors section out of the pie a little bit. To do this, just double-click the large Seniors pie slice (making sure you've only selected the Seniors pie segment, and not the entire chart).

With the Seniors pie segment selected, click the Chart icon in the Inspector palette. At the bottom of the Chart palette is the control you need, which is the Explode Wedge control in the Pie Wedge section (hey, I didn't make up these names!). To move the Seniors pie segment away from the pie, slide the Explode Wedge control to the right, as shown in Figure 3.17. The more you move it, the farther away the segment appears from the pie.

Adding a Table

Now click the fourth slide, which is where you'll create the Production Schedule table. To add a table, click the Table icon in the toolbar. Keynote will automatically place a table in the middle of the screen, as you can see in Figure 3.18.

To edit this, click the table and then go to the Table icon in the Inspector palette. Let's make this table simple, with just two rows and four columns (four quarters with explanation text below them).

Figure 3.16

Updating the pie chart

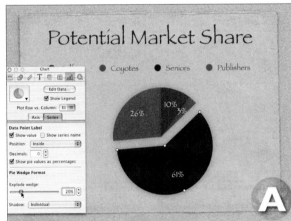

Figure 3.17

Your new exploded pie!

The Table Inspector is where you customize the number of rows and columns, the alignment of the text, and the shape and fill of the table cells. To adjust this table, add four columns and two rows using the Rows and Columns boxes, as shown in Figure 3.19.

Now you need to enter the text for each table element so that it looks like this:

Q1	Q2	Q3	Q4
Redesign	Produce Units	Market	

Let's leave nothing to the imagination and add a money image to the last cell under Q4. Go to the Window menu, and select `Objects.key`. If you accidentally closed the window that `Objects.key` was in, select the Image Library folder. Scroll down to slide 16 and copy the picture of the gold bars. Now go back to the Roadrunner Products presentation, click the Production Schedule slide, click the last cell in the table under Q4, and paste.

Presto! Keynote adds in the gold bars into the cell, nicely resized to fit the table cell area, as you can see in Figure 3.20.

Setting Slide Transitions

How are you doing so far—are you still with me? Good, you are on the home stretch. Now all you need to do is add some transitions between slides and between some of the elements. First, let's add a single slide transition type for all five slides.

Click a slide in the Slide Organizer and then select Select All from the Edit menu or press ⌘+A. If all the slides have been selected, then each slide thumbnail should have a yellow border. Now that you've selected all five slides, click the Inspector icon in the toolbar. Click the Slide icon in the Inspector palette.

Figure 3.19

Use the Table Inspector to adjust the table to four columns and two rows.

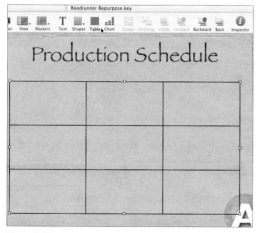

Figure 3.18

Add a table to the slide by clicking the Table icon in the toolbar.

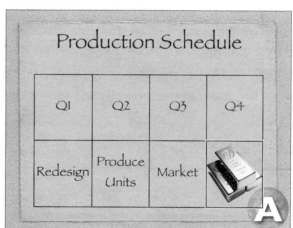

Figure 3.20

Making your point golden: The gold bars are part of the Image library that ships with Keynote.

Figure 3.21

At the bottom of the Slide Organizer is where you set transition type and speeds.

Figure 3.22

You can not only transition between slides, but you can also use builds to add transitions to different objects—from tables to charts.

The bottom control in that palette is the slide's Transition control, where you can set the type and speed of transitions. In this case, select Cube (one of Keynote's nice 3D quartz effects), with a Left to Right transition and a fairly good speed (see Figure 3.21).

That's good for the overall slides, but it would be nice to also have each bullet point come in separately. To do this, click the thumbnail of slide 2 in the Slide Organizer and then select the bullet points within the Slide Canvas.

Now go back to the Inspector palette and click the icon for builds, which is the fifth icon from the left, right next to the Text icon.

Chapter 8 talks more about builds; for now, just know that this is where you control how individual elements come on and off the screen. Set the transition type (the Build Style) to Move In (on the Build In tab). Notice how the small preview screen above the controls in the Build Inspector shows the bullets moving onto the Slide Canvas separately from the background.

To make this slide a bit more interesting, let's have each bullet come in separately. At the bottom of the Build Inspector, use the menus to set the Move In direction from Bottom to Top and the Delivery menu to By Column. Now with each mouse click a new column in the table will appear on the screen (see Figure 3.22).

Finally, let's use the same technique to set a fancy transition for the pie chart in slide 3. Click the third slide in the Slide Organizer and then click the pie. Now click the Build Inspector, set the Transition type to Twirl, and set the Delivery option to By Series. Now each pie segment will spin into place.

One last bit of advice here—keep the transition speeds pretty fast—slow transitions do not make for snappy presentations.

Show Time!

Congratulations, that's it! To see your masterpiece at work, click the first slide and click the Play button in the toolbar. As you click the mouse, you will automatically go through each slide.

In the next chapters, you'll learn about the various controls in the Inspector palette, as well as build some real-world Keynote presentations.

PART II

Keynote Presentations for the Real World

Too often software is designed and tested under theoretical conditions, and most of those conditions ultimately don't apply to the job you need to do right now. Fortunately, Keynote was rigorously tested in a business application for more than a year before it came out. However, you might have difficulty imagining how to *maximize* Keynote to the work you need to do. That's what this part of the book is about—creating real-world projects that introduce you to the finer sections of Keynote.

Chapter 4 **Sales Presentation: Chart and Table Finesse**

Chapter 5 **Class Lesson: Learning with Pizzazz**

Chapter 6 **Artist Portfolio: A Portable Image Gallery**

Chapter 7 **Video Storyboard: Building Slide Actions**

Chapter 8 **Do it Yourself Documentary: Adding Audio and Video Elements**

Sales Presentation: Chart and Table Finesse

Every crowd has a silver lining.—Phineas Taylor (P.T.) Barnum (1810–1891)

Using Keynote for business presentations seems like a no-brainer—after all, this program was originally developed to show Steve Job's Macworld Expo presentations. Yet knowing what buttons to push isn't enough—you can place all kinds of graphics and charts into a presentation and never get your point across to your audience.

In this chapter, you'll see how Keynote handles charts, one of the most effective—and often most poorly implemented—business presentation tools. While you work with charts, you'll create a sales presentation that integrates the slides you create. By the end of this chapter, you'll be well versed at making charts that emphasize your main points.

Creating a Seattle sales extravaganza

Working with charts

Modifying a chart with the Chart Inspector

Tips from the Pros: Gene Zelazny on Making Great Charts

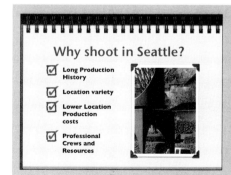

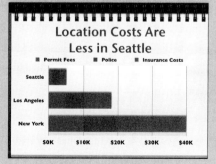

Building a Seattle Locations Sales Extravaganza

To begin, let's build a quick sales presentation for the Film and Video Office of Seattle, my new hometown and one of the most beautiful cities in the Pacific Northwest. Many people have a perception that Seattle rains all the time, which causes mass depression and the consumption of a lot of coffee. Not true! Although it rains often (which is why the area is so beautiful), Seattle is actually not the rain capital of the country, people are happy, and...well...we do drink far too much coffee, but that can be a plus when you are working a 15-hour production day, right?

In this presentation, you'll learn there are many advantages to shooting films and television programs in Seattle—from the variety of locations to the low cost of production, especially when compared to Los Angeles or New York. So, that's the goal; now let's organize the materials before using Keynote. There are three main steps for any presentation: defining the audience and distribution of the presentation, establishing the main points, and formatting the slides.

Step 1: Defining the Audience and Distribution

With every production I do, I tend to start backwards because determining how you will present your show has a major impact on design and production. So even before you figure out the main slide points for this example, it is critical that you answer some key questions. For example, are you talking to a big group or doing a one-on-one presentation? Will you need to hand out a print version of the presentation?

So, one of the first questions you should try to solve is about your audience. Are you talking to a professional audience that can grasp every high-level technical detail, or do you need to explain basic concepts as you go? This determines not only the type of information you present but also the complexity and even the number of slides you plan to show. In this case, let's assume you are talking to professional film and television producers and directors who are looking for new locations for their productions.

Next, you need to figure out the technical variables for the actual presentation. For example, will this presentation be viewed on-screen or projected? An on-screen presentation has an advantage over a projected presentation in that your iBook, PowerBook, or desktop screen is much brighter and has better contrast than a projected image. Consequently, you'll be able to use more complex backgrounds, graphics, and serif fonts within your presentation because you won't have to imagine whether your audience will be able to read the screen from 50 feet away. With Keynote, this means that complex themes such as Parchment, Sandstone, or Crayon Line are usable.

On the other hand, a projected presentation is subject to many variables—such as how much ambient light is in the room, the quality of the projector, and even the distance of the audience from the screen.

Also, before you begin working on your presentation, confirm the information you get. Your presentation's circumstances could have changed or could have been reported incorrectly in the first place.

Finally, once you've made some decisions about your presentation, be aware that you will probably have to modify your show for each group to which you speak. In other words, you don't want to assume that a single presentation will work for every audience. There is nothing as painful as having to watch a "generic" presentation; your audience will know that whatever you are saying has just been "recycled."

For the sake of the Seattle show, let's assume that this will be an on-screen presentation that you can give to a small group of producers or directors on your laptop at a studio office. We could also use this show as a Portable Document Format (PDF) for printing or as a QuickTime file that can be downloaded online. Finally, let's also assume that as film and video professionals the audience will be as follows:

- They'll have very little time to watch a presentation.
- They need a printout of the show.
- They are looking for clearly defined advantages to shooting in Seattle.

So let's start laying out the presentation. Feel free to try this on your own or just read along.

Because this will be a printout as well as an on-screen show, you'll use the Notebook theme. So, open a new file in that theme and apply one of the pictures of Seattle to the "front cover" by following these steps:

1. Create a new document (⌘+N).
2. Select the Notebook theme.
3. Change the first slide to a Photo – Horizontal master.
4. Enter **Shooting in Seattle** as the title on that page.

UPDATING YOUR PRESENTATION QUICKLY AND EASILY

Don't forget that you can update your show by merely changing the theme of your show. For example, let's say you used a theme such as Parchment because you planned on printing your show. If you needed to project this presentation, you could change the theme to Gradient, which will give you white letters on a black background (which is much easier to read than black text on a yellow background).

5. Open the `Seattle Sales Show Images.key` presentation from the Chapter 4 folder on the CD-ROM. In this case, grab an image that shows the Space Needle to use on the front cover (slide 2 from `Seattle Sales Show Images.key`).

6. Save the Keynote file with the opening Shooting in Seattle slide as `Seattle Sales Presentation.key`.

Step 2: Establishing the Main Points

Now you need to figure out what you want to say in this short presentation that will not take more than five minutes of the audience's time.

There are four main points to make in this example:

- You want to dispel Seattle myths, such as "Seattle is the rain capital of the United States."
- You want to show the wide variety of locations available in Seattle compared to Los Angeles or New York.
- You want to give examples of other shows and films that have been shot in Seattle.
- You want to provide financial information that shows how less expensive it is to shoot in Seattle than Los Angeles or New York.

Less is not more! Adding too much information on a slide is too common a mistake. Keep in mind that it takes the same amount of time to present five ideas on one slide as it does to present one idea on five different slides. In his book *Say It With Charts*, Gene Zelazny makes a great point: It is better to separate points than to try and cram them all into one slide. This allows the audience to concentrate on each point as you present it, instead of spending their time trying to read a slide that is too dense with information.

Step 3: Choosing a Chart, Graph, or Bullet Point

Now you can quickly outline the points in Keynote to serve as placeholders for the all the slides to come. After the title slide, these are the points to hit:

Summarize the show This is where you tell the audience what you are going to present. This is an old, time-tested presentation principle: Summarize what you are going to say, say it, and then recap what you've said at the end.

Long production history Long before *Sleepless in Seattle*, Washington and Seattle has been a prime location for film and video productions. Starting in 1933 with *Tugboat Annie*, production companies have used Seattle for a wide variety of motion picture and television projects, from the movie *Assassins* to the hit television show *Frasier*. This is an important point to emphasize.

Seattle location variety Here you need to show, rather than tell about, the great scenery in Seattle. This could be one of several slides that feature pictures of the city.

Lower production costs Compared to New York and Los Angeles, the cost of shooting in Seattle is incredibly low and a great selling point.

Seattle production advantages This will be a bullet chart that includes information about the following:

- Wide streets for easy production access
- Architectural variety
- Waterfront views
- Lush parks
- Easy airport access

Now you need to separate the slides into types. Which points would be better set off as bulleted points? A basic rule of thumb is that anything that implies or demands a comparison is a chart, a list that needs to be checked off works best as a table, and everything else works as bullet points. Like most general rules, feel free to toss out the rules if it doesn't make sense for your production.

In this case, the second and third slides will work just fine as bulleted lists. However, the third slide implies a comparison between New York, Los Angeles, and Seattle, so you'll make that a chart. Finally, the fifth slide is more of a checklist, so you'll make that a table. In fact, you can make the last point of that slide—airport access—its own slide, so you can create a chart comparing the time it takes to get from the airport to the city.

Working with Charts

Because the previous chapter only touched on charts, let's dig into the chart for the third slide, where you compare location production costs for New York, Los Angeles, and Seattle. Because these costs change daily in real life, you'll use some approximate data just for the purposes of creating this chart (in other words, if you are with the film departments for Los Angeles or New York, relax! It's just an example for the book...).

Let's go back to the Notebook presentation, and click the New button to create a new slide. Change the slide master to Title – Top. Now you can add the title of the slide, which is *Location Costs Are Lower in Seattle*. This might sound too obvious, but it's always a good idea to be as direct in your message as possible. Remember, the chart is only there to back up your point, not to make the point by itself. Trust me, you don't want the audience guessing what you are trying to say; chances are it will be just the opposite of what you are aiming for or that you will just confuse them.

Figure 4.1

Replace the generic information created by the Chart Data Editor with the three city names in this example.

Now add the chart by clicking the Chart button in the toolbar. This is nothing new; you did this in Chapter 3, "Putting It All Together: Building a Presentation." In this case, you should stick with the bar chart.

To change the generic chart data, you'll need to type the data into the Chart Data Editor. First, you'll need to set the comparison subjects: Seattle, New York, and Los Angeles. Enter these so that they fill in the names in the first row, as shown in Figure 4.1.

Now enter the columns so that they read *Permit Fees*, *Police*, and *Insurance*. Once you have entered these, add the numerical data so that your data looks like this in the Chart Data Editor:

	Permit Fees	Police	Insurance
New York	10	10	20
Los Angeles	5	5	8
Seattle	1	2	2

Now you should have a bar chart with three groups (Permit Fees, Police, and Insurance) that have three bars apiece (see Figure 4.2).

Although this bar chart is accurate, there are many things you can change to make it more readable. First, let's lose the Bradley Handwriting font; frankly, it's just too hard to read. In addition, let's change the typeface used on the legend, series titles, and scale to a Gil Sans Bold font (see Figure 4.3). To do this, click a text element, click the Fonts palette, and then select Gil Sans Bold from the list of fonts.

Now you need to reduce the font size on the legend because when you changed the font type, it made the *Los Angeles* label too big for the space. Select the Legend text, open the Fonts palette, and use the Size slider to adjust the size to 20. Now to start some real tweaking—it's time for the Chart Inspector.

Figure 4.2

Your chart, with the new subject names

USING KEYBOARD SHORTCUTS FOR CHARTS

While you are working with data in the Chart Data Editor, it's faster to move from cell to cell using keyboard commands than to click in each cell. The following keyboard shortcuts move you around each cell in the editor so you can quickly make changes as needed:

Return Completes an entry in a cell and moves down

Shift+Return Completes an entry in a cell and moves up

Tab Completes an entry and moves to the right

Shift+Tab Completes an entry and moves to the left

Home Moves to the beginning of a row

End Moves to the last nonblank cell to the right in the current row

Arrow keys Moves cells to left, right, up, and down

Modifying a Chart with the Chart Inspector

Stored inside the Inspector palette is the Chart Inspector, which contains all the controls for customizing your chart. Let's take a quick look at this (see Figure 4.4).

There are actually three parts to the Chart Inspector: the top panel, the Axis tab, and the Series tab.

The top area has only four controls:

- The Chart Type button
- The Edit Data button, which opens the Chart Data Editor spreadsheet (the simple cell editor where you enter in your data)
- The Show Legend radio button, which hides or shows the legend of your chart
- The Plot Row vs. Column option, which switches the chart grouping from row to column or vice versa

Click the Chart Type button, and you'll find that Keynote only has eight different types of charts (see Figure 4.5). However, by using the various controls inside the program, you can easily customize your chart. You can only access those controls if the chart is selected; otherwise, they will be grayed out.

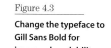

Figure 4.3

Change the typeface to Gill Sans Bold for improved readability.

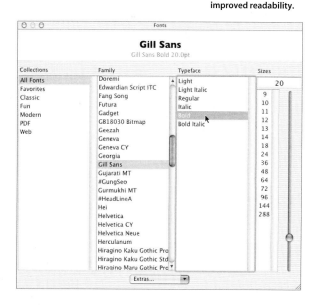

Below the top section you'll find the Axis and Series tabs. The Axis tab is where you format the grid and look of the axes used in your chart (see Figure 4.6).

Clicking any of the four icons in Axes & Border box shows or hides your charts borders. A chart without borders looks really cool, so let's remove the sides of the chart by clicking the left and right sides and "unselecting" them. This now makes a nice, clean look for the slide, with the only horizontal grid lines showing across the chart.

In the next section, you can change the range of the value axis, which in English means that you can adjust the value range within your chart. With this chart still selected, click the Steps arrow so that it reads 5 instead of 4. Notice how the grid increases to five steps instead of four. Also, the value numbers automatically redivide to reflect this change. For the purposes of this chart, enter a range from 0 to 20 and set the number of steps 6 (see Figure 4.7).

Finally, the last box in the Axis tab lets you format the numbers in the value axis. In this case, you want to show that the values are in thousands of dollars. This is a breeze in Keynote; set the Prefix option to a dollar sign ($) and then set the Suffix option to K for thousands. If you have a really large number in your chart, then you can also use a comma to separate the numbers. If you are working in foreign currency, Keynote can also show British pounds, Japanese Yen, a percentage sign, and M for millions, and B for billions.

The Series tab only has two sections: one for the data point label and the other for the bar chart format (which, when you are working with a pie chart, transforms into the infamous Exploding Pie Wedge control from Chapter 3).

The data point label is useful if you want to show the values that each bar or data point represents. However, be careful when you add data point values; although sometimes useful, they often can clutter up your chart.

Figure 4.4

The Chart Inspector (located in the Inspector palette) contains all the controls for customizing your chart.

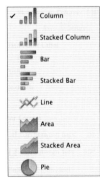

Figure 4.5

Inside Keynote you'll find eight different chart types that you can use within your show—even after you've entered the data.

Figure 4.6

The Axis section of the Chart Inspector is where you'll add or remove grid lines and tick marks in your chart.

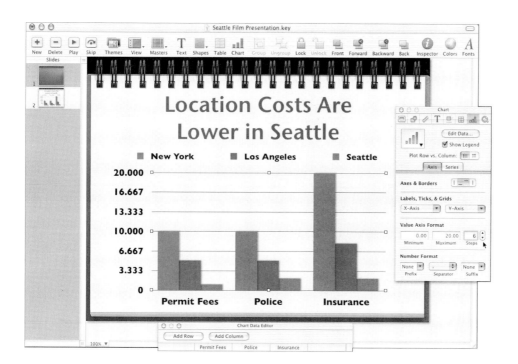

Figure 4.7

Adding or removing steps in the Axis section increases or decreases the value levels in your chart.

To see what this would look like, click the tallest bar (which represents the New York data) and then check the Show Value box in the Series tab. Set the position for the data to Outside. The numerical values for each of the New York bars are now displayed on top of the bars, as shown in Figure 4.8. Again, this looks a little cluttered, so let's turn off Show Value to remove the data values.

Figure 4.8

You can display data figures within or on the outside of the bars.

Like all text in Keynote, you can change the color, typeface, and type style of all the text in a chart by simply by clicking that text and then adjusting it using either the Inspector, Color, or Text palettes.

Close, but No Cigar

The chart so far, as shown in Figure 4.9, has all the elements that you want, but it isn't very effective.

To understand why, count all the elements (except for the labels) you see on the screen. With each of the three groups, there are three bars, making nine data points. This is a problem—you are only trying to get one point across, yet you are using nine pieces of data to show this. Also, the main focus of the chart is the different costs of each cost

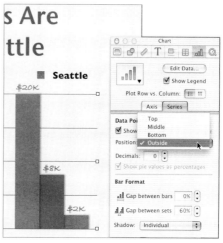

Figure 4.10

The Stacked Column format in the Chart Type pull-down menu is a good chart to show multiple data points in one segment.

segment, rather than what you would spend in those cities. Remember the title of the chart says *Location Costs Are Lower in Seattle* and not *here are the various costs for permit fees, police, and insurance when on location in Seattle, New York, and Los Angeles.* You have to lead your audience to the conclusion quickly and effortlessly.

This is actually a simple fix; you will change the orientation of the chart and then its format. First, let's make some adjustments to put the emphasis back on the cities and not the costs. Select the chart and then go back to the Chart Inspector. Now click the Plot Row vs. Column button so that the right icon is selected. Now this chart shows the costs for New York, Los Angeles, and Seattle grouped together, with the three bars representing the type of costs involved in each city.

This is much better; you can clearly see that Seattle is much cheaper than New York or Los Angeles. However, you can do one better than this by using a stacked bar chart.

With the chart still selected, click the Chart Type button icon and select Stacked Column (see Figure 4.10).

This is much better; instead of nine data points, you have just three—and now without a doubt Seattle is the low-cost leader. To add a bit more pizzazz to this chart, let's add a gradient background and set it up so that the each bar grows from the bottom to the top.

To add the gradient to the background, select the chart by clicking it and then clicking the Graphic button at the top of the Inspector. Instead of going to the Chart Inspector, go to the Graphic Inspector and change the Fill Type from None to Gradient. Now the background has a nice gradient to set each of the bars against, and the bottom-to-top gradient gives a stronger impression of growth.

Figure 4.9

Although the chart has the data elements you need to show, it needs work to make it clear to an audience.

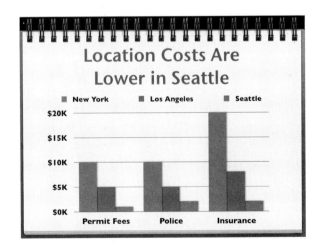

TIPS FROM THE PROS: GENE ZELAZNY ON MAKING GREAT CHARTS

Gene Zelazny is the director of visual communications for McKinsey and Company and has more than 40 years experience working with colleagues and clients to design powerful management reports and presentations. Zelazny frequently presents his ideas at the world's top business schools, including Harvard, Columbia, Cornell, Wharton, Hass, MIT, Oxford, Kellogg, Stanford, Tuck, INSEAD, and others. In his book *Say It With Charts: The Executive's Guide to Visual Communication* (McGraw-Hill, 2001), Zelazny shows how to effectively design, create, and use charts within business presentations. With the following tips, he provides some key information about using charts that will benefit anyone who has ever had to give a presentation:

Make chart titles specific. The key to choosing the appropriate chart form is for you to be clear about the specific point you want to make. Make sure your chart title focuses on the specific aspect of the data you want to emphasize. Don't keep your point a secret; let your message head the chart.

Use pie charts when making "component" comparisons. A pie chart best demonstrates a component comparison. Because a circle gives such a clear impression of being a whole, a pie chart is ideally suited for one purpose: showing the size of each part as a percentage of some whole. If your message contains key words such as *share, percentage of total,* or *accounted for X percent,* then you can be sure you are dealing with a component comparison.

Use bar charts when making "item" comparisons. A bar chart best demonstrates an item comparison. In an item comparison, you want to compare how things rank: are they about the same, or is one more or less than the others? If your message contains *larger than, smaller than,* or *equal,* that is a clue you are working with an item comparison.

Use column or line charts for time series or frequency comparisons. Although a component or item comparison should remain at one point in time, the time series shows changes over time (such as weeks, months, quarters, or even years). Clues to look for in your message are words such as *change, grow, rise, decline, increase, decrease,* and *fluctuate.*

A frequency distribution comparison shows how many items (frequency) fall into a series of progressive numerical ranges. For example, you can use a frequency distribution to show how many employees earn less than $30K, how many earn between $30K and $60K, and so on. Terms to look for that suggests this kind of comparison are *X to Y range, concentration, frequency,* and *distribution.*

Use dot charts for correlation comparisons. A correlation comparison shows whether the relationship between two variables follows—or fails to follow—the pattern you would normally expect. For example, you would normally expect sales to increase as the size of the discount increases. Whenever your message includes words such as *related to, increases with, decreases with, changes with, varies with,* or the converse such as *doesn't increase with,* it's an instant clue that you're showing a correlation comparison.

Finally, to really make an impression, let's make each bar grow separately from each other. Again, with the chart selected, go to the Build Inspector in the Inspector palette.

In the Build Inspector, set the following:

Build Style: Wipe

Direction: Bottom to Top

Delivery: By Set

Now when you play this chart slide back, first the background will fill up from the bottom, and then each bar for New York, Los Angeles, and Seattle will fill upward, which again dramatically emphasizes your point.

Now that your chart is done, you can move onto the other elements in your show, including another chart that displays how much closer downtown Seattle is from a major airport than in New York or Los Angeles.

Once these additional slides are ready to go, you can adjust the timing of the transitions between each slide to make sure the pace moves along. In the next chapter, you'll work extensively with transitions as you build an interactive educational presentation.

CHAPTER 5

Class Lesson: Learning with Pizzazz

Who are you going to believe, me or your own eyes?—Groucho Marx (1890–1977)

Teachers in nearly every grade from kindergarten to graduate school are turning to multimedia tools to enhance the learning experience. Yet most teachers have little time to put together a curriculum, let alone a class presentation. Believe me, I can relate.

In the summers, I teach weeklong media production classes at the International Film and Video Workshops in Rockport, Maine. Because the lessons need to change to fit each class of students, I may have as little as one evening before the next day's class to make a new presentation. In this lesson, you'll use one of my presentations on one of the concepts that can come in handy when preparing elements for Keynote—namely, creating graphics with alpha channels using Adobe Photoshop.

Planning the lesson

Adding details and notes

Preparing the graphics

Using transitions

Tips from the Pros: Paul Hewitt on Educational Presentations

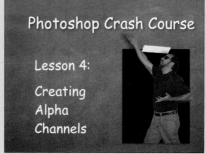

Roughing Out the Lesson

The first step in any presentation—educational or otherwise—is to organize what you plan to say. In the case of this lecture on alpha channels, let's start with the goals:

- Define alpha channels.
- Emphasize that an alpha channel uses 256 levels of gray, black, and white to control transparency.
- Show examples of alpha channels.
- Provide a segue into a hands-on lab.

This will be a short presentation so the students can work with Photoshop as much as possible. So, you shouldn't have many more than 8 to 10 slides. Ultimately you just want to provide a bit of background on alpha channels before getting to the first hands-on lesson.

Let's set this up in Keynote using just the Outline view. First, start a new project (⌘+N) and then select the Blackboard theme (yeah, an obvious one for educational presentations, but the black background is nice).

Adding the Slides and Text

Once the program has loaded, select Outline from the Views pop-up window on the toolbar. Now you'll rough in the presentation by adding slides with their titles.

You can turn a bullet point into a new slide by pressing **Shift+Tab**, which will "un-indent" the bullet point into a separate slide.

Type the following, hitting Return to create a new slide and Tab to indent a bullet point:

Photoshop Crash Course

- Lesson 4:
- Creating Alpha Channels

What's an Alpha Channel?

- The First Among Channels?
- The Envy of the Beta Channel?
- A new cable TV station for dogs?
- The key element for compositing images…

An Alpha Channel:

- Is a 256 Level gray scale image
- Controls transparency
- Can be added to existing graphics

Alpha Channel example 1

Alpha Channel example 2

Show Black and White Alpha Channel example

Creating Alpha Channels

- There are three ways to create Alpha Channels inside Photoshop:

- Cutout the background

- Remove background using the Extract plugin

- Create an Alpha Channel from scratch

To indent further on the outline, press Tab, which indents the next set of bullet points:

Cutting out a background in Photoshop

- To Get Started:

- Launch Photoshop

- Press Command O or go to the file menu and select Open

- Double-Click on "Alpha Channel Tutorial 01.psd"

> If you don't want to build this presentation from scratch, you can also find each step of this presentation (as well as the completed presentation Alpha Channel Presentation.key) on the CD in the Tutorials folder.

You might wonder about some of these text lines; once they are on the Slide Canvas in Keynote they don't all look much like bullet points, do they? That's OK; you're just entering the text quickly for now, you'll fix the formatting in a bit. You should now have an outline that looks like Figure 5.1.

Okay, you've roughed in the presentation; now you need to do some global tweaking.

Adjusting the Overall Look

Several things already are not working with this show, especially when it comes to the size and style of the typeface. Don't get me wrong, the Blackboard theme is a nice design—but being the never-satisfied Mac user that I am, I'd like my designs to go to "11."

So, instead of making individual changes to slides (you'll do that later), let's go ahead and make some master slide changes.

First, let's change the master slide used by slide 1. Right now it is about as tasty as Styrofoam, so let's change it to the master called Title, Bullets & Photo using the Masters pop-up menu on the toolbar (see Figure 5.2).

Figure 5.1

The class presentation roughed out in Keynote's Outline view

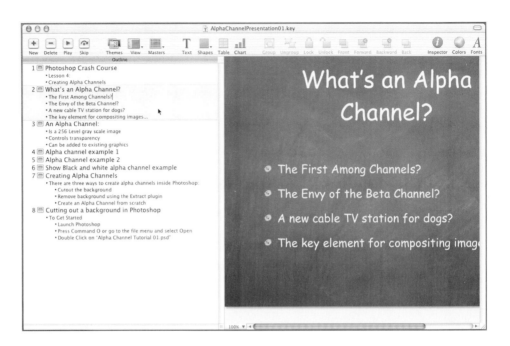

Figure 5.2

Select the Title, Bullets & Photo option as the new master slide for the opening of this show.

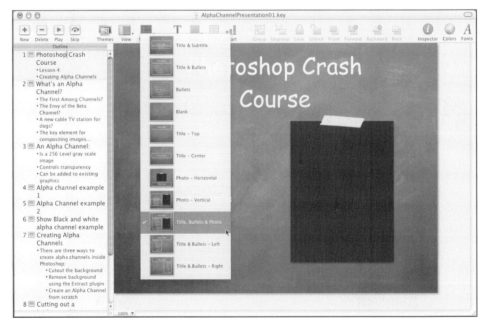

Now, let's make a few global changes to the master slides. Go to the Views pop-up menu on the toolbar and select Show Master Slides. This opens the Master Slide thumbnail drop-down list from the Slide Organizer. From the Master Slide list in the Slide Organizer, select the Title & Bullets thumbnail.

You want to do two things here. First, you want to add a drop shadow to the title of the each slide to help make it pop out of the background. Right now the text seems to blend too much into the background, which I (in my junior designer capacity) think is too bland. So, to change all the title text, simply click the Title Text area and then click the Inspector palette. Inside the Inspector palette, click the Graphic Inspector and then just click the Shadow check box (see Figure 5.3).

With the Graphic Inspector and the master slides open, let's go ahead and add a drop shadow to the title text for the Title – Top master slide and the Title, Bullets & Photo master slide, which should be all you need for this presentation. Obviously, if you were to use other slide types in your show, you would need to adjust those as well.

Now scroll up the Master Slides window and select the Title & Bullets master slide. Here you need to fix the one major flaw in this design, which is the size of the text used for the bullet points. Unless you plan on strapping your laptop around the neck of your audience, you'll need to make the bullet points and text larger.

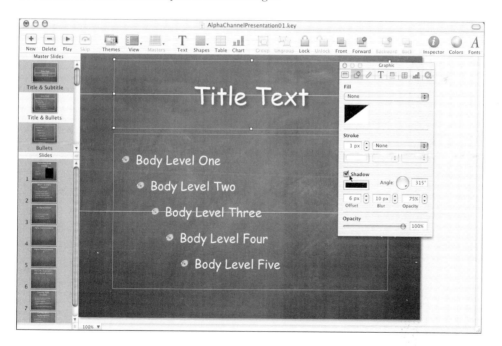

Figure 5.3

Spice up the Black-board theme by adding a drop shadow to the title text.

To increase the text size, click the bullets box (which says *Body Level One*, *Body Level Two*, and so on) and then click the Fonts icon in the toolbar. When the Fonts palette comes up, adjust the size of the bullet text from 28 to at least 36. This goes a long way to making things much more readable. It won't allow you to add as much text onto the screen—but then you shouldn't be using more than a few lines of text per screen anyway. Remember, a bullet point is a summary—not a summation!

> Don't forget to use notes (covered in the next section)! Each slide can have its own set of notes so you remember to bring up as many relevant points and details relating to what is on the screen.

Adding Details and Notes

Now that you've added in a few global changes, it's time to clean up the slides individually.

Starting with the first slide, you'll need to resize and adjust the text on the screen. Here's what you need to do:

1. Make the *Photoshop Crash Course* text one line by clicking it and then pulling on the side handle until it becomes one line.

2. Resize the *Lesson 4* text (which is way too small) from 28 to 48 by clicking the text and then changing the size in the Fonts palette.

3. Remove the bullets because this is a title page and doesn't need them. To do this, select the Lesson 4 text box and click the Inspector palette icon in the toolbar. Now click the Text Inspector, and in the bottom of the screen where it says *Bullets and Numbering*, select None from the pop-up menu.

When you are finished, align the *Photoshop Crash Course* text by dragging it until you see both horizontal and vertical alignment guides, which show you that the text is now centered. Do the same for the *Lesson 4* text.

When you are done, your new first slide should look something like Figure 5.4.

In the second slide, you'll need to again resize the title text box so that the words *What's An Alpha Channel?* fit on one line by pulling on the handle surrounding that text box.

The only other tweak I'd like to do is to embellish the last point to make it stand out even further. Change the bullet to a check mark and also change the color of the text. To make this happen, follow these steps:

1. Select the text on the last bullet point (*The key element for compositing images...*)

2. Open the Text Inspector, click the color box, and select a new color. In this case, select yellow.

3. Next, click the Bullets & Numbering pop-up menu and make sure Image Bullet is selected. Then go to the scroll bar in the lower-left corner of the inspector and scroll to the white check mark. Feel free to pick whatever looks good to you—just as long as it is different from the previous bullets.

Now your second slide should look more like Figure 5.5.

Slide 3 looks fine but a little bland—and these are the main points that you want the students to hang onto throughout the lecture, so they really need to stand out. So let's just add some new bullets from within the Text Inspector—in this case, a bullet image of a red check mark inside a hand-drawn black square that you can choose from the scrolling panel in the lower-left corner. First, you have to select the text. To really make it stand out, in the Text Inspector, unclick the Scale with Text button and set the bullet size to 100 percent, as shown in Figure 5.6.

Finally, to make each line more readable, move the Bullet slider all the way over the right so that it reads 50, which spaces out the bullet points more evenly on the screen. When you are done, click and drag the bullet points so that they are centered on the screen (use the alignment guides to lock the text into the right location). When you are done, slide 3 should look like Figure 5.7.

The last changes you need to make are the same for slides 7 and 8; you want to resize the text boxes and add numbers for the last three bullet points. Resize the titles for each slide using the world-famous "grab-de-handle-und-pull-by-heck" technique and align using the alignment guides.

Figure 5.6

Set the bullet marks to 100 percent in the Bullets & Numbering section of the Text Inspector.

Figure 5.4

The new title slide

Figure 5.5

By changing colors and bullets, you can emphasize different points.

To add the numbers to the bullets, select the last three points. Now in the Bullets & Numbering section of the Text Inspector, select Number from the pop-up menu. Here again you might want to adjust the space between the points to make it more readable, which should look like Figure 5.8.

Adding Graphics

Now you need to add the graphics, which can ultimately make the presentation. As an educator, you need to balance your presentation with audience involvement, information, and some interesting things to look at—otherwise you should just be lecturing. Actually, I'm a bit biased here—I'd rather talk with my students than just lecture at them.

You have four places to add graphics: the opening slide and slides 4, 5 and 6. The opening slide should be something appropriate to the subject, unusual, and somewhat silly. Over the years it seems like a technical presentation works best in an academic setting if you have fun with it right from the start. So let's add an image shot for one of my classes for the Friday Night Wrap party show. In the Tutorials folder on the CD-ROM, drag the EHSpeech.psd file from the CD-ROM onto the Slide Canvas.

The image will be a bit big, so resize it to fit into the black photo space. However, don't send it to the back. Instead, lay it on top with the hand just off of the photo. Now go into the Graphic Inspector inside the Inspector palette and add a drop shadow. This makes the image appear to be outside the frame and slightly above the background, as shown in Figure 5.9.

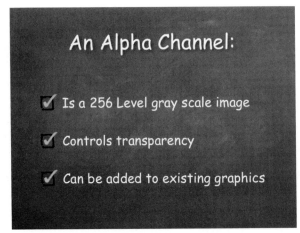

Figure 5.7

Slide 3 now has properly spaced text with newer-bigger-faster bullet marks.

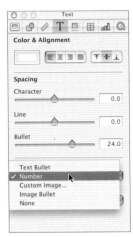

Figure 5.8

Besides bullets, you can also add numbers to different sections or even remove bullet points as needed (as in the first line).

Now let's add images to slide 4, which is where you first show the students what alpha channels can do for images. Click slide 4 to make it active in the Slide Canvas. From the companion CD-ROM, drag two images (`JusticeOriginal.psd` and `JusticeNoBack.tif`) onto the Slide Canvas. Position them opposite each other in the lower part of the Slide Canvas, and change the title to *Look Ma, No Background!* (see Figure 5.10). (These are images from a publicity photo from the Theater Simple production of *Justice*.)

Slide 5 needs to go into more detail about what makes up an alpha channel graphic, so you'll need to add a prepared graphic and some text labels. Click slide 5, and change the title by selecting the *Alpha Channel Example B* title and typing **An Alpha Channel Graphic**.

Adding Really Big Graphics

Now add in the infographic called `JusticeAlphaInfog.psd` from the CD-ROM. You'll need to resize this, so that the sides fit into the Slide Canvas.

This is actually a good time to bring up ways of dealing with Image Giganticus, otherwise known as "My Graphic Runneth Over" syndrome, where you import a graphic that is far larger than the Slide Canvas. This often happens with high-resolution scans and digital camera images, where you could capture images at 150 dots per inch (dpi) or higher. A high-resolution image may seem fine in another graphics program such as Adobe InDesign or Photoshop, but bring that same file into Keynote and it will get scaled up to the point that you might not find a resize handle on the graphic.

Figure 5.9

Leapin' off the page, the author adds a bit of frivolity to the opening of the presentation thanks to an alpha channel image.

Figure 5.10

The first of the graphics slides; slide 4 introduces the concept of alpha channel graphics. Image courtesy of Theater Simple.

Figure 5.11

Selecting Slide Only
from the Views pop-up
window gives you
some room when
working with large
graphic files.

Figure 5.12

Zooming in and out of
the Slide Canvas is a
good way to work with
large, high-resolution
images.

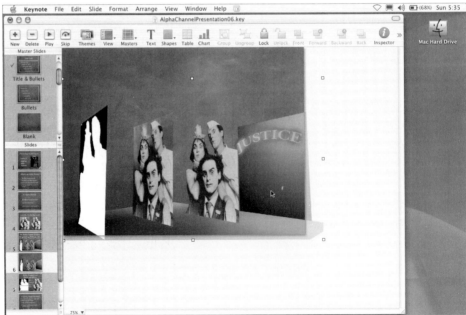

You can deal with this in two ways. If the graphic is just slightly larger than the Slide Canvas, then from the Views pop-up menu on the toolbar, select Slide Only. This clears out the Slide Organizer and gives you a bit more room to work (as shown in Figure 5.11).

However, in the case of the `JusticeAlphaInfog.psd` file, you'll need to do more. Once you've dragged the `JusticeAlphaInfo.psd` file on the Slide Canvas, you can make even more space by changing the size of the Slide Canvas. At the bottom-left corner, there is a small number that says 100%, which is a small pop-up window that allows you to resize the Slide Canvas.

By selecting 75%, you'll reduce the size of the Slide Canvas enough to grab more than one handle on the image (see Figure 5.12). If your image is particularly large, you can go all the way down to 25 percent of the Slide Canvas window.

Adding Graphics Plus Text

Now you need to add some text labels. Using the Text tool, create four text labels:

- Alpha Channel
- Original Image
- Masked Background
- New Background

Once you've entered them, move each of the labels over each image from left to right. You'll need to resize all of the text labels so that they show up on two lines.

The labels look good, but you now need to establish a relationship between all of them. Follow these steps:

1. Click the Text tool and type in a plus sign (+). Use the Fonts palette to make the + symbol fairly large.

2. Move this between the *Alpha Channel* and the *Original Image* labels.

3. Now use the Text tool again and create an equal sign (=) and move that between the *Original Image* and *Masked Background* label.

4. Finally, use the Shape tool to add an arrow pointing from left to right and position that between the *Masked Background* and the *New Background*.

Slide 5 should now look like Figure 5.13.

Figure 5.13

By combining text and graphic elements, you create a relationship between the text and graphic.

Finally, you need to add the graphics for slide 6, which shows the basic principle of alpha channel: the blacker the matte, the more transparent it is. So, add the `JusiticeNoBack.tif` and the `AlphaChannelMask.psd` graphics from the Tutorials folder on the CD-ROM. You'll need to resize both of these to fit them on opposite sides of the Slide Canvas (see Figure 5.14).

Now let's add some arrows to show a relationship between the black-and-white matte and the masked image. In the Shapes pop-up menu on the toolbar, select the line. Position this arrow so that it has one end on the black area near the girl's head and the other end in the same area in the image. With the line selected, click the Graphic Inspector in the Inspector palette.

Here you can add an arrowhead to either the beginning, end, or both ends of the line. Just select an arrowhead in either pop-up menu, and you are all set. To make sure that the arrow isn't lost in the image, change the color of the stroke to a 50-percent gray.

Now just add labels for each arrow, and adjust them to wrap around the shaft of the arrow, as shown in Figure 5.15.

Using Transitions

Now comes the cool part, which is where you use transitions to transform your presentation into a somewhat interesting show.

First, let me mention a few words of warning about slide show transitions. Transitions in slide shows are like using spices in cooking; use too much and your show will unbearable, but use too little and your show will be too bland. This is especially true in an educational setting—after years of television, motion pictures, and even video games, viewing a series of fancy

Figure 5.14

These two images will be the basis for showing how black equals transparent when it comes to alpha channel mattes.

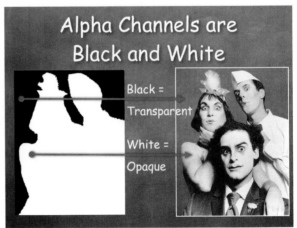

Figure 5.15

The arrows are actually created by applying an arrowhead to a stroke in the Graphic Inspector.

transitions will do little more than illicit a yawn from most audiences. However, if you use transitions precisely to enhance your message, then chances are your audience will be suitably impressed.

Understanding Keynote Transitions

Inside Keynote you have two different kinds of transitions, 3D and 2D. The 3D transitions use Quartz graphics and a graphics standard called OpenGL to provide impressive 3D transitions, such as flips, cubes, and mosaics. The 3D transitions only work between slides.

The 2D transitions are more conventional, where you can have an image "fade in" (dissolve) on-screen or push in from one direction on the screen (move). You can set many of these 2D transitions both between slides and within slides using the Build Inspector.

For more on using transitions with the Build Inspector, see Chapter 7, "Video Storyboard: Building Slide Actions."

Inside the Inspector palette, you can adjust transitions in two places: the Slide Inspector (see Figure 5.16) and the Build Inspector (see Figure 5.17).

Keynote keeps it simple when using transitions; you can really only make two adjustments with any transition, which is the speed and direction of the effect. This is perfectly workable because most of the time you won't need much more in your shows. If you truly need a more sophisticated effect, then chances are your presentation needs more work.

Some 2D effects, such as dissolve, twirl, and drop only have a speed control.

Setting Transitions between Slides

Enough background—add some transitions to the alpha channel presentation. Click slide 1 and then click the first icon on the left in the Inspector palette. In the Transition section, select Cube (see Figure 5.18), set the direction from Top to Bottom, and set the speed about midway. Because this is the first transition (and a fancy one at that), you might as well let the audience enjoy it by letting the transition play slowly.

Save fancy transitions for the beginning and end. I like to add one fancy effect at the beginning of the show, which primes your audience and makes them wonder if you will use it again. And I don't use that transition until the end, which is a nice way to use transitions as "bookends" for your presentations.

Figure 5.16

The Slide Inspector is where you adjust transitions between slides.

Figure 5.17

The Build Inspector is where you adjust transitions between elements on the same slide.

TIPS FROM THE PROS: PAUL G. HEWITT
ON EDUCATIONAL PRESENTATIONS

Professor Paul G. Hewitt really has done it all; he's a former boxer, uranium prospector, sign painter, and cartoonist. Paul began college at the age of 28 and fell in love with physics. Today, thanks to his groundbreaking textbook, Conceptual Physics (Prentice Hall, 2001) his name is synonymous with conceptual physics to educators everywhere.

Paul's approach to teaching involves many classroom demonstrations that both involve and inspire his students. Although he's busier than ever, Paul graciously provided the following tips on how to improve presentations for the classroom:

Good presentations are based around student questions. A great presentation is one that communicates the information that students deem important. The presentation has to answer questions they have or be deeply interesting. If it doesn't answer questions they already have, then it should pose some interesting questions. Then, after they've had time to think and respond on their own, continue.

Tailor your presentation to your students. One must have the ability to tailor presentation to the audience, but, again, if a lecture isn't exciting or otherwise valued, you should consider other modes of imparting knowledge.

During your presentation, do more questioning and less professing. When posing questions, the chief folly occurs when the instructor too quickly answers the questions asked. Tell students to "check your neighbor" by discussing solutions or answers.

Make students the stars of the class. The instructor should guide class activity. Too often the instructor hogs the spotlight and is left with a class of inactivity.

Rehearse your demos before springing them on your classes. Always do this! Not rehearsing your presentation is irresponsible.

Don't underestimate the power of a good presentation... Most teachers underestimate the value of a demo. That's a mistake. Don't use "demos take time to set up" to justify not using them.

...however, use presentations only when appropriate. If demos don't relate to central or valued ideas and they take significant time, then yuk! Demos for the sake of demos are a poor practice. Students value learning more than they value being entertained. That's because their time in class where they're actually learning is, sadly, an exception rather than the rule.

Setting Bullet Point Transitions

As mentioned in Chapter 3, "Putting It All Together: Building a Presentation," you can automatically have bullet points transition within a slide using a variety of 2D transitions. To see this in action, click slide 2, and then click the bullet point box. Now click the Build Inspector, and select Move In from the pop-up menu. In the small preview window in the Build Inspector, you'll now see the bullet points move in all at once from left to right (see Figure 5.19).

To customize this so that only one bullet point moves in at a time, select By Bullet in the Delivery pop-up menu. Keep in mind that when you play back the slide show, you'll still need to click the mouse to bring out each bullet point. For more on using builds, refer to Chapter 6, "Artist Portfolio: The Portable Image Gallery."

If you'd like your bullet point to show automatically when a slide appears on the screen, unselect First Build Requires Click in the Build Inspector.

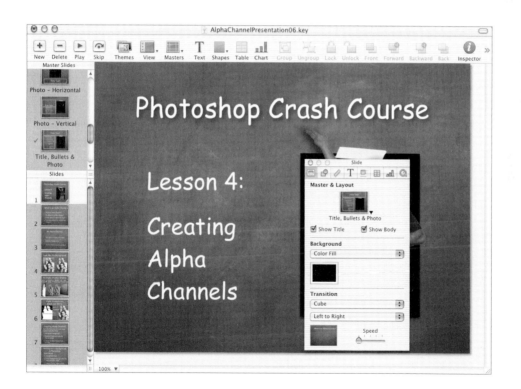

Figure 5.18

Once you've selected Cube, the preview thumbnail in the Transition section automatically displays what that transition will look like.

Setting Graphic Element Transitions

Figure 5.19

You can transition bullet points within each slide using the Build Inspector.

Finally, let's step through adding transitions to graphics using the Build Inspector. (Chapter 6 discusses this in more detail.) For now you'll just walk through the process and examine the final `Alpha Channel Presentation Final.key` file to get more ideas on how to use transitions within the presentation.

Click slide number 6, the Alpha Channels are Black and White slide. During the lecture, if you want to animate the arrows connecting the black-and-white matte with the masked image, then follow these steps:

1. Click the Build Inspector.

2. Click the top arrow.

3. Set the Delivery method to Move In and set the Direction to Left to Right.

4. Click the Black=Transparent text box.

5. Set the Delivery method to Dissolve.

6. Repeat steps 1 through 5 for the second arrow and the *White=Opaque* text.

Now when you play the slide and then click first, each arrow wipes across the screen from left to right; with the next click, the text label appears. What's especially nice is that setting up the slide this way allows you to reveal only the information you want to your students while you are talking.

> Grab back their attention with the blackout key. Too often your students will get caught up in trying to read the slide instead of paying attention to the lecture. You can shut this down by pressing the B key, which will instantly black out the screen. When you've finished discussing your finer point with the class, just hit B to bring the presentation back on-screen.

You can do dozens of other combinations of transitions for each element and slide in your show. Check out the `Alpha Channel Presentation Final.key` presentation included in the CD-ROM, which shows the types of transitions that you built in this chapter—and several others designed to enhance the lesson.

CHAPTER 6

Artist Portfolio: The Portable Image Gallery

Imagination is more important than knowledge.—Albert Einstein (1879–1955)

A digital portfolio for photographers or artists is a great way to show your work. With Keynote, you can make portable demos to show your clients, which you can run during a show or even display on the Web. The "key" to success is how you import your graphics into Keynote.

This chapter covers how to import and edit graphics so you can make the best portfolio possible to showcase your work. We'll also build a sample portfolio of a digital artist's work.

Importing files

Editing and converting graphics

Building a portfolio

Tips from the pros: Mikkel Aaland on Digital Portfolios

Importing Files

Keynote is one of the most graphics-friendly presentation programs on the market. In addition to full alpha channel support, Keynote can import a wide variety of media file formats.

With Keynote, you can import the following formats:

- Still images, such as PICT, PSD, GIF, TIFF, JPEG, PDF, and MOV

- Moving images, such as QuickTime and Flash

- Audio files, such as AIFF and MP3

Many technical documents, books, and Sanskrit rolls document the minutia of each file format. (I once owned a book on graphics file formats that was bigger than a phone book. I eventually found it useful when propping open a door.) However, let's sort these formats out in a way that makes sense, which is by file size: large and small.

Why file size? Simple—Keynote is an on-screen presentation tool that imposes some basic media format limitations. For example, although you can import graphics that are extremely high resolution (all the way up to 4000×4000 pixels for super high-resolution images), Keynote can only effectively display images at a maximum 1024×768 pixels. So if you bring in a super high-resolution image, you'll just have to resize it to fit Keynote's Slide Canvas—and you'll have added an unnecessary burden on your Mac's graphic processing.

Furthermore, the pixel size of a slide show in Keynote can be either 800×600 pixels or 1024×768 pixels (see Table 6.1).

Consequently, using images that are larger or higher resolution will not provide a better image in your show. Instead, you'll provide more work for both you (you'll have to resize all your high-resolution images) and your Mac (it has to push around a much bigger graphics file). It would be better to use formats that are smaller yet still provide you with the resolution and quality you need.

Using Large Media File Formats

Large media file formats contain the most resolution (be it video, audio, or image), which means they are larger to work with than other file formats.

On the still image side, the larger file formats are Photoshop Document (PSD) files and Tag Image File Format (TIFF) files. Both of these formats can contain multiple layers, which can increase the file format size. A Photoshop file that contains three layers is actually three documents rolled into one.

Table 6.1

Keynote Media Limitations

MEDIUM	MAXIMUM RESOLUTION
Audio	16-bit, 44.1 kHz
Video	QuickTime, 320×240 pixels
Graphics	800×600 or 1024×768 pixels

TIFF is actually a much older format than PSD; Aldus, Microsoft, and Apple developed it in the early days of desktop publishing. Like Photoshop's PSD file, a TIFF file is also a high-resolution file. The main difference is that TIFF can also contain some lossless compression and an alpha channel.

Both the PSD and TIFF formats can also support alpha channels, so these are good formats to use if you plan to print your presentations and need to have the images be as crisp as possible. These files are also good to work with if they have been reduced to screen resolution (but more on that later).

> A PICT file can be either large or small, depending upon the resolution at which it was saved. Although it was once the defacto image format on the Macintosh, these days the PICT format is not as commonly used in graphics programs; instead, more programs support saving files in TIFF or PSD formats. In fact, MacOS X has abandoned PICT, replacing it with the more flexible PDF format.

Adobe's Portable Document Format (PDF) is a somewhat variable format. Adobe Acrobat PDF files can incredibly compress text and graphics into a small package that a variety of computers can read. However, you can also save high-resolution PDF files for printing at a service bureau, which bloats the PDF file to a much larger size than Keynote can comfortably handle. So, when importing PDF files, make sure the size and resolution of the file works for your presentation side.

> Any PDF file that you create with the Print dialog box of any MacOS X application will work just fine in Keynote.

On the video and audio side, QuickTime and Audio Interchange File Format (AIFF) files are the larger culprits. Although QuickTime can also be small—it all depends upon the COmpressor DECompressor (codec) used to compress the original video or audio footage. One of the most common codecs used in digital video these days is DV (also called *DVCPro 25*), which is the native format that your digital video camera uses when it records video. When you connect your digital video camera to your Mac via a FireWire connection, the video is stored on your Mac in DV (or DVCPro 25) format.

QuickTime movies in the DV format can be quite large, and generally Keynote is not well equipped to play these full-screen video files.

On the audio side, AIFF files are actually uncompressed digital audio files. AIFF is nearly the identical to the audio files used on audio CDs, so the fidelity of these files is quite high. So, although you can bring AIFF files into Keynote, it's best to keep them small—such as for specific dialogue or sound effects that are critical to your application.

Using Small Media File Formats

So, which files are smaller and easier for Keynote to digest? On the still graphics side, Joint Photographic Experts Group (JPEG) and Graphics Interchange Format (GIF) are the low file size leaders. Because of their ability to compress or limit colors, both are popular graphics formats for the Web. The nice thing about JPEG files is that they can also contain alpha channels, so you can cleanly composite them against a Keynote background.

GIF files generally tend to not reduce as well as JPEG files, but graphics with solid bright colors reduce down nicely as GIFs. This is because you can reduce the number of colors used in GIF files within applications such as Macromedia Fireworks and Adobe ImageReady (which is now included with Adobe's Photoshop program) so that you display only the colors needed to display the image.

On the media side, QuickTime and Flash are the two moving-image leaders. "What's this?" you're thinking, "Didn't you also lump QuickTime into the large media format category?" Guilty as charged—but QuickTime is less of a media format than it is a media "suitcase." You can save your QuickTime movie as dozens of different audio, video, and graphics formats, all of which are part of QuickTime's structure.

QuickTime is one of Apple's greatest innovations and one of the best digital media formats on the planet. This is because QuickTime is infinitely updateable, and it works at the system level so that any application can send files to and from any other application—as long as they can both read and write files as QuickTime files.

One of the most recent additions to the QuickTime "list o' formats" is MPEG-4, a new video compression technology based upon MPEG-2, which is the format used to compress movies for playback on DVDs. The major difference is that MPEG 4 can be many times smaller than other video codecs (such as DV) and yet maintain a high degree of image fidelity. So, a QuickTime movie that uses the MPEG 4 codec could be a great, small-sized addition to a Keynote presentation. Another plus: In different media applications, you can save QuickTime movies with alpha channels, so your background could show through the transparent parts of an animated logo.

Another great small media format is Flash, which Macromedia developed for web-based animation. Consequently, Flash is compact and clean. You need to watch out for this format, though, because not all Flash movies will play inside of Keynote. Particularly, any interactive Flash animation will not play inside of Keynote.

On the audio side of things, MP3 is the better audio format to use than AIFF. MP3 (which actually stands for *MPEG Layer 3 Audio*) can reduce digital audio files to a fraction of their original uncompressed size. For example, you can reduce a 1 megabyte stereo AIFF file down to just 35 kilobytes as an MP3 file—and it will still sound acceptable!

Remember, every graphic and file you add has to be pushed around by Keynote and your computer's Central Processing Unit (CPU). The smaller the media, the faster and smoother your show will play.

Converting Unsupported Files

Unfortunately, not every file you work with can be immediately imported into Keynote. However, there are several ways around this problem; in some cases, you can use other utilities that come with the MacOS X system.

Converting to PDF

PDF is a format that is built into MacOS X, in that any OS X application can "print" to a PDF file. To do this, you simply select Print from the application that you want and then click the Save As PDF button, which shows up in any MacOS X Print dialog box, regardless of the printer, as shown in Figure 6.1.

To select a specific page or pages in your document that you want to import, change the Pages radio button from All to Current Page, From/To, or Page Range.

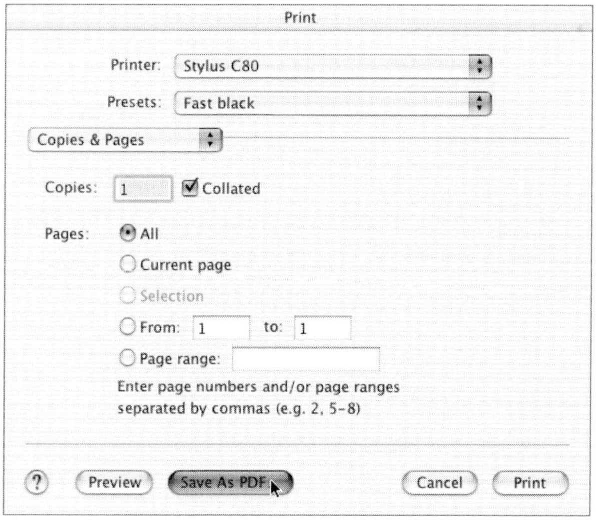

Print
Printer: Stylus C80
Presets: Fast black
Copies & Pages
Copies: 1 ☑ Collated
Pages: ⦿ All
○ Current page
○ Selection
○ From: 1   to: 1
○ Page range:
Enter page numbers and/or page ranges separated by commas (e.g. 2, 5–8)
(?) (Preview) (Save As PDF)   (Cancel) (Print)

Figure 6.1

Using the Save As PDF feature in the MacOS X Print dialog box is a great way to import files that are not compatible.

Converting to QuickTime

Another way to import your graphic file into Keynote is to save your file as a QuickTime document. Many programs have export features that allow you to convert your file to QuickTime, which you can then directly bring into Keynote.

You can save the QuickTime movie as many different formats, which could affect the playback of your Keynote program. In general, it's a good idea to use a few tried-and-true codecs when exporting files. For still images, you should use the Photo-JPEG or Animation codec, which keeps alpha channel information and retains small sizes. For video or animation, stick to the Sorenson 3, MPEG-4, or Video codecs.

Figure 6.2

Photoshop can convert graphics to a variety of formats.

Converting Files Using Third-Party Conversion Programs

Finally, you can always rely on some other commercial programs to provide a bridge between your media format and Keynote. On the Mac, there are at least three great programs for doing media conversions: Adobe Photoshop, Equilibrium Technologies DeBabelizer, and Discreet Cleaner.

> This is not an exhaustive list of third-party programs. I could go on and on with all the options, but that's not the point of this book. Please forgive me if I've left out your favorite!

Using Photoshop and Photoshop Elements

In addition to being one of the most popular image-editing programs, Adobe Photoshop has long had the ability to convert to and from many graphics formats. To do this in Photoshop or Photoshop Elements, simply select File → Save As and then select which format you want to save the file as (see Figure 6.2). Presto—instant new format! Keep in mind that you can directly import Photoshop files into Keynote, so most times you can just save your new file as a PSD file.

> At the same time you convert your graphic into a format that Keynote can use, you can also add an alpha channel to mask out the background.

Using DeBabelizer

DeBabelizer was one of the first graphics conversion programs on the Mac and PC that could not only convert graphics to and from a variety of formats but could also process hundreds of graphics simultaneously. Today Photoshop covers most of the conversions that DeBabelizer can handle, but DeBabelizer still does one feature much better than Photoshop—batch processing (see Figure 6.3).

Using DeBabelizer, you can convert hundreds of graphics at one time using scripts that you create to change the format, adjust the brightness, and dozens of other parameters within your image. If you need to convert many still images, then DeBabelizer is definitely worth trying.

Using Cleaner

Discreet's Cleaner program has been a defacto standard for compressing digital video files on the Mac. Cleaner is much like Debabelizer in that its primary function is to convert one media type to another. Even though Cleaner can convert still images, its main strength is its ability to convert audio and video files (see Figure 6.4).

Cleaner provides many different adjustments during the conversion or "re-encoding" process. While creating a daily news webcast, I used Cleaner to not only improve the quality of the streaming video uploaded to the Web but also to create RealVideo and MPEG versions of the show simultaneously. Even though these conversions can take some time, Cleaner lets you batch process the files. So, I set up a batch file with all my parameters, started the processing before I went home for the day, and then came back and checked the results in the morning. Cleaner is a great product to have if you need to do media conversions.

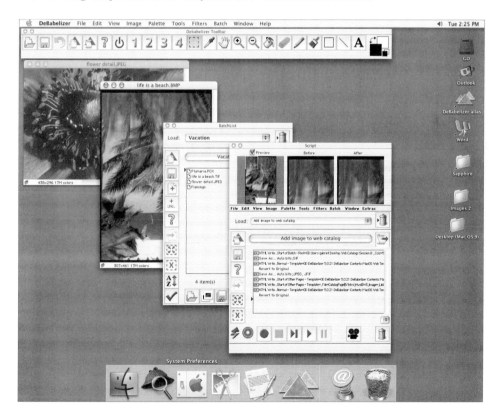

Figure 6.3

DeBabelizer from Equilibrium Technologies is a great graphics batch conversion tool.

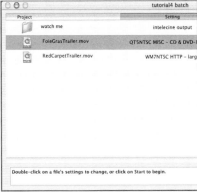

Editing Graphics

Now that you have your graphics in your show, can you make any adjustments to them? Well, yes and no—but mostly no. Compared to PowerPoint and other programs, Keynote still relies heavily on other programs such as Photoshop to be the main graphics-editing application. For example, there isn't even a simple cropping tool inside of Keynote to help trim the sides of your photos.

However, there are three ways you can adjust images within Keynote:

Layering, where you move one image in front of another.

Resizing, where you increase or decrease the size of an image.

Rotation, where you can angle an image at any degree.

The layering controls are the Front, Forward, Back, and Backward buttons that you can add to the Toolbar using the Customize Toolbar feature. Both resizing and rotating an object are controlled using the handles on the object. These controls won't help you much if you need to adjust the brightness or color of your images; to do that, you should work with Photoshop, DeBabelizer, or other image-editing programs.

Building a Portfolio

To get you started toward creating your own portfolio, let's construct a mini-portfolio for Jeffery Beckstrom. Jeff works with the City of Seattle doing web management, but he's also a great location photographer. In this mini-portfolio, you'll show some of his work, which should give you a few ideas on how you could present your work. The goal for this project is to give potential clients a sample of the kind of work that Jeff does.

For the mini-portfolio, you will include the following information:

- A title slide
- A skills page
- Three sample slides
- An end title slide

Usually you would also want to put contact information in the show, but Jeff has requested that you not do this because he's having far too much fun maintaining the City of Seattle's website.

Sounds easy, doesn't it? Well, it is (although you will also build a custom master slide and do some fancy transitions for the three slides). To get started, create a new presentation in Keynote (⌘+N) and select the Notebook theme.

Next, select the first slide and set its master to Title & Subtitle, which is the first master slide on the Masters pop-up menu in the toolbar. You could also have used the Photo – Horizontal & Title master, but for now let's use the Title & Subtitle. I like the Notebook cover metaphor, so keep the "cover" intact.

You now need to add a title to the presentation, so in the Title text box, type **JEFF BECKSTROM**. I used all caps here on the opening page because it really makes Jeff's name stand out, ensuring readability from several feet away. Unlike a book or magazine—where all caps can be glaring—using all caps sometimes with very few lines on screen can add interest.

Next, type some info about Jeff in the subtitle line:

WEB PRODUCER

LOCATION PHOTOGRAPHER

Use the alignment guides to center both text boxes. When you are finished, your title slide should look something like Figure 6.5.

The skills page is a simple bulleted list, but you should spice it up a bit with one of Jeff's photos. Click New on the toolbar and then change the new slide's master slide to Title, Bullets & Photo. This gives you space to place text and show one of Jeff's photos at the same time.

In the Title Text box, type the following:

JEFF BECKSTROM • SKILLS

For the bulleted list, type the following:

LOCATION PHOTOGRAPHY

QUICKTIME VR PRODUCTION

WEB PRODUCTION

I'm really not wild about the default bullets that come in this theme, so let's change the bullets on this slide to a box with a check mark. Remember, you do this by selecting the Text dialog box and then changing the bullet type in the Text Inspector section of the Inspector palette (if you are confused on where this is, refer to Chapter 2, "Working with Keynote," which goes over each Keynote tool).

When you have typed the information, use the alignment guides to center everything so that it looks something like Figure 6.6.

Now let's add the photo. From the companion CD-ROM, drag the image called `Alley.jpg` from the Chapter 6 folder onto the Slide Canvas. It will be a bit small, so click and drag one of its handles to fill the photograph area. Once you've done that, while the Alley image is still selected, click Back to send the image into the photo frame. Now your skills page should look something like Figure 6.7.

Figure 6.5

The opening title for the presentation, which also has the benefit of also being the end title

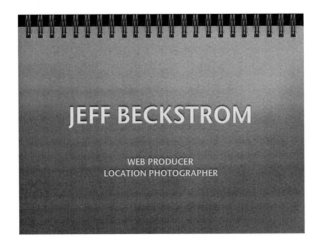

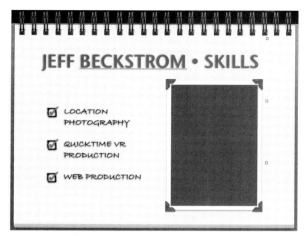

Figure 6.6

The skills page with the text added

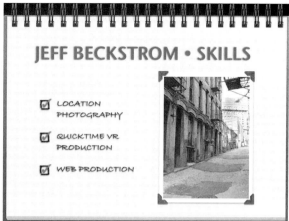

Figure 6.7

The skills page with all of its elements

Stylistically this page is fine, but you can really jazz it up with some nice build transitions. If it is not already open, open the Inspector palette and click the Build tab. To set the title to come in first, followed by the Alley photo, and then have each of the bullet point lines come in separately, follow these steps:

1. Click the *Jeffery Beckstrom* text and then, in the Build In section of the Build palette, select Flip as the Build Type and Bottom to Top as the Direction. Keep this relatively quick as a transition because you don't want to keep the viewer waiting to see Jeff's name.

2. Click the `Alley.jpg` image inside the picture frame, and then in the Build In section, set the Build Type to Scale, and the Direction to Down. This adds a nice zoom out on the image and yet still keeps it within the frame.

3. Finally, click the bulleted text and set Dissolve as the Build Type and By Bullet Group as the Delivery method (see Figure 6.8).

For the slides that show Jeff's photos, you can add his name to a master slide, so each photo slide will be identical. Select Show Master Slides from the Views pop-up menu on the toolbar, click the blank slide in the Masters section of the Slide Organizer, and then click the New button in the toolbar. This gives you a new master slide with which to work.

You want to add Jeff's name here, but it would be nice to keep it subtle so you don't distract from his photos. So, let's create an embossed look. To do this, follow these steps:

1. Click the Text button in the toolbar.

2. Type **Photos by Jeff Beckstrom** into the text box.

Figure 6.8

To get each bullet point to come in separately, make sure you set the Delivery to By Bullet Group.

3. With the *Photos by Jeff Beckstrom* text still selected, click the Graphic Inspector and then click the radio button for Shadow.

4. Finally, select all the text and click the color button in the Text Inspector. Set the text to white.

Because the white text is on a white background, you'll see only the drop shadow, which gives a nice embossed look to the text. Be sure to center the text at the bottom of the Slide Canvas so that the name is out of the way, as shown in Figure 6.9. Once you've done that, then double-click the name of the new master slide and rename it to *Jeff's Photos*.

Now that you have the master slide, click slide 2 (the skills slide) and then click New from the toolbar. Set the master slide to Jeff's Photos using the Masters pop-up menu.

You could have the photos randomly appear from within one slide or have multiple slides with one image. This is the plan: Show all three images but have each successive image build over the top of the previous image. The goal is to create a stack of photos that you can smoothly build up. This could take some time, but let's do it the easy way:

1. From the Chapter 6 folder on the companion CD-ROM, drag the file `Kerrypark03.psd` into Keynote and place it on the upper-left side of the Slide Canvas.

2. Add a drop shadow to the image by clicking Shadow in the Graphic Inspector.

3. Next, select this slide in the Slide Organizer, copy, and then immediately paste it into the Slide Organizer. This gives you an exact copy of your third slide.

4. Click your new fourth slide, select the `Kerrypark03.psd` image, and in the Graphic Inspector, reduce the opacity down to about 40 percent.

Figure 6.9

A nicely embossed master slide for the photos.

5. Now drag the `Kerrypark02.psd` file onto the Slide Canvas and place it on top and in the middle of the image.

6. Add a drop shadow to this new image.

7. Copy and paste this slide and repeat steps 3 through 6, only this time drag `Kerrypark01.psd` to the lower-right side of your slide.

When you've finished, your fifth slide should look like Figure 6.10.

This may seem like a bit of extra work, but it gives you many options when it comes to transitions. You can have each slide do a slow wipe from right to left, so at the same time that the new image is shown, the previous image gets more transparent. It's a subtle effect, but again it gives a nice bit of depth to an otherwise flat screen.

Finally, copy and paste the first title slide and drag it to the end of the show. You can find a QuickTime movie that shows the finished product in action on the CD-ROM in the Tutorials folder as `Jeff Beckstrom Portfolio.mov`. Refer to it after you've done your own version and see how the two compare.

Preparing Your Portfolio for Delivery

You now have an example of how you can structure your portfolio. However, before you get started, you really need to plan on how you will present your portfolio to your audience. The following are a few suggestions on formats and delivery:

One-on-one shows In one-on-one shows, you are stepping a client through your digital portfolio, one slide at a time. Keynote is perfect for this just the way it is. Keep in mind that you can also save and print a version of your show as a PDF file or export your program as a PowerPoint or QuickTime file.

Figure 6.10

By layering the graphics on top of each other and then changing each underlying image's opacity, you can add depth the presentation by making the images appear to be on top of each other.

TIPS FROM THE PROS: MIKKEL AALAND
ON PREPARING DIGITAL PORTFOLIOS

 Mikkel Aaland is a photographer, a writer, a web producer, and the author of seven books, most recently *Photoshop Elements 2 Solutions: The Art of Digital Photography* (Sybex, 2002). Mikkel's documentary photographs have been exhibited in major institutions around the world, including the Bibliotheque Nationale in Paris and the former Lenin Museum in Prague. Mikkel graciously provided some tips for anyone interested in creating their own digital portfolio, especially on what you need to look out for as you start your project.

Understand your project before you get started. Knowing where you're going with your project is critical. You purpose influences the kind of images you ultimately decide to use. Determine how much, if any, image preparation applies to and inspires the overall look and feel of the project. If you're vague about your goal, everything you do—from choosing the right image to the final design of your project—will be difficult. You'll find yourself constantly making decisions without focus or clear intent, and the odds are good that your final piece will not command attention.

Determine your audience. When determining who your audience is, remember that the closer you can identify a specific group, the easier it will be to tailor your message and create an appealing work. It's best to visualize a small group of friends, relatives, or colleagues seeing your work. You can write their names on a piece of paper and create a "profile" of people. Much like a professional researcher might do, ask yourself the following: What do these people actually need? How can my work help them achieve this need? What is the best way of providing this information to them?

Get organized. If your digital media project uses more than a few dozen images, or if you obtained images from many sources, you must be particularly well organized. You'll need a viable system such as an image database for logging and tracking valuable content as it moves through the various stages of your project and special software to help catalog and organize the images once they are in digital form.

Use schedules to help limit your endless possibilities. In the digital world, schedules and deadlines are especially important. Anyone who has spent time working on an image with Photoshop or creating an image with Synthetik Software's Studio Artist knows there are limitless possibilities for refinement. A picture can always be a little better, a painting more realistic. A deadline becomes a boundary, a way to say "Enough!"

Nonstop slide show Keynote is still not set up to automatically move from one slide to another in native form, so you'll need to convert your entire presentation to a QuickTime movie. The next chapter covers all the various strategies for importing and exporting QuickTime movies.

For now, just know that you'll probably need to export your Keynote presentation to a 15-frame-per-second movie. Once your Keynote show is a QuickTime movie, you can have it continuously run by selecting Movie → Loop. If you are using QuickTime Pro, you can even have your looping movie play back at full screen.

Web-based demo On the Web, the bigger the file size, the less likely it is that your clients or fans will want to see it. Although you could upload a small QuickTime movie version of your show, it would probably be best to just save your show as a PDF file. PDF files can be remarkably small, yet they can also maintain the quality of your images.

In the next chapter, you'll look at another creative application; you'll use Keynote to help plan video and film productions.

CHAPTER 7

Video Storyboard: Building Slide Actions

Television: A medium. So called because it is neither rare nor well done.—Ernie Kovacs (1919–1962), comedian and television pioneer

Professional video and film production is not cheap; depending upon the production, you can spend thousands of dollars per minute. To save time (and a lot of money), filmmakers often create storyboards to show what is going to happen in each stage of a shot. Keynote is a wonderful tool for this; it allows you to have a steady flow of images from scene to scene. Furthermore, the Build feature makes Keynote an incredible tool for filmmakers. In this chapter, you'll build part of a storyboard from a film script.

Introducing storyboards

Creating a storyboard

Building with builds

Tips from the Pros: Steven Katz on Storyboarding

Getting the Story Behind Storyboards

So, just what is a storyboard? Essentially, a storyboard is a pictorial representation of the events in a film. Here's another way of looking at it: A storyboard is to a film as sheet music is to a performance. Both provide the artists with a guide as to where things are going and where to add emphasis.

Chances are you've seen quite a few storyboards growing up—remember comic books? They are a great example of using images to show a linear story. In fact, *graphic novels,* a new genre of comics, have become an industry unto themselves because of the cinematic imagery and stories they tell.

A storyboard helps producers and directors get a handle on how the film will look and flow from scene to scene. This is especially important when on the set, where dozens of different elements will compete for your attention and distract you from your original concept of a film.

In a storyboard, you need to use fast images or phrases to remind you of what you are shooting for—basically "a rough map" of your production.

Often these storyboards display three or four images on one sheet of paper from top to bottom, with notes explaining each scene. Other directors such as Steven Spielberg will use an entire page for one image, just to provide more detail for the scene.

With Keynote you can create something even more interesting, which is an electronic storyboard that can show transitions and movement within a scene.

In the past, moving storyboards were called *animatics*. These days anything related to the design of a film (including storyboards) is called *previsualization*.

Besides screenwriting, storyboarding is one of my favorite parts of movie making, *preproduction*. In preproduction, the sky is the limit: You can make whatever kind of movie you want to whatever scale you want. Why? Simple—because it is just on paper or on screen and you haven't spent a dime yet, you can do whatever you want.

Creating a Demon Encounter

So let's create a storyboard sequence. I've taken the liberty of getting one started; open `Demon Encounter.key` from the Chapter 7 folder on the companion CD-ROM.

This is a storyboard sequence from a new horror anthology television series called *Nightlife*, which is yet another shameless derivative concept from such great things as Joss Whedon's *Buffy the Vampire Slayer* television show and Laurell K. Hamilton's *Anita Blake, Vampire Hunter* novels. If you haven't seen or read either of these, then shame on you—you should always make time for genre fiction, especially when it is fun.

In this sequence, Anne, the heroine, is looking for clues or evidence in the alley behind a warehouse. Naturally, she finds more than she is expecting, namely a bit of nastiness called *Kismet*, who is not exactly human. It is supposed to be a tense "monster-creeping-up-on-the-girl" sequence to give the last part of the sequence the proper, well, kick.

Once you've opened the `Demon Encounter.key` show, click the second slide, which should show you the establishing shot of the sequence (see Figure 7.1).

I created the images in this storyboard using two 3D Mac animation programs: Curious Labs Poser 4 for the characters and Vue d'Esprit 4 from E-on Software for the alley background (which originally was a 3D scene called *The Homeless* created for E-on Software by 3D artist Eran Dinur). Both of these are excellent Macintosh 3D tools, especially for those who are somewhat 3D animation challenged.

Using Poser, I created two characters—Anne and Kismet—and posed them in different positions and at different camera angles. I used Poser to then build or "render" the images complete with alpha channels. This is critical because you want to be able to adjust the characters against the 3D backgrounds rendered in Vue d'Esprit.

In slide 2, Anne is fairly large against the background, which makes it look like she's already midway down the alley. Fix this by clicking her and dragging her so that the top of her head is at the top of the door in the upper-left corner of the image (see Figure 7.2).

Now resize her by dragging the middle bottom handle up, shrinking her so that her top foot just touches the floor of the doorway. Once you've done that, drag her over to the middle of the sidewalk, so her front foot is just over the first crack in the sidewalk (see Figure 7.3).

Figure 7.1

The opening long shot (LS) of the sequence shows Anne walking down a lonely alley.

Figure 7.2

Drag Anne so that her head is at the top of the doorway.

Resizing elements is a powerful way of positioning 2D elements to provide an illusion of depth. You could have just as easily made it look like she was farther up the alley by scaling her larger.

Keep in mind that you could have used any graphic or photo here—as long as it has an alpha channel. For example, you could just as easily taken photographs of an actor in different positions against a white wall. Once you've loaded the photos into your Mac, you could then use Photoshop to delete the background using an alpha channel.

Adding a character to a background is just the start of the storyboarding fun with Keynote. What truly sets Keynote apart is the ability to use the Build tool.

Building with Builds

Previous chapters touched on it, but let's take a closer look at the Build tool, which is an essential Keynote feature. You'll need to use it when creating storyboards or other presentations and adding transitions to multiple elements inside of one slide.

Builds simply determine the order and transitions of the different elements in a single slide. All of your build controls reside in the Build Inspector, which like all good things resides in the Inspector palette.

Inside the Build Inspector, you'll find two additional tabs: Build In and Build Out. These control how each element enters and exits the slide. Like the Slide Inspector, the Build Inspector also has a transition type (the Build Style menu), a direction, and a speed control. The main difference is that you won't find any 3D transitions in the Build Inspector transitions—these are straight 2D transitions such as dissolves, moves, and so on.

The most critical feature is the Order pull-down menu, which sets the order in which everything appears. This is also a good place for everything to go wrong in your storyboard; different elements can appear completely in the wrong order. If this happens to you, don't panic—just check the order of each element in the Build Inspector.

Figure 7.3

Anne is now properly resized so that she looks like she is just starting to walk down the alley.

Simulating Camera Focus

Now let's add some builds into the storyboard. With the Demon Encounter.key show still open, click slide 4. What an amazingly black screen! There is actually a lot going on in this scene—just select View → Show Notes. At the bottom of the Slide Canvas, you'll now see a description of the scene:

> CUT: ALLEY FRONT CU. MCU of ANNE walking farther down the alley. Camera changes focus, showing KISMET as he fades in, crouched on the ground.

In English this means you've cut from the previous scene, moving directly from the last scene without any transition. The Alley Front CU. MCU is the location (CU stands for close up, and MCU stands for medium close up), which is a shot of Anne framed at about midchest.

You could just show this scene as it would look like when complete, but using Keynote you can show more of what this scene would look like over time, including a simulation of the camera effect.

To make things easier, I've compiled all the images you'll need to create this scene in a file on the CD-ROM called Tutorial Storyboard Images.key. Open this file, and drag the Tutorial Storyboard Images window to the side, so you can easily click back and forth between both programs, as shown in Figure 7.4.

CREATING KEYNOTE STORYBOARD TRANSITIONS

As you know, the Slide Inspector offers a variety of great transitions within Keynote, which can add a nice style to a typical presentation. However, for the purposes of storyboarding, forget about all of them except None, Dissolve, and Move or Wipe. These simulate the most typical transitions found in film and video, which are the cut, dissolve, push, and wipe transitions. Each of these types of transitions has specific uses:

None or Cut   The None option, or a cut transition, is the shortest way from one scene to another. This is the transition you need to use when you are moving from one camera angle to another in the same scene. You can also use this to transition to a different scene, which can be jarring but is acceptable.

Dissolve   The Dissolve option, where one scene gradually fades into another, is a transition used to show time passing or to soften the transition between different scenes. You can also use a dissolve between different camera angles in the same scene, which has the effect of making time pass more slowly or quickly, depending on to which scenes you transition.

Wipe or Move   Both of these transitions are best used to move to a different scene. Using a wipe or push transition is typically used as a "meanwhile, back at the ranch" kind of transition where you want to separate a scene from what preceded it.

Figure 7.4

By keeping the Tutorial
Storyboard Images and
Demon Encounter
shows in separate parts
of the screen, you can
easily switch back and
forth between the two
so that you can copy
and paste images.

Let's set the scene first by clicking and dragging the background image in slide 5 of the Tutorial Storyboard Images.key show onto slide 4 of the Demon Encounter show (see Figure 7.5).

The background alley image should nicely fill up the Slide Canvas, with no space at the top, bottom, or sides. Once you have that in place, select Arrange → Lock, or press ⌘+L to lock the background down. The reason you want to do this is so you don't accidentally click and move the background while you are adjusting the positions of your characters.

Now that you have a background, add the characters. You can't just drag the image of Anne over slide 4 because Keynote will just create a new slide of Anne rather than placing her image in slide 4. To get around this, follow these steps:

1. Click the MCU of Anne from slide 6 in the Tutorial Storyboard Images show.

2. Now select Edit → Copy or press ⌘+C.

3. Paste the image into slide 4.

Now do the same for the Kismet character; copy him from slide 7 of the Tutorial Storyboard Images show to slide 4 of the Demon Encounter show. When both characters are on the Slide Canvas, position them so that Anne is in the left-third of the screen, and Kismet is crouching in the top-right third of the screen. To position Kismet behind Anne, click his image, and then select Arrange → Send Backward or press ⌘+-. Now slide 4 should look something like Figure 7.6.

Now add the fake camera focus in slide 8 of the Tutorial Storyboard Images show, which is simply the same MCU image of Anne, only blurred using a Gaussian blur filter in Adobe After Effects. You can do the same type of effect in Adobe Photoshop; I just used After Effects because I also wanted to adjust the alpha channel around the character.

When you copy in the blurred Anne above the regular Anne, the images might be a little off, which you need to fix to really create the illusion of a rack focus. A rack focus is a cinematography term in which the camera man focuses the lens on first one subject in a scene and then refocuses to bring attention to something that had been out of focus. In this example, we are simulating what it would look like if the camera initially had Anne in focus, and then did a "rack focus" so that Anne is blurred and Kismet is in focus. For the pupposes of storyboarding, we only need to show the one move from Anne in focus to Anne blurred. Line up the two Annes by simply clicking and dragging the blurred Anne above the regular Anne until the yellow horizontal and vertical alignment guides both show (see Figure 7.7).

Now move the blurred image behind the nonblurred Anne by again selecting Send Backward or by pressing ⌘+-.

Now you build. To make this work, follow these steps:

1. Dissolve the nonblurred Anne away.

2. Fade in the image of Kismet.

Figure 7.5

The new background for slide 4

Figure 7.6

Anne and Kismet placed into slide 4

Figure 7.7

Keynote's alignment guides not only line up individual elements but they also automatically help you line up similar sized objects with each other.

Now, let's start with Anne. Click the unblurred Anne, open the Inspector palette (unless it's already open), and click the Build Inspector.

The Build Inspector will show a preview of the slide. The first thing you want to do is turn off the First Build Requires Click option; instead, you want the first build to start immediately after the transition without waiting for a click.

1. The idea is for the image to fade out, so click the Build Out tab.

2. Select Dissolve from the Build Style pop-up menu.

3. Use the Speed slider in the bottom-right corner to adjust the speed of the transition. The farther to the right you pull the slider, the faster the transition. Generally, camera focusing happens pretty slowly, so move the Speed slider all the way over to the left.

As you can see, the top layer now dissolves to reveal the bottom blur layer. However, because both images are perfectly laid on top of each other, the effect is that the original image just got blurry, as shown in Figure 7.8. Cool, no?

Now let's fade in Kismet:

1. Click the Kismet figure.

2. Click the Build In tab in the Build Inspector.

3. Set the Build Style to Dissolve.

4. Set the Order to 2.

5. Set the speed about midway on the slider.

This makes sure that the first action is where you fade to the blurred Anne, and the second action is where Kismet fades in.

You need to make one last adjustment to this slide, which is more of an aesthetic point. Kismet looks too bright in this scene. You can't adjust the lighting of the scene, but you can change his opacity so that he blends into the background a bit more. Click the Graphic Inspector and adjust his opacity down to about 56 percent, which looks much better.

Now click the Play button in the toolbar to see the result. Your slide should show a fast fade from a focused Anne to a blurred Anne, followed by a slightly transparent Kismet fading into the background.

Using Builds, Transitions, and Alpha Channel Graphics

Now let's tackle slide 3, which takes advantage of the Build feature, transitions, and alpha channels.

First, here's the scene you want to portray:

FADE: MS ALLEY SIDE: ANNE continues down the alley. Hearing a sound, she pauses and looks to her left as she walks past. After she moves past, KISMET floats into the alley, hanging in midair and then fading away.

Figure 7.8

By fading between two different versions of the Anne graphic, you can simulate a camera defocusing effect, which is also called a *rack focus.*

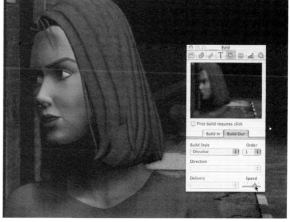

So you have four actions to show:

1. Anne moves down the alley.

2. Anne pauses as she hears a sound.

3. Kismet floats into alley.

4. Kismet fades away.

 Let's start with the background, which you're going to do a bit differently this time. Open the CD-ROM and find the two files `Alley Side (door).psd` and `Alley Side (floor).psd` (see Figure 7.9). The background is split into two files with their own alpha channels, which will give you some interesting options later.

In the Demon Encounter show, click slide 3. First, click and drag `Alley Side (floor).psd` onto the right side of the Slide Canvas. Second, do the same for `Alley Side (door).psd`, only positioning it on the left side of the Slide Canvas. It's important to do this in the right order (but you can always fix it later if necessary). Position the Alley Side (door) image so that the top of the graphic is at the top of the screen, with the door around the middle of the screen. Now move the other side of the alley into position so that it completes the image. To make things a bit easier, there are two white lines on each graphic; to hook the pictures up, just line up the white lines on top of each other, as shown in Figure 7.10.

What you've just done is add two layers to the Slide Canvas, which you can use to simulate a background with depth. Once you've lined up the background images, keep them from being moved around by locking both of them (clicking them and pressing ⌘+L).

Figure 7.9

By splitting up the background and giving each one an alpha channel, you can create some nice foreground and background plates in Keynote.

Figure 7.10

Use the white lines in the graphic to line up the two parts of the background.

Next, bring your `Tutorial Storyboard Images.key` file back up, copy the image of Kismet standing from slide 4, and paste it into slide 3 of the Demon Encounter show. His Big Badness now appears in front of the door. Thanks to the two backgrounds, you can now place him behind the door. With Kismet still selected, select Arrange → Send Backward or simply press ⌘+-. Now Kismet's left arm vanishes behind the door (see Figure 7.11). If you clicked Send Backward again, he'd disappear entirely, having been moved behind the `Alley Side (floor).psd` graphic.

Using this technique of layering graphics with alpha channels, you can create all kinds of interesting foreground and background elements that your characters can move in front of or behind to give a greater sense of depth to your storyboard.

Copy and paste the image of Anne from slide 3 of the Tutorial Storyboard Images show into slide 3 of the Demon Encounter show. She should now be on the left side of the Slide Canvas so that you see the brick wall behind her.

Now let's add some motion to this scene. With Anne still selected, click the Build Inspector, select the Build In tab, and then do the following:

1. Click the Build In tab and set the Build Style to Move In.

2. Set the Direction to Right to Left.

3. Set the Speed slider almost all the way to the left, as you want her to slowly move across the screen.

Keynote automatically numbers the builds, so starting a Build In with one element is 1, another Build In is 2, and the next action is 3.

That moves her into the scene for the pause. Now let's move her out:

1. Click the Build In tab and set the Build Style to Move In.

2. Set the Direction to Right to Left.

3. Set the Speed slider all the way to the left.

Now Anne moves in and out of the scene. Click Kismet to add him the scene:

1. Click the Build In tab in the Build Inspector.

2. Set the Build Style to Move In.

3. Set the Direction to Left to Right.

4. Set the Speed slider to the second notch from the left.

Now let's have him move out:

1. Click the Build Out tab.

2. Set the Build Style to Dissolve.

3. Set the Speed slider all the way to the left for a nice slow dissolve.

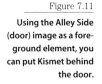

Figure 7.11

Using the Alley Side (door) image as a foreground element, you can put Kismet behind the door.

Notice how this changes the order for each build. With the final Build Out for Kismet, the build order is up to 4, which represents the four actions you've created with the Build Inspector.

Now you want to keep the tension up, so you cut to slide 5, where you see a reverse shot (from Kismet's perspective). I created these by just turning the camera around in Poser and rendering a picture of both Kismet and Anne. In the `Demon Encounter.key` file, I've already set up a build transition for Kismet so that he moves upward into the frame, making it look like he is rising from his crouched position in the previous slide.

In slide 4, you cut back to Anne's perspective with a tighter close up. Using the original image of Kismet that I created for slide 3, I created a blurred image to simulate a tight focus on Anne (see Figure 7.12). What's nice about this is that any director of photography would see this image from your storyboard and know exactly what kind of shot you are looking for (and even what lens they will need to use to get this look).

For slide 7, you move to the reverse shot again, only this time with a different image of Anne that shows her fearfully looking behind her (see Figure 7.13). The only thing to note is that the transition on slide 6 to slide 7 is None. Why? Because you want to simulate a cut, which is the most common kind of transition. A cut also is just the kind of abrupt transition that keeps the viewers on edge.

Cutting to slide 8, you have the typical reaction shot, where the heroine breathes a sigh of relief, having seen nothing. Now, this is a slight break from tradition but still a good use of Keynote as a storyboarding tool. Slides 8 and 9 are actually one shot, in which two moves happen. First, you have the MCU of Anne and then you zoom out to a medium wide shot, just

Figure 7.12

Using a blurred version that you scaled up, you can create a tight focus on Anne with the demon Kismet coming up right behind her.

Figure 7.13

Anne looks back, but there's nothing there. Moving to this slide uses a cut transition, which is the same as no transition.

Figure 7.14

Set your slide transition to Scale and set the Direction to In to simulate a camera zoom.

as Kismet lands in front of Anne. To approximate this camera movement, you can set the transition from slide 8 to slide 9 to Scale and then set the Direction to In (see Figure 7.14). Of course, this isn't the exact look, but again you want this storyboard to just provide broad strokes for those involved, so they can better understand how you are approaching the script.

Slide 10 moves you behind Anne to see Kismet's expression from over Anne's shoulder (see Figure 7.15). This is another example of reusing elements to help build your scene. The background image is the same shot of the alley used in slides 5 and 7; I just resized it to make it appear that the viewer is both closer to the wall and farther into the alley. You could just as easily reposition it so that the windows were higher or even drag it back so that the alley is farther behind the two characters. How you set up the scene is completely up to you. Thanks to the flexibility of Keynote, you can keep rearranging positions of scenery and characters until you are satisfied.

Slides 11 through 13 are close ups that you'll use to cut back and forth between during the conversation between Kismet and Anne (see Figure 7.16). Again, all you've done is to resize the image of Kismet from the front and the image of Anne that you first saw in slide 6. Keynote can resize things quite nicely, but it is also a good idea to not keep giant graphics in each slide. To that end, I made separate files that showed Kismet and Anne from the chest up and from the front. This way I didn't have to resize either character so large that only 20 percent of their image (such as their face) is showing on screen. Notice how you can also simulate the growing tension as, with each slide starting with slide 11, you move closer into both subjects.

Figure 7.15

Using only one new element and several resized elements, you show Kismet confronting the heroine.

IT'S NOT MINE, IT'S NOT YOURS, IT'S *OURS*.

One of the other wonderful side benefits of storyboarding is that it opens up the discussion with your collaborators (such as the director of photography, actors, and so on). You may deviate completely from what you originally came up with, yet the benefits you get from openly working with other people to find an idea that blends the best of all perspectives can be impressive.

Naturally, the heroine is anything but helpless. When you cut back to a medium shot in slide 14, Anne jumps up with a powerful kick to the front. Once again you rely on the handy Move In transition in the Build menu, with the direction set to Bottom to Top (see Figure 7.17). This also works well because it starts the movement with Anne off the screen and then moves her into position. You could have also played this scene differently by cutting to behind Kismet so that all you see is Anne's wind up and delivery.

Finally, I decided to cut to a medium close up of Kismet, with a pained expression on his face for the last slide of the sequence (see Figure 7.18). This is a great example of trying to get your point across with a storyboard. You could just as easily have cut to a wide shot that showed Anne's foot connecting with Kismet's groin, but stylistically, I think it is better to just show the impact from his facial expression. By cutting to his look of pain just as the kick lands, you have only his expression to tell you how much her kick hurt—and you let the audience imagine how effective the blow was. Is this the way you would direct this scene? Maybe not, but at least you have a solid visual reference to discuss as you try to find the best way to approach the story.

Figure 7.16

Using scaled-up versions of the characters, you can show some nice tension between the characters.

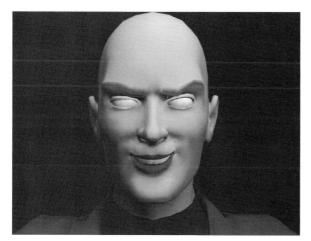

Now let's see the show. Click the first slide in the Demon Encounter show and then click the Play button. Don't forget to keep either clicking the mouse or pressing the spacebar to keep the show going. If your mouse-clicking finger is sprained at this point, you can also refer to the QuickTime movie version of this sequence (`Demon Encounter Final.mov`).

TIPS FROM THE PROS: STEVEN KATZ ON STORYBOARDING

S.D. Katz (Steven D. Katz) is a film director and writer who contributes to a variety of publications, including *Scenario* and *Millimeter*. Steven is also the author of the best-selling book *Film Directing Shot by Shot: Visualizing from Concept to Screen* (Michael Wiese Productions, 1991) and *Film Directing, Cinematic Motion: A Workshop for Staging Scenes* (Michael Wiese Productions, 1998), which is the definitive book on film design. To give you a better idea on storyboarding, Steven shared some tips to get you started using storyboards:

A storyboard should emphasize the most important things in a script. Close your eyes and imagine the most important scenes in your script. Chances are you'll have something come up visually. Think to yourself "What one frame would I need to see all the action?" Start with the simplest scene and work to the most complex.

Digital cameras are great storyboarding tools. Digital cameras are one of the great boons to storyboarding. You could get a few actors, shoot different shots with a camera, and then convert those frames into digital images, which you can put into your storyboards. Drawing is good for those who can draw, but a digital camera is just fine for those who can't.

Don't get bogged down by the storyboarding process. Keep things simple. You don't need to be able to draw; you can use stick figures. If you are shooting *Lawrence of Arabia,* then that's different—you probably need detailed, high-quality art. However, the majority of things are shot in rooms and locations that are readily available. If it is taking too long for the tool to do what you want, then you need use another tool or method. Also, don't get overwhelmed with trying to storyboard every single shot in your movie. If you can do 30 percent of your movie, then you are way ahead of the game.

Give yourself a to-do list. You will build up many materials and shots in the process of creating your storyboard. Get organized before you get started; make sure you know where your images are located, keep track of what shots you need to show, and so on. Develop an organization system so that you can save yourself headaches later.

Figure 7.17

Using the Move In from Bottom to Top command in the Build menu, you help Anne make her point.

Figure 7.18

In the end, Kismet gets a big kick out of talking with Anne.

This is just a small example of the kind of storyboards you can do with Keynote. By changing the order of the images, as well as the transitions of each slide or even each element, you can really play with the flow of a scene.

On the companion CD-ROM is a file called `All Storyboard Images.key`, which contains all the images that appeared in the final sequence you built. Feel free to try out different images in different slides or even completely change the order to make the scene play out the way you'd like it to look. For example, what if you used mostly close ups or more distance shots—how does that affect the scene?

In the next chapter, you'll really put the squeeze on Keynote as you create a mini-documentary/promotional video using Keynote and iMovie.

CHAPTER 8

Do-It-Yourself Documentary:
Adding Audio and Video Elements

In documentary you do not shoot with your head only but also with your stomach muscles.
—John Grierson (1898–1972), British film producer and founder of the documentary
film movement

Just about the only limit to what you can create with Keynote is your imagination. Keynote can even be a great tool for self-marketing, where you create presentations to showcase yourself or your interests. In this chapter, you'll expand on that idea with a mini-documentary/promotional digital video clip that you'll create using Keynote, Adobe Photoshop, iMovie, and a scanner. Although this chapter's project is specific to a theater group, you could just as easily apply it to anything you want to promote, from a wedding to a martial arts organization.

Introducing Theater Simple

Prepping the project

Adding fancy transitions

Adding video

Adding audio using iMovie

Exporting your show

Tips from the Pros: Multimedia Marketing

Introducing Theater Simple

Theater Simple is the brainchild of Llysa Holland and Andrew Litzky, two amazing actors I've known for more than 20 years. The goal behind Theater Simple is to create excellent theater regardless of how much money you have to work with.

Over the years, I've seen them put on incredible productions that would put Broadway shows to shame, yet they do it with nearly no budget. Winning awards and audiences from Seattle to Australia (and quite a few places in between), Andrew and Llysa are shining examples of the creative spirit at work.

Yet even shining examples have to succumb to the drudgery of constantly marketing themselves. Every theater festival, arts grant, and contest entry requires custom promotional material, all at a moment's notice. Andrew and Llysa have a website, but it includes only still images and text describing each show and the theater troupe. So why not create downloadable movie files that they can update as needed that combine text, images, and video clips?

This leads us to this chapter's promotional video project. Llysa has provided some great materials to use:

- Dozens of still images from their productions
- Several videos of their shows
- Text from the website

The goal is to take all of this material and combine it with a short presentation that describes each show and gives the viewer a sample of what the show looks like when fully produced.

Using some imagination and a few production skills, I turned Keynote into an image compositing, animation, and video production machine. For this book I included a copy of one of the videos I did for them on their show *The Master and Margarita,* which I've called `Master and Margarita Keynote.mov`. You can find this in the Chapter 8 folder on the companion CD-ROM.

As you play the file, you'll see a lot of animation, sound effects, music, and even a full motion video clip. The following sections show how I created the video.

Prepping the Project

Like all creative projects, the first thing you need to do is to get organized. I not only logged in all of the material that Llysa provided but also took notes on where the productions where held and which year they were produced. When you are working with dozens of images, sounds, and so on, it is easy to lose track of their locations and formats. By taking a bit of time to document everything, you will save yourself hours of pain later.

Setting Up the Keynote Project

Next, we set up Keynote in preparation for the project. Specifically, we need to do two things:

- Create a custom slide size
- Create a new theme

Select File → Slide Size, and you'll see a dialog box that allows you to choose the height and width of your project. For the Theater Simple project, set the width to 720-pixels wide by 480-pixels high, as shown in Figure 8.1.

The reason for this will become clearer when you start adding sound effects and the like. For now, just know that 720×480 happens to be the size of a frame of digital video.

Creating a Custom Theme

The 12 themes in Keynote work just fine for most presentations, but you can also completely customize a theme for your own shows. I put off this section until now because it is a lot easier to do once you've mastered some basic Keynote operations. For this show, you're going to create an all-black theme that will be the reverse of the White theme.

Creating an all-black theme is important for two reasons: First, black can hide imperfections in an alpha channel (in other words, if there is still some "dirt" in the mask, then it won't show up as much). Second, many of the images Theater Simple provided have dark or black backgrounds, so providing a black-on-black background will give a better depth to the image. In this case, the images appear to be floating in a black background so that the images blend more readily into the background.

Figure 8.1

Instead of using the typical 800×600 or 1024×768 slide sizes, the Master and Margarita Keynote show uses a 720×480 slide size.

Finally, and most important, you want as much black in the image as possible to improve the final compression in the QuickTime movie that will contain the final project. Image compression codecs (such as MPEG-4 or Sorenson Video 3) reduce the size of images by taking out redundant image information. So, instead of saving every blue pixel in a blue sky, a codec such as MPEG-4 only captures the different blue pixels and duplicates the others as needed. Needless to say, this can drastically reduce the size of a still image or movie; however, the more you compress an image, the more likely it is that the compressed media will not resemble the original.

> You don't have to use only black; any solid background will do. However, the more you use one color, the better your compression will be.

To create a custom theme, you must go through four steps:

- Changing all master slides
- Setting your default text type and style
- Setting the default chart type
- Saving your theme

There is good and bad news to each of these steps. First, the bad news: Making a custom theme can be tedious work because you have to manually change over every font and background on each master slide. The good news is that it isn't *hard* work, and—once completed—your custom theme will always be available to you via the Themes window.

Starting Your Custom Theme

Open a new Keynote presentation, and select the White theme. I like using this theme to start custom presentations because it's easy to track changes in the background and in the text used. To create an all-black theme you need to change every master slide so that the background is black and the text white. If this sounds pretty straightforward, it is—you just have to do it for every slide master:

1. First, click the Views icon in the toolbar and select Show Master Slides. Nearly all the work you need to do to create the custom theme will happen in the master slide area.

2. Next, click the first slide, which is the Title & Subtitle slide.

3. To change the text, select it and the open the Text Inspector.

4. Change the color of the text to white.

5. Now, click the Shape tool icon in the toolbar and create a square that will completely cover the Slide Canvas.

6. Set the color of the square to black in the Graphic Inspector and remove the stroke.

7. Finally, select the square and send it behind your white text by selecting Arrange → Send to Back.

Your first master slide should now have a black background and white text for the Title & Subtitle (see Figure 8.2). This is what you need to do for each master slide to create a full custom theme. Of course, you could just do the master slides you need now, but if you do it all now you don't have to do it again.

Formatting Chart Types in a Custom Theme

Next, you can set the chart type. If you don't plan to use any charts with your custom theme, then you can skip this part. If not, all you do is create a master slide with a chart. To do this, follow these steps:

1. Duplicate the Blank master slide by selecting it and then choosing Edit → Duplicate. Make sure it has the black square as the background.

2. With the new Blank master slide selected, click the Chart icon in the toolbar.

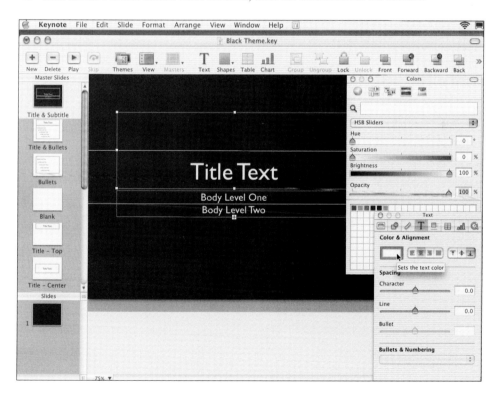

Figure 8.2

To start customizing the theme, you need to change all the master slides so that they have a black background and white text.

3. Using the Object Inspector and Color Inspector, adjust the colors of the text and chart bars to better suit the dark background. (I used bright contrasting colors with a white drop shadow to help add depth.)

4. When you are finished adjusting your chart, set this chart as a default for the theme by selecting Define Defaults for Master Slides and then selecting Define Column Chart for Current Master (see Figure 8.3). If you want this chart style to apply to all the master slides, then select Define Column Chart for All Masters.

Setting Text for a Custom Theme

Only two more steps are left in creating the custom theme. All the master slides have white text and black backgrounds, and you've created your custom chart. Unfortunately, every time you add text on the screen now you'll have black text on a black background. To fix this, follow these steps:

1. Click the Text icon in the toolbar. The text will show up in the center of the screen, with only the block outline of the text visible.

2. Now open the Text Inspector and change the color of the text to white.

Figure 8.3

Once you've defined the chart type, this chart opens automatically anytime you add a chart in your new theme.

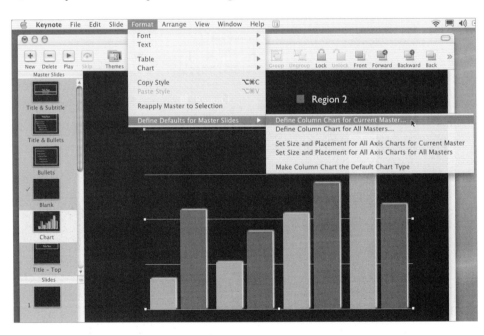

3. If you want to make changes to the font, then open the Font Inspector and adjust the type and size according to your preferences. (For the black theme, I increased the Gil Sans font size to 60.)

4. Finally, select Format → Define Defaults for Master Slides → Define Text for All Masters (see Figure 8.4).

Saving a Custom Theme

Now all that is left is to save your theme. Do this by selecting File → Save Theme. This saves your theme, complete with master slides, default chart, and text styles. The next time you open Keynote, your new theme will appear in the Themes window so you can access it from within Keynote.

You can add a title to your theme by creating a blank slide and then adding text that has the name of your theme. Remember to make the text large (nearly big enough to fill the entire screen).

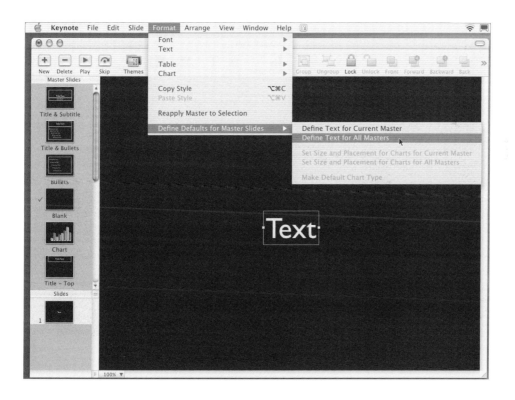

Figure 8.4

Once you've defined the text style by using the Define Text for All Masters command, each time you apply text it will use your new default settings.

Scanning

Once you set up the slide size and new black theme in Keynote, you need to start digitizing all of your images. Although you can use any scanner, for this project I used an Epson Perfection 2400 Photo scanner to scan in all the images that Llysa provided. The great thing about this model is that it can scan slides, transparencies, and just about anything you throw at it. The ability to handle a variety of still image types really came in handy; Theater Simple provided a variety of 8×10 photos, 35-millimeter slides, and a few 4×5 transparencies.

However, regardless of which scanner you use, when scanning images to use in Keynote, you need to keep a few things in mind.

- Keep the image to 72 dots per inch (dpi). In these days of low-cost but high-resolution scanners, it's easy to go nuts and scan in a 2,400dpi image. This is a total waste of time because Keynote uses the Mac's screen resolution of 72dpi—anything higher will appear huge on the Slide Canvas.

- Don't make your images more than 1.5 times larger than the Slide Canvas. Again, you don't want to swamp the Mac's processor and Keynote with too much image data to move around. If you scan in your image no larger than 1.25 times the size of the Slide Canvas in the largest direction, then you'll be fine.

So, a good scan size for an 8'×10' photo that is destined for an 800×600-pixel slide show is 1000 wide×750 high.

This gives you plenty of room to move your image around, but it isn't impossible for Keynote to push the image around the screen.

Editing in Photoshop

Once the images were scanned in, I removed their backgrounds so that I could layer them together in Keynote. Naturally, I used Adobe Photoshop, which is the best image-editing application on the planet.

> Yes, I'm a bit biased about Photoshop, having used it when it wasn't even a professional program—just a utility supplied with a Barneyscanner professional scanning system. Even back then I was able to create professional results with Photoshop, which in that case meant creating color separations for *Publish* magazine. That's what I was able to do with Photoshop version 0; with today's program, there are few limits to what you can do.

In Photoshop, I first did some image adjustment so that the black backgrounds were not washed out or too low contrast. You can do this in a dozen different ways in Photoshop; I've always been comfortable using the Levels feature (Image → Adjustments → Levels).

Next, I removed the backgrounds on each of the images and applied an alpha channel to the image. Again, there are dozens of ways to do this. I used Photoshop's Extract plug-in, which does a nice job of removing a subject from the background. Once you've opened Extract from the plug-in's menu in Photoshop, you trace around the outside of an image and then use a paint bucket fill for the inside of that image. Extract then uses a custom algorithm to detect the edge of your image, delete the background, and pull your subject out of the background (see Figure 8.5). The Extract plug-in is not fool-proof, and you'll need to work with the image to cleanly separate your subject from its background, but it can save you a bit of time.

Once the background was removed, I created an alpha channel by selecting the empty background and then adding a layer mask that "hid the selection." This is a critical step because without an alpha channel mask, your image will not have a transparent background in Keynote. Another way is to simply create an alpha channel from scratch by painting in the transparent areas in the image (see Figure 8.6). Again, there are about a dozen ways to do this in Photoshop; for more information, check out any of the great Photoshop books from Sybex, including *Photoshop 7 Savvy* by Steve Romaniello.

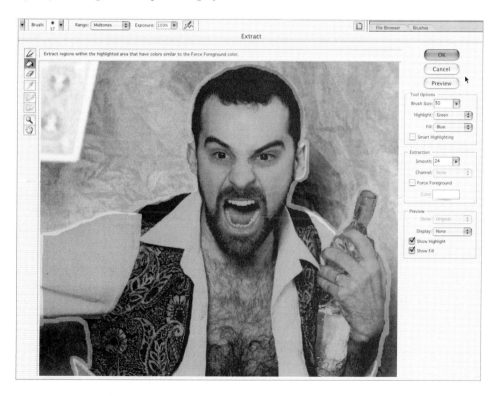

Figure 8.5

Using Photoshop's Extract plug-in is a fast way to remove backgrounds from an image.

Figure 8.6

Using the dozens of
tools in Photoshop, you
can create an alpha
channel for your graph-
ics. Here I created an
alpha channel from
scratch.

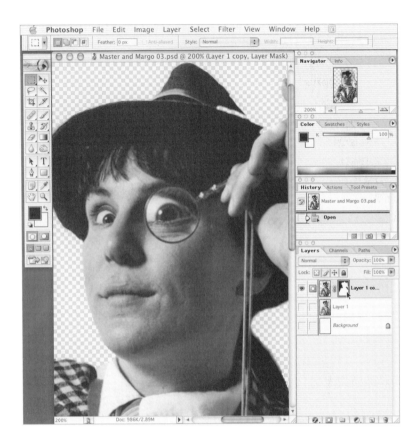

To clean up any material that might have not been removed when you extracted the image,
create a gray background layer behind the image. This helps locate and then clean up any
residue that might still be in the image.

Converting the Digital Video

Finally, I had to bring the video into the computer. Luckily the video was recorded onto DV
(which stands for *digital video* or, in some circles, *digital versatile*) tape, so all I had to do
was transfer the footage from the DV deck to my Macintosh via a FireWire cable.

I used Final Cut Pro to bring in the footage, but you can also use Apple's iMovie (which is
free) to import the footage. Once it was on my Mac, I added a quick opening and closing title,
as well as an opening transition. The video clip was the final element I needed, so I started
building the project.

If you want to add video footage to your presentations but the footage was not recorded on a DV tape, you can still convert your camcorder or VCR video to a digital video signal that you can send via FireWire to your Mac. One great (and inexpensive) product for this is the Dazzle Hollywood DV-Bridge. It's an embarrassing name, but I've found Dazzle makes good products (its DVD authoring package is still the low-price/big-on-features leader on the Windows side of things).

Setting Up Fancy Transitions

To help you understand a bit better, open and follow along with `The Master and Margarita Sampler.key` file in the Chapter 8 folder on the CD-ROM.

The mini-presentation needs to have four main parts:

- As quickly as possible, we need to give a quick synopsis of the play's story.
- We need to mention some of the awards that the show has won to add interest.
- We need to show the video clip.
- We need to give contact information at the end of the show.

To keep things simple, you can put each of these points on one separate slide, so already you are up to four slides. You'll also add three slides: a Theater Simple logo slide, a title slide for *The Master and Margarita* play, and an empty black slide at the end of the show. Why the last slide? This is so that when you export to a self-contained QuickTime movie, you'll be sure to have a clean black screen at the end instead of a slide caught at the tail end of a transition.

Making Title Elements Transition In

For the opening logo, I just use three elements:

- A red circle stretched into an oval
- The *theater simple* text
- The *PRESENTS* text

To set this up, you'll use three builds on slide 1:

1. Selecting the oval, I used a Flip transition on the oval (from Bottom to Top, which you set in the Build In order section of the Build Inspector as 1).

2. Then you can scale the *theater simple* text in front of the oval using Build Style → Scale. Set the text to 2 in the Build In order.

3. To make the text a bit more readable, add a drop shadow to the text using the Graphic Inspector. This makes the text stand out against the oval.

4. Next, set the *PRESENTS* text to fade in by setting it to 3 on the Build In order.

5. Finally, select the Cube transition in the Slide Inspector and set it to transition from Bottom to Top so that the entire slide does a nice three-dimensional cube move to the next slide.

The second slide also has three elements:

- The *The Master and* text
- A picture of Llysa from the show
- The *Margarita* text

Here again, you can use the Build Inspector to add separate elements into the screen. There are three separate moves:

1. First, *The Master and* text moves in.

2. Next, the picture of Llysa pivots in from the bottom left.

3. Finally, the *Margarita* text fades in.

Each of the internal transitions that I created using the Build Inspector is pretty fast. In the same way that no one ever complains if you finish your presentation early, no one will complain if your transitions are a bit too fast. However, keep in mind that you can turn your audience off if your transitions are too slow.

Building Complex Slide Transitions

If you click slide 3, you'll see that it's a bit of a mess. Six separate elements on slide 3 pop in and out of the slide over time but simply appear to be all over each other on the Slide Canvas. Rather than show each section in different slides, you want to keep everything in one place. The main advantage is that you can add sound effects or dialogue to this slide and not have the audio file cut off by a transition to a new slide.

> Keynote's inability to play a sound file across multiple slides is a major down point for the program. However, by the time you read this, Apple may have an update that fixes this limitation.

I do a lot of image compositing, so juggling multiple image files in one space like this is not difficult. However, if you find organizing a slide like this overwhelming, it helps to make up a table to plot when things occur.

For example, first figure out the order that things will display on the screen:

1. The stage image

2. The text *The Story*

3. The *Story description* text

4. Woland dancing image

5. Summary text

6. Llysa and James image

Now that you know the order things appear, you can fill out the rest of your table with the appropriate information. Just keep these two things in mind:

- If you want an element to leave the screen, then you need to provide a Build Out transition.

- The next element you want to see has to have a Build In order that follows the Build Out of the previous element.

With this in mind, Table 8.1 shows how to set up slide 3.

To create the proper order for each clip, you'll need to first click the image and then set both its transition type and order in the Build Inspector. Notice how I had the story description text move in as number 2 of the build but had it move out as number 4. This allowed the image of Woland dancing to fly across the text before it disappeared, which I did just because it made the sequence a bit more fun. I also did this effect at the end where the image of James and Llysa pops up in front of the text and then drops back down. The difference was that I didn't set a Build Out for the summary text, hence it stayed after James and Llysa appeared and disappeared.

One last note: While you are building with multiple elements on the screen, don't forget to use the Build Inspector's preview window to help sort things out, as shown in Figure 8.7.

ELEMENT	BUILD IN NUMBER	TYPE	BUILD OUT NUMBER	TYPE	
Stage image	No build		No build out		Table 8.1
Story text	1	Drop	No build out		**Setup for Slide 3**
Story description text	2	Move In	4	Twirl	
Image of Woland dancing	3	Move In	5	Dissolve	
Summary text	6	Flip	No build out		
Llysa and James image	7	Move In (Bottom to Top)	8	Move In (Top to Bottom)	

Figure 8.7

**If things get too clut-
tered on screen, keep in
mind that you can still
see how things will
appear over time in the
Build Inspector's pre-
view window.**

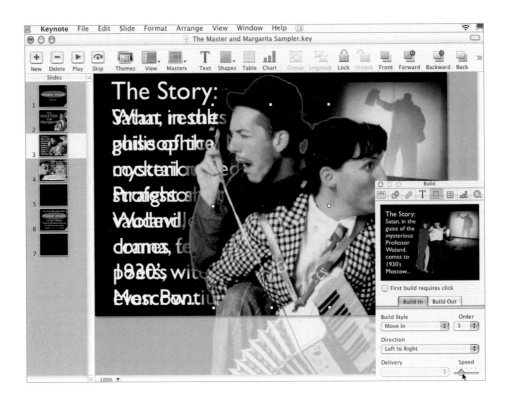

Figure 8.7

If things get too clut-
tered on screen, keep in
mind that you can still
see how things will
appear over time in the
Build Inspector's pre-
view window.

Cheshire Cat: Transitioning an Image in Stages

Slide 4 (the awards slide) takes a cue from the storyboard chapter (Chapter 7, "Video Storyboard: Building Slide Actions") by combining three similar images in the same slide. In addition to the text bubble and the text on the awards, I used the same image of Llysa and James
as Behemoth the Cat and processed them three ways.

- One regular layer with the background removed

- One layer with only the eyes and mouth on James showing (left)
- One layer with Llysa only (right)

Once I placed the first image of both Llysa and James, I then resized and positioned the other layers on top of the first image. I then send each layer behind the first. After that, it was just a matter of positioning the text and then setting the order of the build. With slide 4 done, I could add the video clip to slide 5.

Adding Video

Adding video into your Keynote presentation should be straightforward—just click and drag your QuickTime movie clip onto the Slide Canvas and you are done, right? Unfortunately, there is only one problem with this: QuickTime video playback in Keynote is not great.

Specifically, although you can play back a full-screen video clip in Microsoft's PowerPoint program, the original version release of Keynote starts to seriously choke if you use a video clip larger than 25 percent of the screen. Apple improved QuickTime playback significantly in Keynote 1.1.

However, if you find your full-sized movie file is giving Keynote troubles, not to worry. You can still use full-screen movies in your Keynote presentations—you just have to export the whole presentation as a QuickTime file.

Another alternative, if you really need to play back a digital video clip inside of Keynote, is to create a full-screen QuickTime movie using the Apple MPEG-4 codec. I was able to place a full-screen version of the Master and Margarita Keynote file into the Keynote presentation by doing this. The original DV QuickTime file was around 590 megabytes (MB), but after a resaving it using the MPEG-4 codec, the file squeezed down to just 39MB. The image quality isn't quite as good, but the playback is much smoother. However, even then you might have problems if the Macintosh computer you use doesn't have enough horsepower to smoothly play back the movie file.

After adding the video file (by doing the click and drag just as described earlier) and completing all the production on the contact slide (slide 6), you are ready to export the presentation. To do this, select File → Export. The next dialog box gives you three choices:

- QuickTime
- PowerPoint
- PDF

Don't forget to embed your movie. If you move your Keynote presentation to another computer and want to retain the movie, make sure you embed that movie in your Keynote file. To do this, select the Copy Movies into Document check box when you are in the Save dialog box.

After picking QuickTime from the Export dialog box, you then get a new dialog box, where you have some important choices to make in the upper Playback Control and lower Formats sections.

The Playback Control section gives you two choices: Interactive Slideshow or Self-Playing Movie (see Figure 8.8). If you want to create a version of your presentation that you could control—in other words, a version that you could click through at your own pace—then you select the Interactive Slideshow option. This simply compresses all the graphics together but gives you the ability to click forward one slide at a time.

For this project, choose the Self-Playing Movie option. Once a user plays the movie, then the show will just play through. You set the timing of the show using the Slide Duration and Build Duration controls, which sets the amount of seconds between actions.

You'll want to set the duration for both of these rather low. For example, for the Master and Margarita Keynote project, using a Slide Duration of 2 seconds and a Build Duration of 2 seconds is almost too slow! The reason is that Slide Duration primarily counts the time between slides, especially when there are many builds inside a slide. So, a slide that has six builds with a 2-second Build Duration and a 2-second Slide Duration will actually take 14 seconds (six builds times two seconds plus two seconds for the slide duration). Hence, adding additional time to the Slide Duration will make for a slooooow show.

Deciding which format to pick is easy because this chapter uses iMovie to add audio to the presentation. Skip past all the preset options, and go directly to Custom. Once you are at Custom, you have some more choices to make. For these purposes, you want to keep

Figure 8.8

The QuickTime Export dialog box in Keynote is where you can setup up a variety of options in your QuickTime movie file, including the timing of slides and builds and whether you want the movie to continuously loop.

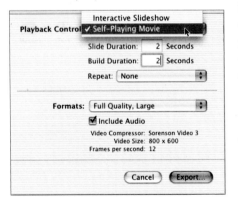

your presentation at the original size (720×480, which as you remember is the native size of digital video files) and use as little compression as possible but also be compatible with iMovie or another other video editing application that can use multiple audio tracks.

The best QuickTime format for exporting to a video editing application is DV/DVC PRO–NTSC, which is the standard DV codec. Using this codec will lower image resolution a bit, but you will also have complete compatibility with nonlinear editing systems such as Final Cut Pro, Final Cut Express, or even iMovie.

Finally, if your movie has stereo sound, it's not a bad idea to compress that down to one channel if you plan to add more audio. iMovie only has a few audio tracks (which is where you place additional audio files) to work with, so compressing your stereo file down to mono gives you more tracks with which to work. Once you make your selections, the Custom QuickTime window should look like Figure 8.9.

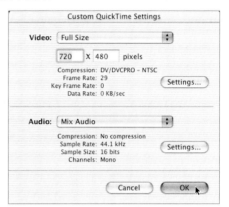

Figure 8.9

Use the Custom Quick-Time Settings window for exporting your Keynote presentation as a QuickTime movie file that can be used with video editing applications.

Once you've set up the export, click OK and then set the name and destination of your QuickTime movie. Just one more OK to click, and Keynote starts exporting your show. You can see Keynote's export progress in the small preview window, which slowly plays the show frame by frame while exporting.

As soon as the show finishes exporting, bring it into iMovie for some quick audio additions.

Adding Audio Using iMovie

iMovie is a great little video editing application on the Mac—it not only gets the job done for simple productions, but it comes at a great price (free!). iMovie has the ability to edit multiple audio tracks. So, for these purposes, it is just fine. Using iMovie, you are not held back by Keynote's inability to play a sound or music (or even multiple sounds) behind more than one slide at a time.

You could also do this same editing, with a lot more control over volume, panning, and so on, using Apple's Final Cut Pro or Final Cut Express editing products.

For the Master and Margarita Keynote project, bring in the exported Keynote application by dragging it into the Clips bin inside iMovie. It takes a few minutes for iMovie to digest your presentation.

Once it's in iMovie, a small thumbnail will show up in the Clips bin. Drag that to the timeline, which will show a long clip at the top.

After this, it is a matter of adding some background music and a few sound effects. For the background music, I used an instrumental piece from a musical that I'm writing. I had a copy of this piece in iTunes, so I was able to easily access that file from the Audio section of iTunes.

To emphasize the transitions within the slide, I added several sound effects (a "boing" sound when the *The Story* text drops in, a film projector sound before the video plays, and so on). The audio section of iMovie (beginning with version 2) also allows you to fade sounds in and out, so I was able to fade the background music out before the video starts playing (as shown in Figure 8.10).

Exporting Your Show

With the sound effects and music in, all that is left is to export the file from iMovie. You have a variety of options from which you can choose, including outputting your presentation to video using the DV output setting, outputting to DVD using the iDVD export option, and outputting to various formats of QuickTime. Because you are going to export this as a QuickTime movie, you'll want to customize the settings. First, choose File → Export; second, from the Formats pop-up list, choose the Expert Settings mode.

Figure 8.10

iMovie is a great tool you can use to add sound effects and background music to your Keynote presentations.

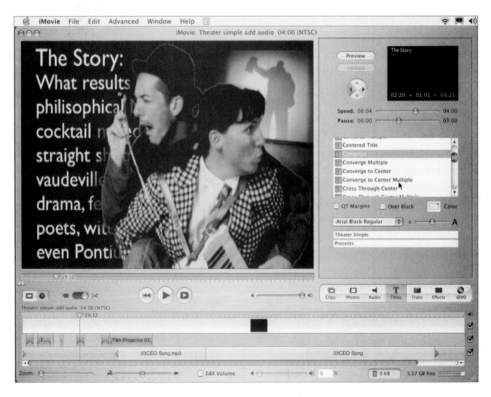

TIPS FROM THE PROS: ERIK HOLSINGER ON MULTIMEDIA MARKETING

It's time once again to mount the soapbox of Interactive Marketing Mayhem, with tales of desperation , hope about the evil necessity of entrepreneurship—self marketing. Over the years I've created everything from interactive magazine shows for Apple Computer CD-ROMs to animated web ads. The principles and limitations with these projects are similar, as are the pitfalls. The first thing you need to do before you begin creating your marketing presentation in Keynote is to take some time with some paper or your favorite word processor and plan out everything about your marketing project. By setting a few directions before you get started, you can maximize the success of your Keynote marketing presentation:

Who is your audience? This seems obvious, but you need to know everything you can about the people viewing your show. Are they prospective clients, and if so, are they the ones who will make final buying decisions? This requires a more specialized presentation and probably a personal visit. However, if you are doing a broad marketing tool, then you should avoid specifics such as costs or delivery times.

How is the presentation getting to the audience? Will they see it on their own computer, or will you display it on a monitor that they will pass by (such as in a trade show)? This determines many things, from the size of your text to the compression that you use when exporting a QuickTime version of your show. Generally, if you can control the playback circumstances and equipment, then you can push show sizes and complexity to the limit. However, if you can't control the circumstances, then make sure your show will playback on even the most meager Macintosh or Windows computers because chances are someone important will try to play your show on a machine that belongs in the Smithsonian.

Do you have a workable production schedule? Be realistic here; too often you can start working on a project thinking that it will take you X amount of time when it fact it can balloon out of control. For example, if you plan to add graphics, how many of those will you need to edit to adjust sizes or create alpha channels? Think carefully: Do you have a set deadline for the project, and if so, do you have any other projects or events that will conflict with it? If you do have a deadline, can you get the project done with style, or will you be rushing to complete everything at the last minute? The bottom line is that if you have to concentrate on several jobs at once, chances are they all will suffer. Pick a time when you can focus on your marketing show (even if only for a few hours).

Be entertaining—quickly. There is a long-standing rule of thumb about presentations and audiences that applies well to just about every type of show. If you can grab an audience's attention in the first 10 seconds, then you've got them until the 30-second mark; if you keep them interested at 30 seconds, then you've got them until one minute; if they are still thrilled at one minute, then you've got them for two to three minutes; you've enthralled your audience at three-and-a-half minutes, you can keep going until around five-and-a-half minutes. After five minutes, unless you can show Catherine Zeta-Jones doing a production number or a politician doing a dastardly deed, then you can count on losing your audience. Remember, even movie trailers generally last about a minute.

This opens the same kind of dialog window, where you have three areas you can set: Video, Sound, and Prepare for Internet Streaming (see Figure 8.11). Click the Settings button, and you'll see a pop-up menu that shows the different codecs you can use to compress your video. Although there are several different ones you can use that work well (such as the Sorenson Video 3 codec), the one you'll want to use for Keynote presentations is MPEG-4.

The reason MPEG-4 works especially well for Keynote is that the pure backgrounds and colors used by Keynote are easily compressed by MPEG-4 and yet still retain their quality. Although every presentation will require different compression settings, generally you'll have good results by using the Medium or High setting and setting the frame rate to 15 frames per second (as shown in Figure 8.12).

The other setting you will need to pay attention to is Limit Data Rate To. In general, for downloading off the Web you want to keep to a data rate of 35 kilobytes (KB) to 60KB per second, but a movie playing back from a CD-ROM can sustain a much higher data rate such as 100KB to 200KB per second.

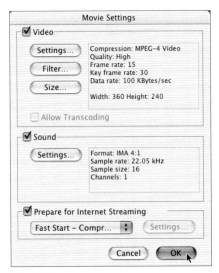

Figure 8.11

The Movie Settings dialog box

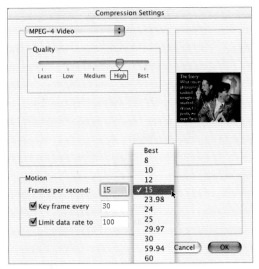

Figure 8.12

Exporting your sonically enhanced Keynote presentation from iMovie to MPEG-4 works well if you keep the Quality slider at Medium or High and also limit the frame rate to 15 frames per second.

Finally, you can also compress the audio to further reduce the size of your file. I've had good luck compressing both music and voice using the IMA 4:1 audio codec, which reduces the audio in a nearly lossless way down to 25 percent of its original size.

Ultimately you'll need to experiment with different settings to find the right balance between image qualities, smoothness of motion, and file size.

I've included two different versions of the Master and Margarita Sampler file. Notice that even though the large movie is twice the size of the small movie, thanks to the MPEG-4 compression it is only 24MB. With some work you could reduce this in size even further by reducing the size of the movie and the number of frames while increasing the amount of compression used.

So, there you have it, a mini-promotional video that uses Keynote as the primary compositing and media organization tool. Imagine doing the same for a wedding, where you use all the images and media from the ceremony to put together a mixed media wedding album. Just about anything that uses still images, audio, and video—from baby showers to important projects—are prime candidates for a Keynote production. All it takes is Keynote, a few other hardware tools, a bit of imagination and some patience.

PART III

Keynote Meets World

Congratulations, you know Keynote—now you've got to work with it beyond your own desktop. There's more to preparing a presentation than your software; you must be able to interchange files with other applications, especially PowerPoint. And then there's the entire purpose of your work: getting your message out to an audience, whether in person or in various types of output.

In this part of the book, we'll look at everything you need to know to work with Microsoft products, project your presentation, and produce your show for others through slides or print.

Chapter 9 **Keynote in the Networked World**

Chapter 10 **Keynote on the Road: Peripherals and Projectors**

Chapter 11 **Slide, Print, and Video Output**

CHAPTER 9

Keynote in the Networked World

It takes more than three weeks to prepare a good impromptu speech.
—Mark Twain (1835–1910)

Try as you might, eventually your island of Macintosh technology has to venture out into the real world. This chapter talks about that most obtuse of technological worlds, otherwise known as the Windows PC, paying special attention to Keynote's evil twin, Microsoft PowerPoint.

Using PowerPoint and Keynote Together

Exporting Keynote to PowerPoint

Importing PowerPoint to Keynote

Getting files from Windows PCs

Discovering where Keynote hides files

Tips from the Pros: John Rizzo on Mac/Windows File Compatibility

Comparing PowerPoint and Keynote

When Keynote first came out, the press proclaimed Keynote to be the "PowerPoint killer"—a new presentation application that would steal some of Microsoft's thunder. Yes, it did look impressive—after all, it prompted me to write a book about it! Still, as with many high-tech journalistic conclusions, this was based upon too little information and too many assumptions.

The bottom line is that Keynote will not replace PowerPoint any time soon—even on the Mac platform. Why? A couple of reasons:

- PowerPoint is bundled with Microsoft Office, the most ubiquitous productivity software package in the world.

- PowerPoint is cross platform, which historically has not been something in which Apple is interested.

- PowerPoint has the advantage of having gone through many versions, and Keynote is still a new product.

This last point is important because PowerPoint has many features you won't find in Keynote, and in some cases (such as QuickTime movie playback), PowerPoint is far superior to Keynote.

Because PowerPoint is here to stay, it is a good idea to find out how the two can work together. If you work on a Mac in a standard office environment (that is, with a mix of Macs and Windows computers), then chances are someone will throw you a PowerPoint file that you'll have to add to your Keynote presentation.

To better understand how to make this work, let's compare PowerPoint and Keynote.

Figure 9.1

Welcome to the machine: PowerPoint for OS X's interface is bristling with tool palettes, many of which offer more precise control over presentations than Keynote.

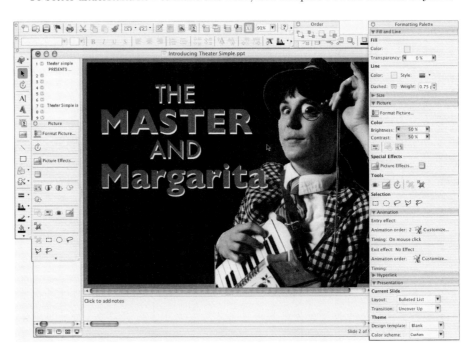

Interface Differences Reflect Feature Differences

Once you get past the price comparison, the main difference between PowerPoint and Keynote is in the amount of features you will find in PowerPoint. Looking at PowerPoint for OS X, you'd think you'd entered into a CAD (Computer Aided Design) program by mistake (as shown in Figure 9.1).

Instead of just one toolbar, PowerPoint has 18, each of which you can customize. These toolbars range from global controls, such as transitions or hyperlinks, to subtle controls that adjust the direction of an object's drop shadow.

Like Keynote's Inspector palette, PowerPoint has a main Formatting Palette, which you use to precisely format your slide. However, unlike Keynote's Inspector palette, PowerPoint's Formatting Palette has dozens of controls for fine-tuning your display, as shown in Figure 9.2.

Why bring this up? Am I going through a massive feature-envy spell? Actually, the reason is simple: I want to emphasize that PowerPoint has far more adjustments to keep track of than Keynote does. In other words, when you move presentations back and forth between PowerPoint and Keynote, you'll have a harder time converting PowerPoint presentations into Keynote presentations than the other way around. Keynote simply doesn't have as many features or controls that you'll have to convert. For example, Figure 9.3 shows the same presentation inside Keynote that Figure 9.1 showed in PowerPoint.

Table 9.1 breaks down the differences between PowerPoint and Keynote. Plus (+) signs indicate where one program has an advantage over the other.

Obviously there are many more differences between the two programs, but—given how often technology changes—it would be futile to detail every contrasting feature. From my perspective, there are really only three key differences between the two programs: graphic formatting, media control, and layout control.

Graphic Formatting

Keynote has a marked advantage over PowerPoint in its ability to handle alpha channel graphics and anti-aliased graphics—even when they've been resized (as shown in Figure 9.4). Power-Point can still only display a basic transparency, as opposed to the smooth alpha channel transparencies of Keynote (discussed later in this chapter). When doing graphics-intensive presentations, Keynote gives you far more options on what you can bring into your show.

Media Control

When it comes to media, however, PowerPoint handles video and audio files much better. You can run audio files all the way through your PowerPoint presentation and also smoothly play back full-screen video files. This would have come in handy for the mini-promotional movie you developed in Chapter 8, "Do-It-Yourself Documentary: Adding Audio and Video Elements"; you could have added sound effects on each slide and still have used a separate audio file for the background sound effect.

Figure 9.2

PowerPoint's Formatting Palette has dozens of features that you can use to design your presentation.

Table 9.1

**Comparing Keynote
and PowerPoint
Features**

KEYNOTE	POWERPOINT
Uses a thumbnail or Outline view on the left side.	+ Has separate outline, slide, slide and outline combo, and slide sorter views.
Slides are designed to move in a linear format (from the beginning to the end), but can move to different points if needed.	+ Slides can move in linear format or in nonlinear format (skipping back and forth to different points in the presentation) using hyperlinks.
+ Can accept a wide variety of graphics formats.	Can accept a limited variety of graphics formats.
+ Can play back movies, sounds, and Flash animation.	Can play back movies and sounds.
Can play back full-screen movies, even in native Digital Video (DV) format.	Can play back full-screen movies, even in native Digital Video (DV) format.
Sounds cut off when transitioning to next slide.	+ Sounds can play throughout the entire length of a slide show.
+ Can use alpha channels in graphics to create transparent backgrounds.	Can only create a one-color transparency.
+ Can export presentations to QuickTime, Portable Document Format (PDF), and PowerPoint.	Can only export different varieties of PowerPoint documents, Portable Document Format (PDF) documents (using the built-in PDF printing capability of Mac OS X), and still image files.
+ Uses alignment guides to position text and graphics consistently.	Uses an Alignment tool to position text and graphics but doesn't have a global alignment guide.
Can create transitions between multiple items on one slide.	Can create transitions between multiple items on one slide.
Only works under MacOS X.	+ Works on MacOS, MacOS X, and all varieties of Windows.
+ Is easy to use.	Has a steep learning curve.

Layout Control

Keynote's greatest strength lies in its ability to control the layout of each slide. Not only does each Keynote theme standardize how to treat bullets, graphics, and text, but also it is easy to maintain consistency thanks to the built-in alignment guides. This is one area where Keynote is much better than PowerPoint, which still requires users to judge alignment between slides by sight.

Figure 9.3

**By comparison,
Keynote's interface is
much sparser.**

If you have both programs on your Mac, you have the best of both worlds in presentation software. For example, you could use Keynote's Outline view and alignment guides to organize and lay out all the text on your slides. Then you could export your Keynote presentation to PowerPoint, where you could add graphics and multimedia files such as full-screen video and an audio track for your show. The only caveat is that you won't be able to take advantage of alpha channel graphics.

Keynote anti-aliased alpha channel graphic

PowerPoint single-color transparency, no anti-aliasing

Figure 9.4

When it comes to graphics, Keynote's ability to use alpha channel graphics gives it a major advantage over PowerPoint.

Exporting to PowerPoint

Recognizing that working with PowerPoint is a critical point for professional presenters, Apple made has made it relatively easy for users to get PowerPoint shows in and out of Keynote.

Keynote has PowerPoint as one of its three different main export formats. The export will include all the graphics, text, and media you use in your show. Generally, this works without a hitch, but you'll find the differences between the two programs can come out in interesting ways (as you'll see in the following sections).

To export your Keynote presentation as a PowerPoint show, select File → Export and then click the PowerPoint radio button, as shown in Figure 9.5.

Let's look at the areas where you'll have problems when sending Keynote presentations to PowerPoint.

Alpha Channels

PowerPoint doesn't support alpha channel graphics; instead, it shows Keynote's alpha channel graphic with a transparent, but not anti-aliased, background.

The first way you'll become aware of this is when your nicely anti-aliased graphic develops a nasty edge when you move into PowerPoint, as shown in Figure 9.6. There is no good fix for this other than to grin and bear it. Because PowerPoint only uses a single color (such as 100-percent white), any anti-aliasing in the image from alpha channels becomes a hard edge around your image.

This doesn't mean you can't use any graphics with alpha channels—you just have to use them with a bit of caution. For example, you can still use the Horizontal and Vertical Photo master slides in the different themes of Keynote when you export them to PowerPoint. You'll just need to do some tweaking to make it work.

Figure 9.5

Exporting to PowerPoint is one of Keynote's three main export options.

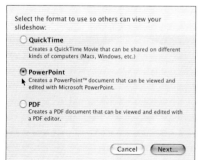

Select the format to use so others can view your slideshow:

○ **QuickTime**
Creates a QuickTime Movie that can be shared on different kinds of computers (Macs, Windows, etc.)

● **PowerPoint**
Creates a PowerPoint™ document that can be viewed and edited with Microsoft PowerPoint.

○ **PDF**
Creates a PDF document that can be viewed and edited with a PDF editor.

Cancel   Next...

Figure 9.7

Bringing in a Keynote
presentation, such as
the Presentation Tips
show, is straightfor-
ward. The only problem
is that the graphic is
no longer in the
picture frame.

Let's take our beloved, and overused, Presentation Tips slide show and see what the title
page looks like when you bring it into Microsoft PowerPoint X for OS X. As you can see, it
looks pretty much like the original, but the graphic is not behind the picture frame (see
Figure 9.7).

Figure 9.6

In PowerPoint, the
backgrounds in alpha
channel graphics are
transparent but not
anti-aliased. This leaves
a noticeable white line
around the subjects.

If this were Keynote, you'd just hit the Back button on the toolbar and send the image behind the picture frame. Unfortunately, PowerPoint doesn't work that way. When you imported the Presentation Tips show into Keynote, it sent the background graphic that contains the picture frame to the Slide Master layer, which is similar to Keynote's master slides. The difference is that you can't interact with master slide items in a hierarchy from the slide level—you have to change things at the master slide level.

Figure 9.8

Use the Slide Master command to get at your background graphic layers in PowerPoint.

Before you do this, though, you need to cut the picture from the page by first selecting the image and then selecting Edit → Cut or pressing ⌘+X. Now you need to bring the graphic into the master slide layer.

To get at the master slides in PowerPoint, you need go to View → Master → Slide Master, as shown in Figure 9.8.

Once you are at the Master Slide level, your text will revert to *Click here to set text.* Because you've already cleared off the photo, you need to paste it back in by using the Edit → Paste command or by pressing ⌘+V. Now you can use the Send to Back feature to move the road picture behind the picture frame. All you have to do is find it...among the many palettes cluttering up the screen.

This is definitely one area that Microsoft just doesn't have a clue about—adding 100 palettes to an application does not make for a good time, especially when you have limited screen real estate. Apple has the better approach: Display only the tools you need and not overwhelm you with too many choices.

Figure 9.9

PowerPoint has craftily hidden the back/front controls for adjusting the layering order of graphics in the Drawing toolbar under the Arrange heading.

The PowerPoint equivalents of the back and front controls are located in the Drawing toolbar. To access this, you need to go once again to the View menu, and this time move down to the Toolbars section and then select Drawing. At the far left of the Drawing toolbar, you'll find a nifty little feature called *Arrange*, as shown in Figure 9.9.

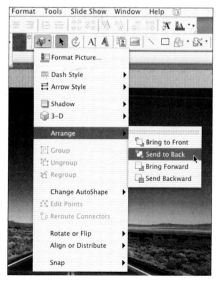

Now click the road picture and click Send to Back in the Arrange menu. Presto! Your picture is now back behind the picture frame and ready to use, as shown in Figure 9.10.

The only problem with this arrangement is that you'll see that the edges of the picture frame are no longer smooth, thanks to PowerPoint replacing the alpha channel with a one-color transparency.

Drop Shadows

When you bring in images from PowerPoint with drop shadows, they shine when Keynote turns the flat shadows to smooth, realistic drop shadows. However, you won't get the same reception when you take your Keynote file to PowerPoint. When imported into PowerPoint, all shadows that are slightly transparent and blurred become solid and sharp edged, as shown in Figure 9.11.

Again, there is little you can do here; however, the solid drop shadow is not always a bad thing. Check out an image from the same presentation, which uses a drop shadow behind the *An Alpha Channel* text.

Although not as smooth and sexy as the drop shadow you created in Keynote, it still serves the same purpose, which is to make the text stand out from the background.

A good rule of thumb is to try and keep drop shadows as close to words as possible. Also, because you can't soften the shadow, unless you are working with a square graphic image, don't use drop shadows on alpha channel graphics.

Transitions

As you know, Keynote's slick three-dimensional transitions put it in a class by itself—especially when it comes to exporting PowerPoint presentations. PowerPoint has no three-dimensional transitions, so it makes do the best it can. Generally, PowerPoint will interpret the Cube, Flip, and Small/Large Mosaic transitions by the direction that they are moving. So, a Cube move from top to bottom changes into a Push from top to bottom. Obviously, this isn't nearly as interesting, but then it is one of main selling points for Keynote over PowerPoint.

When it comes to two-dimensional transitions, PowerPoint and Keynote actually get along quite well. You'll find that a wipe in Keynote works just fine in PowerPoint. However, fancy downward transitions such as Drop transitions are simply treated as downward movements.

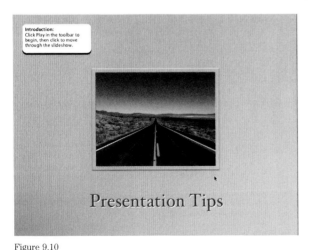

Figure 9.10

The restored image

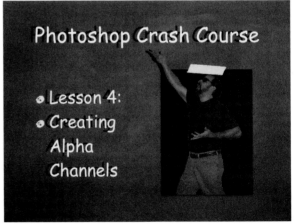

Figure 9.11

Moving images with drop shadows from Keynote to PowerPoint is not a pretty sight. The drop shadow becomes solid, not blurred, which makes the text more difficult to read.

DISSOLVES OF DEATH

One of the absolutely worst transition conversions from Keynote to PowerPoint is the Dissolve transition. PowerPoint still uses a horrible pixilated dissolve that should have been outlawed when it first appeared in Macromedia Director. Stop the madness—just say no to PowerPoint dissolves.

Table 9.2 compares how Keynote transitions work in PowerPoint. This chart doesn't list actual PowerPoint transition names but uses the type of movement you can expect inside of PowerPoint.

Importing from PowerPoint

Getting a PowerPoint presentation into Keynote is a relatively easy operation, but it can have mixed results. To import a PowerPoint file, simply press ⌘+O and then select your PowerPoint file. You can also just drag the PowerPoint document and drop it on top of Keynote's Dock icon. If your PowerPoint file is in the proper format, then Keynote will be able to open it immediately.

That's the good news; you can get PowerPoint into Keynote. Now for the bad: You can also count on reformating that presentation once you bring it into Keynote. The necessary changes can range from subtle (replacing bullet symbols) to major (fixing smashed graphic files).

Let's look at the areas where you'll have problems when bringing PowerPoint presentations into Keynote.

KEYNOTE TRANSITION	POWERPOINT BEHAVIOR	Table 9.2
Dissolve	Dissolve (pixilated)	**How Keynote Transitions Work in PowerPoint**
Move In (from left to right)	Move in (from left to right)	
Move In (from top to bottom)	Move in (from top to bottom)	
Drop	Move in (from top to bottom)	
Flip	Appear	
Pivot	Appear	
Scale (up)	Scale down	
Twirl	Appear	
Wipe (left to right)	Wipe (from left to right)	
Mosaic (3D)	Mosaic (2D)	
Reveal	Reveal	
Fade Through Black	Fade Through Black	
Motion Dissolve	Dissolve (pixilated)	
Scale Up	Appear	
Twirl	Dissolve	
Push	Push	

Bullets

In all the tests I've run in sending documents from PowerPoint to Keynote, the one consistent problem is with bullet points; inevitably, you are going to have to reformat the PowerPoint bullets with new bullets. There are actually two separate problems with bullets: one of which you can fix and the other you will just have to accept. First, every text bullet that comes in from PowerPoint gets replaced with a z or n in Keynote (see Figure 9.12).

Figure 9.12 is pretty typical; bullets just get tossed aside. You can just click the bullet text on the left, go to the Text Inspector, and then replace the bullets with an image or text bullet of your choice.

GETTING FILES FROM WINDOWS PCS

You should keep the following things in mind when you are thrown files from the shadowy world of Windows PCs. These are general tips, which means they should work most of the time; inevitably, the closer your deadline looms, the more likely it is that these tips will not work. Sorry about that—it's just standard formula of Fear + Need + Technology = Glitch.

- Use Mac Office X to convert PC documents. Microsoft Office on the Mac can convert just about any file that a PC user might send to you. This includes PowerPoint for Windows XP because generally the Mac and PC versions of PowerPoint are compatible with each other.

- Use generic text. If your file is coming from a Linux, Unix, or Whatever-nix platform, have them send you plain ASCII files, which you can convert and open in TextEdit.

- Use .ppt files (not .pps) for Windows PowerPoint files. PPS stands for *PowerPoint Show*, which is a self-contained presentation file that automatically launches into a show mode, rather than launching into the PowerPoint application for editing. Keynote turns a blind eye to .pps files, but you can get around this by simply changing the file extension from .pps to .ppt, which is the standard for PowerPoint files.

- Microsoft does a pretty good job of maintaining compatibility between Microsoft applications and Microsoft system platforms, so a Windows XP (or earlier) version of a .ppt presentation has a better shot at being read either by the Mac version of PowerPoint or even directly into Keynote.

This brings you to the second bullet "issue." Unfortunately, you won't be able to do the same with the second bulleted list shown in Figure 9.12—no matter what you do, Keynote will not recognize a second bulleted text list.

However, you can cut and paste that text into the first bullet list and then resize it to show both lists, using color to differentiate the two bullet sets, as shown in Figure 9.13.

Cropped PowerPoint Graphics

You've already learned about the problem with using alpha channel graphics when moving from Keynote to PowerPoint. Now let's talk about the joy of working with PowerPoint graphics in Keynote. There's one major piece of advice you must give anyone who wants you to convert his or her graphics-intensive PowerPoint presentation to a Keynote show.

Tell them these five words with as much emotional intensity as you can without having them call for help: *Do not crop your images!*

One of the great missing tools in Keynote is a crop tool. Although you can resize images, there is no tool for eliminating those parts of the image you just don't want to see. I hope this will be corrected in future versions of Keynote, not only because it is a real handy tool but also because not having this capability causes amazing havoc when importing cropped graphics from a PowerPoint presentation, as shown by the "squashed" image in Figure 9.14.

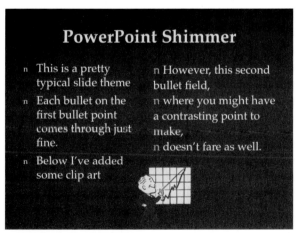

Figure 9.12

Here's a typical PowerPoint slide that uses two different bulleted lists. The first one comes out okay in Keynote, but the one on the right lost its indentation formating.

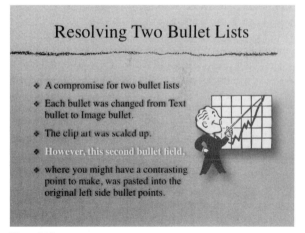

Figure 9.13

The compromise when dealing with two different bullet lists: You can paste the second list into the first, resize, and then use colors or different font styles to set the two lists apart.

What Keynote is doing is taking the cropped shape of the image from the PowerPoint data fileand then scaling the entire original picture into the same space. This is about as useful as putting a screen door on the outside of a submarine, but there it is. And now the punch line—you can't fix this. The only way to repair the damage is to get the original file that was used in the presentation, resize it, and then replace it, as shown in Figure 9.15.

Figure 9.14

Holy pancake, Batman! The image from PowerPoint on the bottom, which was originally cropped, is now badly stretched.

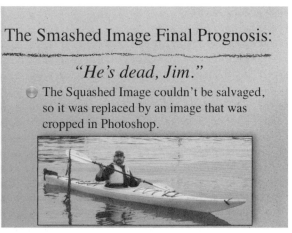

Figure 9.15

The only solution to the squashed cropped image dilemma is to replace the original image of the waterlogged author.

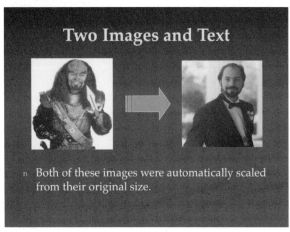

Figure 9.16

If images are scaled, but not cropped, in PowerPoint, they will look just fine when they come into Keynote.

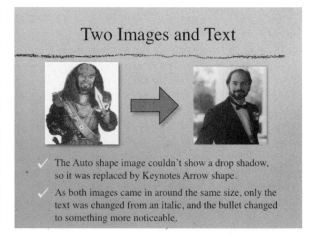

However, if the PowerPoint presentation uses images that were scaled down or up to fill a space, then you should be fine. Figure 9.16 shows a slide from PowerPoint that kept the size and proper aspect ratio of the images just fine.

Color in Charts

PowerPoint charts generally come in just fine, but the colors in the chart will generally not match the colors used in your theme. Luckily, Apple provides an easy way to reset colors in a slide. This is a handy thing to know, so you might want to follow along to change the chart colors to match the Crayon Line theme.

Go to the Chapter 9 folder in the CD-ROM and then open the `PowerPoint in Keynote Examples.key` file.

When this opens, click slide 9, which is an original PowerPoint slide that shows a pie chart. This is a pretty generic pie chart that you'll find in most PowerPoint presentations.

You'll change the chart's background and fonts by dragging a Crayon Line–themed master slide onto slide 9. In this case, drag the Title–Top master slide from the Masters pop-up menu, as shown in Figure 9.17.

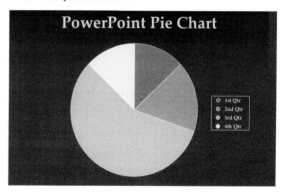

Now your chart slide will change over to the Crayon Line theme, but your chart is still in the solid and definitely unsubtle PowerPoint colors. To fix this, visit the Image Library, which you select in the File menu. When the Image Library window opens, open the file called `Chart Colors.key`.

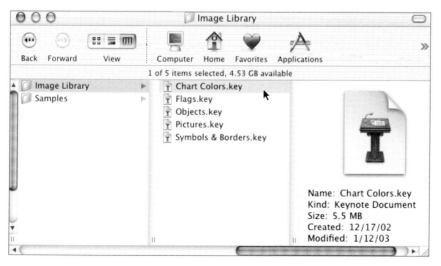

Figure 9.17

To change your charts' background and text styles, drag the Title–Top master slide on top of slide 9.

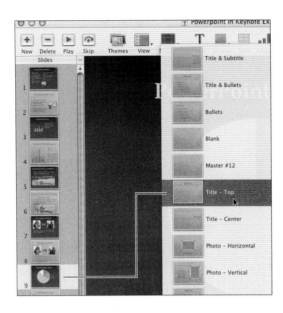

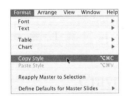

When this opens, click slide 10, which contains all the colors used in the Crayon Line theme. Click the yellow square, which is the second one from the right, and then select Format → Copy Style.

Now go back to the `PowerPoint In Keynote Examples.key` file and click the yellow slice of the pie, which is the largest slice in the pie. With the yellow pie slice selected, choose Format → Paste Style.

The yellow background, complete with texture, is now in the yellow slice, which blends it in nicely with the theme. You can also use colors or textures from other themes—it's entirely up to you. After resetting the colors, you can add drop shadows, explode the pie, or even size the legend text, as shown in Figure 9.18.

For IT Managers: Where Keynote Puts Files

For those happy few whose job it is to keep Macs in the office working, this section provides a quick list of where Keynote keeps various files. This could come in handy when a user changes the directory that the Image library is in, can't find where their presentations are, or just generally tries to "take user error to a whole new level."

- Documents are located in:
    `/Users/Documents/Keynote documents`

- The Image Library and the User Samples are located in:
    `/Library/Application Support/Keynote`

- Keynote themes are located in:
    `/Users/[username]/Library/Application Support/Keynote`

Two other tech notes: First, for custom themes to show up in Keynote, they have to be placed inside this folder:

`Users/User Name/Library/Application Support/Keynote`

Second, the `.key` file is not a file but a package. Inside the package are all the graphics and media used in the Keynote presentation, as well as a `presentation.apxl` file and two folders (one for thumbnails and one for smaller images, such as the tape image used in the Blackboard theme). The `presentation.apxl` file is a good one to remember because it contains all the positioning, formatting, and timing information for a Keynote presentation, but it is a tiny file. So, if a salesperson needed to get an updated presentation while on the road—but that update didn't need any new graphics—then you (the fearless IT manager) could simply send them the new `presentation.apxl` file instead of the entire presentation.

To get at the `presentation.apxl` file, click a Keynote file and then right-click (or Control+click) it, which opens a contextual menu. Select Show Package Contents from the list. This opens the Keynote package; now all you need to do is select the `presentation.apxl` file.

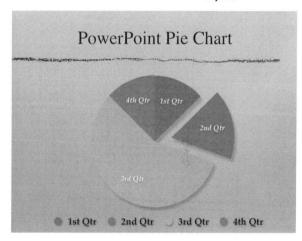

Figure 9.18

The PowerPoint chart after a bit of recoloring and reformatting in Keynote

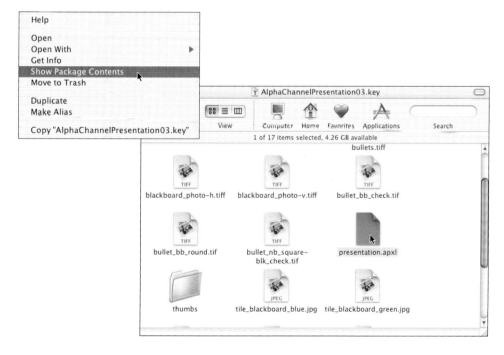

TIPS FROM THE PROS: JOHN RIZZO
ON MACINTOSH AND WINDOWS FILE COMPATIBILITY

John Rizzo, this book's fearless technical editor, happens to be one of the most knowledgeable Macintosh experts on the planet. I started working with John back in 1988 when the late, great *Macintosh Today* magazine first launched. Since then, John has written hundreds of articles on Macintosh technology for various magazines and websites, as well as several books, including *Thinking OS X* (Morgan Kaufmann, forthcoming), *Macintosh Windows Integration* (Morgan Kaufmann, 1999), and *How the Mac Works* (Que, 2000).

John shares the following tips for sending Keynote files (or other files) between Macs and Windows PCs:

Watch out for TIFF files. Some TIFF files are encoded specifically for either MacOS or Windows. Most programs can read the TIFF file despite this formatting, but a few can't. When in doubt, use a program such as Photoshop to convert the file to another format or to a format that is specific to the platform to which you are exporting.

Keep filenames short. The MacOS X specification states you should be able to use 255 characters per file. However, not every Mac application can handle this. To be safe, try to limit the filenames you use on Windows to 31 characters or fewer; otherwise, your filename could get truncated.

Beware of e-mail encoding. If you are a Mac user who is e-mailing a file to a Windows user, MIME/Base-64 almost always works, and Apple Double also works. However, beware of BinHex because it will often cause havoc on the PC side—your recipient will often just end up with garbled text.

Stick with fonts that Windows users will have. Unless you know your recipient has a specific Mac typeface or PostScript typeface, stick with the fonts you find in Microsoft Office. For example, if you use Arial, you are in good shape; however, Copperplate on the Mac needs a substitute on a Windows PC because it doesn't exist.

Use high-contrast screens when exporting Keynote shows to PCs. Windows-based computers use a darker gamma setting for their displays, so make sure your QuickTime movie or PowerPoint exports have high-contrast graphics. Otherwise, your subtle Keynote design will just look dim.

CHAPTER 10

Keynote on the Road:
Peripherals and Projectors

There are three roads to ruin: women, gambling, and technicians. The most pleasant is with women, the quickest is with gambling, but the surest is with technicians.
—Georges Pompidou (1911–1974)

In this chapter you'll learn how to show your Keynote presentation in the real world, whether for a small sales presentation or to a crowd of several thousand. First, you'll need to understand the components behind showing your presentation, including everything from remote controls to projectors. Then you'll look at using different Apple laptops with Keynote. Finally, you'll explore what you need to know to successfully set up a presentation in a remote location.

Preparing for presenting on the road

Using OS X presentation peripherals

Understanding projectors

Using Apple laptops with Keynote

Setting up a Keynote presentation system

Tips from the Pros: Selecting AV Companies

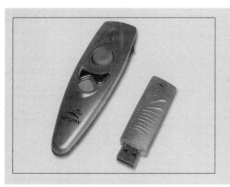

Understanding the Perils of the Road

The projector didn't show up. There is no screen on which to project your presentation. The audio/visual (AV) company has every cable—except the one that works with your system. Truly, there is nothing like giving a computer-based presentation to a crowd to let you know that technology is not your friend. I've given presentations to small and large groups all across the country, and the only consistency is that some technical glitch will try to derail an otherwise smooth presentation.

For example, one year at Macworld Expo I was asked to speak at a vendor demonstration. So I prepared my slide presentation, which also used a custom DVD of my work, and even brought a hard drive that had a bunch of digital video examples (see Figure 10.1).

However, when I got there, the computer system couldn't read the DVD, there wasn't enough space to load on my presentation to the internal hard drive, and the custom application drivers were incompatible with my hard disk. So instead I just spoke without the slides and used the DVD player on my laptop to show many examples of how I used the vendor's product. Ultimately it was successful because I was able to tailor the session to the audience, answering the many questions that were raised by the work I showed.

This is a typical situation, especially when you are not in control of the AV equipment where you are presenting. This chapter explores the various external tools you will probably use when projecting your Keynote presentations to others. Although this chapter won't prepare you for every eventuality that you'll encounter, it will give you a better idea as to what to expect when bringing your Keynote presentations on the road.

Figure 10.1

The author does a last-minute save for a Macworld presentation that was nearly destroyed by incompatible technology. Can you see the fear dripping off his brow?

Using OS X Presentation Peripherals

One of the best things you can do in any presentation is to make eye contact with your audience. Unfortunately, if you are driving your Keynote presentation from the keyboard or mouse, then you are also behind your laptop. To solve this, professional presenters (such as Steve Jobs) use remote-control devices that emulate a mouse but allow them to move around on stage and stay in front of the audience.

These devices work just like your remote control for your television or VCR by using infrared signals to communicate with a receiver module. The difference is that the receiver module is connected to the USB port on your Macintosh, so the controller information travels directly to the Mac's processor.

There are a number of devices on the market for this, but one of the most popular brands is Keyspan, which puts out two different remote controllers: the Digital Media Remote and the Keyspan Presentation Remote.

The Digital Media Remote is a simplistic controller that uses push buttons to control mouse movement (see Figure 10.2). In general, this controller is best used where you have little mouse action needed—just a mouse click to move your Keynote show forward.

The remote I prefer to work with is the Keyspan Presentation Remote, which uses a thumb toggle in the center of the controller (see Figure 10.3). The advantage is that you can use the thumb toggle to push the mouse around, so its performance is more "mouse-like." The Keyspan Presentation Remote also has a built-in laser pointer, which can be handy when you are trying to highlight a specific point on the projection screen—or want to drive your friend's cat insane playing "Catch the Red Dot."

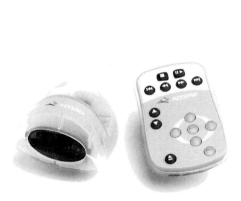

Figure 10.2

Keyspan's Digital Media Remote and its infrared receiver module

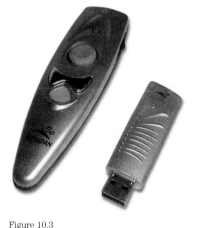

Figure 10.3

The Keyspan Presentation Remote

STEVE JOBS AND CONTROLLER X

Steve Jobs also uses a remote controller during his presentations, but it is a custom controller—often using third-party products as a base—that the Apple team engineered specifically for Steve. This ensures that all the peripheral equipment that Steve works with will be compatible and that the controller doesn't clash with any other presentation controllers in the area.

The only caveat about using these remote-control devices is that you are dealing with infrared controller technology, which is far from infallible. First, you'll need to make sure you have line of sight between your controller and the receiver. If your controller can't see the receiver, then your Mac won't get any signals. Also, if anyone else is using the same remote control for his or her computer, you could find that your machine triggers at the same time. This happens rarely, but it can happen.

Examining Projectors

Projection technology has improved dramatically over the past few years. Where in the past you'd need a team of technicians to deliver and set up a projection system, today you can carry a powerful projection system in your briefcase that you can set up in minutes.

That's the good news; the bad news is that it is not easy picking the right projection system. You could rent or buy a projector for your shows, but you'll still have to sort out hundreds of products from many different vendors. Even your favorite Macintosh mail-order catalogs now have pages devoted to selling projectors—so which one do you choose? Before you figure out which model to choose, you should determine whether you should buy or rent your projector.

Actually, the question as to whether you should buy or rent is an easy one. I've always been a big fan of keeping overhead low, so I tend to rent equipment when possible. With the cost of good small projectors starting at $2,500, it's better to rent a projection system if you are using it occasionally. Renting AV equipment also gives you several advantages:

Cost Rental fees are often only a few hundred dollars a day, compared with many thousands of dollars you'd need to purchase a projector.

Technology Projector technology is improving every year, so the great system you purchase today will pale in comparison to the projectors that will come out next year. Remember, your local AV company has to keep up with the latest technology to stay in business—you may as well take advantage of this.

Scalability Buying a small projection system won't help you when you need to show your Keynote presentation to hundreds of people. By renting, you can get exactly the right projector for your presentation.

Maintenance When you rent, you are not responsible with fixing any problems with the projector that will occur over time, such replacing the projector bulbs—which can be incredibly expensive.

However, there are also some good reasons to purchase a projector. You should buy a projector if any of the following are true:

- You give enough presentations either in the office or remotely that the cost of rental would be equal to or greater than the cost of purchasing.

- You often need a projection system for impromptu or last-minute presentations, and you just won't have the time to book a projector in advance with an AV house.

- You want a projection system that you can also use at home to project big-screen movies.

- You feel so good about this book that you decide to reward the author by purchasing for him a top-of-the-line, High Definition Television (HDTV)–compatible projector (okay, not as good a reason, but it was worth a try).

Understanding Projector Specifications

Before you buy or rent your projector, you need to decode the specifications that projection vendors use to categorize their products. Of all the different specifications you'll see, you should pay attention to three main areas: lumens, contrast ratio, and native resolution.

Lumens

Lumens or *ANSI lumens* are a measure of how much light passes through the projector's lens and then onto the screen. This should measure how bright your projector will be, right? Unfortunately, this measurement is deceptive, and more often than not it is inaccurate.

Recently I did some work comparing five different projectors for a client, including testing. During those tests, it became painfully clear that projector manufacturers' published lumen output level and what projectors actually could output were very different.

For example, Brand X projector stated that it had an ANSI lumen rating of 1,000, and Brand Y only had an ANSI lumen rating of 800. Brand X is better than Brand Y, right? That's what I thought—until I put the two together and really measured their outputs. During this test I knew something was wrong—the supposedly dimmer Brand Y projector was nearly twice as bright as the Brand X projector! As it turns out, the Brand Y projector actually was pretty close in its ANSI lumen output specification; it was putting out around 700 ANSI lumens. However, Brand X was only putting out about 50 percent, or 500 lumens, of the light level it claimed, making it nearly 200 lumens dimmer than the other projector.

The reason for this major discrepancy comes in when the vendors test their projectors. Some vendors will take the projector, put it in a "light-tight" room with black walls and then measure its output. I don't know about you, but I don't remember the last time I gave or sat through a presentation given in a completely blackened room, so this test is not exactly "real world."

The bottom line is that you should use the ANSI lumen rating only to establish major differences between projector systems. Chances are, the difference between a 1,000-lumen projector and a 1,200-lumen projector could be slight. However, you should easily see the difference between a 1,000-lumen projector and a 3,000-lumen projector, so if you need a brighter projector, the brighter 3,000-lumen projector is the way to go.

Furthermore, only use a projector's ANSI lumen specification as a start for comparison— not as the final determining factor. Also, when in doubt, see if you can get a demo of the unit you are interested in—just to be sure things are really as "bright" as they seem.

Contrast Ratio

You'll find some pretty impressive contrast ratio figures with projector systems, some of which are really...well, laughable. Let me put this in perspective for you.

When you talk about contrast ratios, you are measuring the distance between black and white—or within an image, the darkest and the lightest range. Each medium in communications technology can handle only so much of a contrast range (see Figure 10.4).

Figure 10.4

Putting contrast ratios in perspective

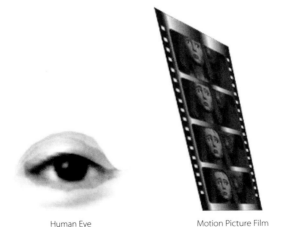

Human Eye
1000:1

Motion Picture Film
100:1

Video
30:1

FORMAT	RESOLUTION	DESCRIPTION	
SVGA	800×600 pixels	SVGA is a shortened version of the real name for the standard, which is *Super VGA*.	Table 10.1
XGA	1024×768 pixels	XGA stands for *Extended Graphics Array*, which is a high-resolution graphics standard that IBM introduced around 1990.	**SVGA vs. XGA**

So, the higher the contrast range, the more realistic and pleasing the image that the projector will display. However, keep in mind that the contrast ratios are also measured inside that infamous black box, so the vendor's specification might not be a good real-world measurement.

Native Resolution

Just about the only specification worth paying attention to is the projector's native resolution. This is the maximum screen size that the projector can display without scaling, which means that any resolution higher than the native resolution will be electronically enlarged.

This electronic scaling is not always a bad thing, however; today many projectors can nicely enlarge images with little image degradation. Still, it's good to be aware of this because some projectors simply cannot display anything other than their native resolution.

There are two native resolutions to keep track of: SVGA and XGA. Although there are a few other video and graphic formats, these are the two main ones you'll need to be aware of when projecting your Keynote presentations (see Table 10.1).

As you can see, it is no accident that the two preset slide sizes in Keynote are 800×600 and 1024×768. Generally, you are safest keeping your presentations down to the 800×600 display size because this is the most common display resolution for most mid-end to low-end projectors.

Exploring Projector Types

Within the projector market today, you'll find four main types of projectors to purchase or rent. Which one you use will mainly depend upon the size of your audience and the size of your budget. The four projector types are LCD, DLP, CRT, and Light Valve, described in the following sections.

Most newer projectors on the market can handle both video and computer signals. However, some older models handle video only, so be sure to check that your projector can also handle computer video signals.

LCD

Liquid Crystal Display (LCD) projectors have been around for a long time, so there are a variety of models from which to choose. These projectors generate a Mac's image onto an LCD screen and then project that image.

There are dozens of LCD projectors on the market. Although it can be a bit confusing as to which model to pick, the good news is that LCD technology has improved drastically over the past five years. For example, the LCD projectors from Epson have been consistently good performers (see Figure 10.5).

Generally, LCD projectors are bright, but they can suffer from slightly lower resolution and can be slow when updating the image. This can cause what is called *ghosting*, where a moving image such as a cursor leaves behind fading images of it as it moves across the screen.

LCD projectors are good for smaller presentations, where you are presenting to five to 15 people at a time. When you move to a screen size that could accommodate more than 40″ or so, you'll find that the image becomes too dim to see properly.

DLP

One of the newest projector technologies around is DLP, which stands for *Digital Light Processing*. DLP projectors are amazingly bright yet often are as small or smaller than typical LCD projectors. For example, HP's xb31 DLP projector puts out an incredible 1,500 ANSI lumens, but it only weighs about 3.5 pounds (see Figure 10.6).

DLP projectors are different from LCD projector technology in that they use thousands of tiny, sensitive mirrors on a semiconductor chip called a *digital micromirror device* (DMD). Inside the projector, a super-bright lamp shines light through a fast-spinning color wheel, which changes the light from red to green and then to blue.

Figure 10.5

Epson's 811 LCD projector offers XGA resolution and 2,000 ANSI lumen performance.

DLP projectors have better image resolution and color clarity than most LCD projectors and have even higher contrast ratios and image brightness.

On the downside, the newness of the technology makes DLP projectors much more expensive than LCD projectors. Also, because of the brightness of the lamp used, DLP projectors can be almost too hot to handle after running for a few minutes. Vendors handle this in one of two ways; they build the case so that it doesn't transfer all the heat to your hands, or they build in a fan noisier than an aircraft carrier. One vendor (who shall remain nameless) chose to build a noisy fan on the company's super-small DLP projector, which nearly makes the projector unusable. After all, what's the point of doing the presentation if your audience can't hear you over the projector's fan?

> Speaking of noisy fans, you might want to avoid using a PowerMac G4 as the computer driving your presentation. To keep those new Mac components cool, some of the new G4 Power-Macs have fans so loud that they could give a vacuum a run for the money.

CRT

The oldest technology on the market is Cathode Ray Tube (CRT), which uses separate projection tubes for the red, green, and blue signals. You will mainly find these systems in rental houses because they are both large and require ongoing maintenance. Figure 10.7 shows Sony's G-90 CRT project.

The main benefit to using a CRT projector is that it can provide a sharper image with better contrast ratios than LCD screens. Furthermore, because it uses the same kind of display technology as your TV set, a CRT projector can often display moving video much better than LCD projectors.

Figure 10.6

Small yet super bright, HP's xb31 DLP projector is a great example of DLP projector technology.

DLP Digital Cinema

DLP Digital Cinema projectors are high-powered projection systems that combine CRT and DLP technology. Digital Cinema projectors are used when you need to display huge images, such as the video playback at music concerts or sports events. Chances are you won't be running out to buy one of these systems—the starting price for systems such as the Barco SLM-R8 Performer is a cool $55,000 (see Figure 10.8).

There are even Digital Cinema display systems that are slowly but inevitably working their way into movie theaters, such as the Barco DP 50, which was used to screen the digital version of Lucasfilms' *Star Wars: Attack of the Clones* at the Cannes Film Festival a few years ago (see Figure 10.9).

Figure 10.7

Sony's G-90 CRT projector is a good example of a CRT projection system, which has three separate lenses for the red, green, and blue signals

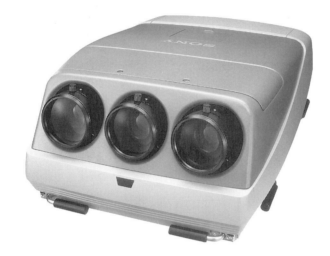

Figure 10.8

The Barco SLM-R8 is a DLP projector for use in mid-sized theaters. Putting out an awesome 8,000 ANSI lumens, the SLM-R8 can project an image up to 33 feet wide.

However, although it is still expensive, when you need to present your show to an audience of 40 or more, you can rent DLP Digital Cinema projectors (or their older, less powerful cousins, the Light-Valve projectors) for a few thousand dollars a day. The important thing to keep in mind is that these are complicated systems that require several hours to set up and test, so you will need to plan on extra charges for setup and a specialized technician for this type of projector.

Picking a Projector

There you have it—everything you wanted to know about projectors but were afraid to ask. I'd love to be able to tell you exactly which projector you should get, but it really depends upon the presentation you are giving, the size of your audience, and your budget.

However, you should make sure your rented or purchased projector has the following technical aspects:

Figure 10.9

Costing a bit more than some houses, the Barco DP 50 uses both CRT and DLP technology to project an image that is nearly as good as a standard 35-millimeter movie projector.

DVI or VGA input   These are the inputs you need to connect the computer Red-Green-Blue (RGB) signal to the projector. If you don't have a DVI output on your Mac, don't exclude the projector—just get a VGA to DVI adapter.

XGA resolution   This will make sure you have a 1024×768 image, so your larger-screen Keynote presentations will not be squeezed into an SVGA 800×600 pixel space.

High horizontal scan frequencies   Another way to be sure you are not getting stuck with a video projector (instead of what you need, which is a data projector) is to make sure that the projector can handle higher horizontal scan frequencies. Many Macintosh displays are set around 70 hertz (Hz), but some Mac display cards can output as high as 85Hz or even 90Hz. A video-only projector usually will not be able to go above 60 Hz.

The final rough way to figure out what projector to get is the size of your audience and the ambient light conditions in the location where you will do your presentation.

Essentially, the larger your audience, the more powerful a projector you'll need.

If you are giving a presentation to five to 15 people, then an LCD projector should work just fine. If your group is larger than this—say, up to 40 people—then you'll need to project a much larger image, which would probably require a CRT or high-end DLP projector. Finally, if you need to give a presentation to 40 or more, then you should plan on a Digital Cinema projector.

The main factor that will affect your projector decision (besides budget and audience size) is ambient light. Your LCD projector might be perfect for a small audience. However, if there is a lot of light spilling into the room where you are presenting, then the projected image will be washed out. You can cure this by moving the projector closer to the screen and brightening the image—but you also reduce the size of the image, making it harder to see.

The only real way around this problem is to use a projector that is slightly brighter than you might need for the group. So, if you know that you will need to make a presentation in front of 15 people but it could be in a really bright room, you might consider using a CRT data projector instead of a CRT for maximum image quality.

Using Apple Laptops with Keynote

In his Macworld keynote speech, Steve Jobs called 2003 the year of the laptop. Apple has done a phenomenal job designing a great line of notebook computers. For many years I used a PC-based laptop because Apple had not released a laptop with enough power and a reasonable price point to make the switch worthwhile.

This changed with the release of the G4 PowerBooks, which boast near desktop performance in sleek Titanium wrappers. These days I'm hooked—the G4 PowerBooks are one of the best laptop investments I've ever made.

Naturally, Keynote works with Apple laptops nicely, taking advantage of MacOS X and the laptops' built-in graphic capabilities. There are a few things you should keep in mind when working with the different Apple laptop models, mostly how they handle graphics and external displays.

The following sections deal with getting graphics out of your PowerBook, not audio. For all of the PowerBooks and the iBook, the audio is sent out to external speakers or mixers via the headphone output jack, which is a stereo mini-jack.

Using Keynote and the iBook

The iBook is a slick little machine with a decent amount of computing power. Unlike its big G4 siblings, the iBook uses a slower G3 processor. Although this is fine for most applications, the graphics-intensive computations in Keynote can cause the iBook to stumble.

Projecting images from the iBook is possible—as long as you have the right adapter. As you can see from Figure 10.10, the iBook doesn't have a standard VGA output port for connecting to an external monitor. To connect to a projector, you'll need the Apple VGA display adapter (which should come with the iBook), which fits into the Video Out port.

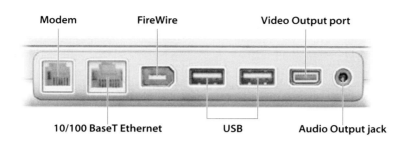

Figure 10.10

The iBook can connect with projectors using its Video Output port— but only as long as you use the Apple Video to VGA adapter.

The only other thing to keep in mind is that the 32 megabytes (MB) of video Random Access Memory (RAM) that the iBook uses might not be enough to drive both its internal LCD display and an external projector. One way around this is to connect the external display, power up the iBook, and then close the iBook cover while it is booting. This will make the external display the main display and also reserve all of the iBook's graphics hardware for that display.

Using Keynote and the 12″ PowerBook

The 12″ G4 PowerBook is a dandy little machine—it's small, sleek, and oh-so powerful. Packing an 867 megahertz (MHz) G4 processor, the 12″ PowerBook can handle just about any production task—especially Keynote presentations. Even though it only has a 12″ LCD screen, the native resolution on the 12″ PowerBook is 1024×768 pixels, which Keynote can accommodate nicely.

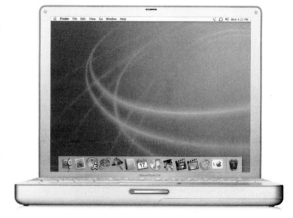

Like the iBook, you are limited to about 32MB of video RAM. However, the 12″ G4 video processor—an NVIDIA GeForce4 420 Go—is a much more powerful graphics processor. Consequently, you should have no problem running two monitors at the same time. However, if you run into problems, try reducing the resolution on the 12″ PowerBooks LCD screen from 1024×768 pixels at millions of colors to 800×600 at thousands or 256 colors. This will take some pressure off the graphics chip during your presentation.

The 12″ PowerBook also needs the Apple VGA display adapter to hook into an external VGA-based projection system.

Using Keynote and the 15″ PowerBook

The 15″ PowerBooks are true workhorses—I've used mine for everything from writing to editing videos on location. In general, there is little that you can't do with Keynote and a 15″ PowerBook.

The 1 gigahertz (GHz) 15″ PowerBook has double the video RAM of the 867MHz PowerBook, so using 1GHz and future, more powerful models will allow you to use two displays at one time.

For those of you who just want to use the PowerBooks screen to show your presentations, you'll need to make a few adjustments. The LCD display for the 15″ PowerBook G4 shows a full-screen image at 1152×768 pixels, which is a bit larger than the 1024×768 maximum size set by Keynote. To fill the entire screen, you'll need to reset your display resolution in the display's system preferences. To do this, click the Monitors icon in the Finder and then select 1024×768 (see Figure 10.11).

Keep that Apple DVI to VGA adapter handy when doing remote presentations. Although some projectors can accept a DVI video cable into their input ports, many on the market can still only handle VGA connectors.

Using Keynote and the 17″ PowerBook

The 17″ PowerBook, the first of its kind, is one of the hottest machines that Apple has ever released. It also can handle just about any Keynote presentation you throw at it. The 17″

PowerBook has 64MB of video RAM, along with the NVIDIA GeForce4 420 Go video processor.

In this situation, you'll also need to keep your DVI to VGA adapter that comes with the unit because many projection systems on the market still use a VGA input port.

Finally, the native display on the 17″ PowerBook is 1440×900 pixels, so you'll need to resize your screen down to 1023×768 to completely fill the 17″ PowerBook's LCD screen.

Setting Up a Keynote Presentation System

Let's look at a basic Keynote presentation system. In this example, you'll use a PowerBook G4, a projector, and a remote mouse. Here's how you hook it up:

1. With the PowerBook turned off, attach the DVI output from the back of the PowerBook to the DVI input on the projector. If the projector doesn't have a DVI input, then you'll need to convert the DVI output port to a VGA port using the Apple DVI to VGA adapter. Turn on the projector.

2. Boot up the PowerBook. After it boots up, open the monitor's display window. Click the Arrange tab. You should now see two monitors: the internal PowerBook LCD screen and the projector, which appears as another monitor.

3. Make sure the PowerBook is set as the primary display (where the MacOS X menu bar shows up). If this is not on the PowerBook monitor in the Arrange window, then change this by dragging the menu bar from the projector monitor to the PowerBook monitor.

> If you are demonstrating software applications, it's a good idea to arrange the projector "monitor" so that it is above or on the appropriate side of the PowerBook LCD screen. By setting up the monitors this way, when you move the cursor from one screen to the next, it is easier to track.

4. Next, connect the remote mouse by plugging in the USB receiver to any available USB port on your PowerBook. If your vendor recommends it, you can also plug in the receiver while the PowerBook is turned off.

5. If you are connecting to any external speakers or to an audio mixer, you will need to plug in the audio cable to the stereo mini-jack headphone port.

When everything is properly hooked up, it should look something like Figure 10.12.

Using Dual Displays

Generally, the newer PowerBooks, and eventually even the iBooks, will be powerful enough to have both the laptops' LCD screens open at the same time as the projector. Using two monitors in Keynote gives you two major advantages.

First, you can view your notes on one screen while having only the slide displayed on the other screen. Second, you get the entire Keynote interface on the monitor that shows the notes, so you also can see what slides are displaying.

Figure 10.11

To have your Keynote presentation fill up the entire LCD screen on your 15″ PowerBook, change your display settings to 1024×768.

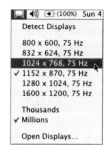

Figure 10.12

A typical Keynote
presentation setup
with a projector

PowerBook DVI output   **TO**   **Projector DVI or VGA input**

Headphone jack   **TO**   **External speakers or mixer**

To set up Keynote to use two monitors, select Keynote → Preferences. At the bottom of the Preferences window, click the Display on Secondary monitor and Show Notes Separately radio buttons.

That is it—now Keynote will play just the slides on the projector while showing you the full interface with your notes on your PowerBook (see Figure 10.13).

Setting Up Projector Placement

The only other factor you'll need to adjust is how far away the projector is to the screen. This distance is called *throw distance,* and it is key to understanding how far to place your projector.

WORKING WITH A VIDEO PROJECTOR

As mentioned earlier, some projectors can only project video. If you should get stuck with one of these instead of a data projector, then you can also send the video output of the PowerBook to the projector. For the best results, connect your PowerBook to the video projector using an S-Video cable. The S-Video signal separates the color and the brightness within a video signal, making the image much sharper than the standard single RCA or composite video output.

There are many formulas about how to work this, but again this will depend up on your individual circumstances. You might get away with placing a projector farther away from the screen when in a darkened room but find you'll need to move closer when there is too much ambient light.

A good place to start is knowing what the maximum size your projector can display and then working backward as to whether that it is big enough (or too big) for your audience.

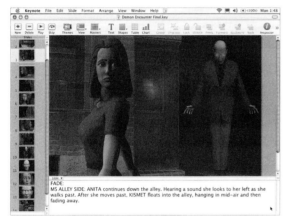

Monitor shows slides with notes

Projector shows only slides

Figure 10.13

By setting Present On Secondary Display and Use Alternate Display to View Slide Notes, you can see your Keynote slides with notes on one monitor while sending the projector only the slide images.

Another nice online utility is on the Projector Central website at `http://www.projectorcentral`
`.com/projection-calculator.cfm`, which is a handy calculator for determining if your projector will fit into the place where you plan to give your presentation (see Figure 10.14). All you
do is enter in the projector model and the distance to screen or the image size, and the calculator will tell you whether you'll fit.

Working with AV Companies

If you are planning a large presentation and it's in a remote location, you'll need to work
with another company to provide you the AV equipment you'll need to project your Keynote
show. If you've never done this, don't be alarmed—it is no more difficult than arranging a
caterer or a photographer for a wedding. The key to successfully working with AV companies
is clear communication.

When to Start Planning

One of the first major mistakes that people make when working with AV companies is to wait
until the last minute to order their equipment. This can result in not getting the equipment
that they really need or even not getting any equipment at all.

Figure 10.14

Projector Central's
Projection Calculator is
a handy utility for mak-
ing sure your projector
will work with your
presentation space.

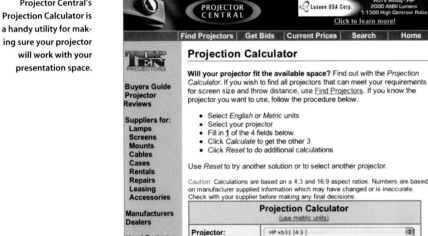

ANSWERS, NOT ASSUMPTIONS

According to AV company agents, nothing is worse than talking to someone who only knows a few of the details regarding the presentation. If you have someone call for you, make sure they have all the information that they need, such as presentation date, time, duration, and a detailed list of required AV support.

You need to contact and start working with your AV company as soon as you have all the main details about your meeting—namely, when it is, how long it lasts, and what type of activities will require AV support.

For major rollouts, such as one of Steve Jobs' keynote presentations, the trade show planners at Apple will work with their vendors for months to make sure that the multiple video, streaming media feeds, and multiple monitor presentation systems are in place. This may seem like a long time, but given all the things that can go wrong—from having to create custom tools to renting specific equipment—it's best to start working as far ahead as possible. At the least, you should call the AV company at three weeks before your presentation's start date.

Picking Your Equipment

Your AV support person will want to know as much about your presentation as possible in order to recommend the proper equipment for your show. You should be able to answer the following questions:

1. How long is your presentation?
2. What type of computer will the presentation be shown on?
3. What computer program and computer operating system are you using?
4. Is there any sound in your presentation?
5. Will there be more than one person presenting?
6. Do you plan on having external video playback (such as a sales video tape or DVD)?

Question 1 is something only you will know, but err on the side of telling the AV company that your presentation will run a bit longer than you might have originally planned. For a five-minute presentation, say 10 minutes just in case you run long. The AV company will pad their technician's time accordingly, so you can be sure you are covered.

TIPS FROM THE PROS: ERIK HOLSINGER
ON SELECTING AUDIO/VIDEO COMPANIES

My love/hate affair with presentation technology goes back decades to when I was in charge of AV operations for a San Francisco Bay Area AV rental house. During my tenure there, I planned and set up everything from simple slide projection systems to major shows complete with four or more video projectors, computer-controlled slide systems, and a partridge in a pear tree. This was invaluable later on when I'd have to arrange for presentations and work with AV companies all over the country. Finding the right AV company is critical to a successful presentation; if you don't have the right company helping you, you could end up trying to show 300 people your presentation using just your iBook.

As with any industry, in the AV rental market there are both reputable companies and members of the Brotherhood of Incompetent AV Operators, Incorporated. The following tips will help you try to sort out the good AV guys from the losers:

Talk to the chamber of commerce. Call the chamber of commerce in the city you will be presenting in or talk to an association related to your business for their recommendations on a good AV rental house. It's a good idea to talk to someone who has worked with the AV company.

Talk to several AV companies. Not all companies offer additional services, such as free pickup and delivery or reduced labor costs. Look for the company with the best price and the best deal.

Find out if the AV company owns the equipment it is renting. Because of the sophistication of the equipment, setup can take longer for someone who doesn't work with it frequently.

Review AV bids for hidden costs. Never sign off on a lump-sum bid. A major hidden cost is labor, such as setup and delivery, which can add from $50 to $1,000 to the daily rental rate.

Questions 2 and 3 are easy enough; simply give them the model of Macintosh laptop you are working with (including amount of RAM and processor speed), Keynote presentation program, and tell them you are running under MacOS X (be sure to include the version number). This might seem like a lot of extra information, but chances are your AV company has done this kind of presentation before, so they will have a good idea of what will and will not work with their equipment.

Question 4 is an important one. If you do plan to use sound in your presentation, the AV company will need some special gear to make this happen. First, it will need a long enough cable to reach from the public address (PA) system to your machine. Then it will need a special adapter that will convert from a low-impedance XLR connector (which is the standard type of connector used in professional sound reinforcement systems) to a high-impedance stereo mini-jack. It definitely has these cables in stock, but you need to inform the company so it knows to bring it to your show.

Finally, questions 5 and 6 are straightforward—just provide details of everyone who plans to give presentations and a full list of their presentation materials (including video cassettes, DVDs, laser discs, CDs, and so on).

When it comes to picking the type of projector you need, work with the AV company to determine which type of projector would best fit the room in which you plan on giving the presentation. Remember, local AV companies spend a lot of time at the various convention and meeting locations in their towns, so they will have a good idea as to what the size, lighting, and other conditions exist in your meeting location. Just let them know how many people will be in the audience and also how detailed your presentations will be. For example, if you are doing a simple slide show, then the screen size might not be that important. However, if you are demonstrating a software application, then you will need a screen large enough so that anyone in the back row of the room can make out the program's details.

This should give you a good head start when taking your Keynote presentations to the outside world. Don't forget the most important element of your presentation—have fun. If you have a good time making your presentation, chances are the audience will also enjoy it. In the next chapter, you will see how to transform your Keynote presentations into video, Portable Document Format (PDF), and print documents that you can distribute to the audience after a presentation.

CHAPTER 11

Slide, Print, and Video Output

Making duplicate copies and computer printouts of things no one wanted even one of in the first place is giving America a new sense of purpose. —Andy Rooney (1919–)

Your Keynote presentation was a success, and the audience leaves with a sense of time well spent—but will they remember anything you said? The only way to be sure your presentation leaves a lasting impression is to present your show in some format that the audience can take with them. In this chapter, you'll learn about various things you need to keep in mind as you convert your Keynote masterpieces to analog formats.

Converting Keynote presentations to 35-millimeter slides

Improving print output

Converting Keynote presentations to video

Tips from the Pros: Jesse Busby on Working with Slide Service Bureaus

Transferring Keynote Presentations to 35mm Slides

It may seem like a giant technological step backward, but one day you might need to convert your Keynote presentations to 35-millimeter (mm) slides. Not every place where you plan to give a presentation will have the technology (or budget) available to project your show from your computer. Also, you might be in a situation where you need to archive or provide your show to others who don't have access to the wonders of Macintosh technology. For example, if you develop an entire course curriculum using Keynote, chances are the educational institute that paid for that work will want analog (35mm-slide) versions available for archiving or use by other educators.

Obviously, there are some severe limitations on what you will be able to show once you've converted to 35mm slides. For the record, once you are in 35mm slide mode, you:

- Cannot show any complex two-dimensional or three-dimensional transitions
- Can only show dissolves if using two slide projectors with a dissolve controller
- Have limited abilities to show builds
- Cannot play back any video, animation, and music elements—unless using a separate playback unit

Basically, all of your transitions will be cuts, which Keynote calls either "none" or "appears" in the transition menu. Once your first slide is on the screen, the next slide will simply replace it. If you create separate slides for each of the builds in your show, you can bring in the individual elements of a slide one at a time.

So, now that you know and accept the limitations, you have several ways to get your images to slides.

Slides the Easy Way: Using PowerPoint

Pro: This approach takes the least amount of time. Online slide export to a slide bureau is built into PowerPoint.

Con: This approach requires PowerPoint. Exporting to PowerPoint greatly reduces the resolution and image quality of Keynote slides.

The easiest way is to export your slides to Microsoft PowerPoint. In the early years when PowerPoint was first available, its primary purpose was to output to 35mm slides because projection systems were both too expensive and not impressive. Consequently, Microsoft included the ability to send all PowerPoint slides to a service bureau that specialized in taking PowerPoint images and creating 35mm slides.

Like a vestigial tail, the current evolution of PowerPoint on the Mac (PowerPoint for MacOS X) still has this link to Genigraphics, one of the top service bureaus available online to process and output computer presentations to slides. Because this feature is built into PowerPoint, creating 35mm slides is a snap.

To export your Keynote presentation, you'll first need to either own or have access to PowerPoint for MacOS X. Next, you'll need to export your presentation as a PowerPoint file, which is one of the three options under File → Export. Then, open your exported Keynote presentation (which now sports a `.ppt` suffix instead of a `.key` suffix) inside PowerPoint.

> Don't forget to clean up your Keynote presentation prior to export as a PowerPoint presentation to take into account PowerPoint's limitations, such as its inability to show drop shadows and so on. For a more complete list of PowerPoint incompatibilities, refer to Chapter 9, "Keynote in the Networked World."

Once you are in PowerPoint, choose File → Send To → Genigraphics. This opens the Genigraphics wizard, which steps you through the process of defining your slide order. You can even provide your credit card information and the address of where they can ship your slides.

> Creating your slides at a service bureau can take anywhere from a few days to a few weeks, depending upon how much you are willing to pay to get them done. Obviously, the faster the turnaround, the more the Genigraphics service bureau will charge you. If possible, try to allow for up to two weeks to get the best price on 35mm slide conversions.

Slides the Hard Way: Using Grab

Pro: This approach maintains the graphics capabilities and resolution of Keynote images, including showing alpha channels and drop shadows.

Con: For this approach, each slide has to be manually captured.

If you want to keep the entire image processing in Keynote but still need to get your Keynote presentation to 35mm slides, you do have an option. What you'll need to do is create individual screen shots and then send the individual files to a service bureau for conversion to 35mm slides.

There are a number of ways of doing this, but I'm going to propose a way that uses one of the great little utilities that comes with MacOS X: Grab. I've used Grab throughout the creation of this book, which is how I've been able to capture slide images and still show all of the graphics processing used in Keynote. Not only can it quickly and easily handle getting versions of your slides, but it also has an added benefit: It's free.

You'll find Grab in the Utilities folder, which is buried in the Applications folder. This excellent little program has but one purpose in life: to capture Mac screen shots. Grab is incredibly easy to use but still has options in how you use the program: Selection, Screen, and Timed Screen.

To open the Applications folder, select Go → Applications in the Finder or press ⌘+**Shift+A.**

Selection takes a shot of the screen based upon a rectangle that you click and drag on the screen.

When grabbing screen shots, another great Grab technique is to first set up your shot—in other words, arrange the application or folder windows on your screen the way you like. Next, switch to Grab and choose Selection. Now, before you make your selection, press ⌘+Tab, and the previous application you were working in will come to the foreground. Finally, you can drag your selection, and your application will be the active window.

Finally, if you happen to be writing a book on MacOS X applications, then Timed Screen is the mode for you because it can take screen shots of active applications and menus, which can be handy for presentations. Just start the timer and then switch back to your application. Grab will give you 10 seconds to make your application the active application, pull down menus, or adjust your cursor and then take the picture (see Figure 11.1).

You can use any of these options to capture images of your slides, but I think the easiest—certainly the mode requiring the least amount of work—is to use Selection. Using the Selection mode, you can just select your slide and you don't have to worry about later cropping the image in Photoshop or some other image-editing application. The only problem with this technique is that using Selection in Grab is not nearly as accurate as grabbing the whole screen and then just cropping in Photoshop. Still, if you don't have Photoshop and need a quick way to get at individual screens, then this is a good way to go.

Figure 11.1

Using the Timed Screen feature in Grab allows you to capture screen shots of active applications in MacOS X.

To capture your Keynote slides, follow these steps:

1. First, open both your Keynote presentation and Grab.

2. Set your screen resolution so that it is larger than the size of your slides so you'll have some space around the slide to select. Also, make sure that 100 percent of your slide is showing in the Slide Canvas.

3. Switch to Grab and select Capture → Selection.

4. Grab will prompt you to select a section of the screen. I find it easiest to start at the upper-left corner of the slide and drag down to the lower-right corner, as in Figure 11.2. Also, make sure you are just inside the slide when you start dragging so you only capture the slide and not anything outside of the Slide Canvas.

5. When you've finished clicking and dragging to the lower-right corner, then release the mouse button. Grab will present you with the image of your slide, complete with drop shadows and alpha channel transparencies—the works (see Figure 11.3). Finally, save your slide file by selecting File → Save in Grab or by pressing ⌘+S.

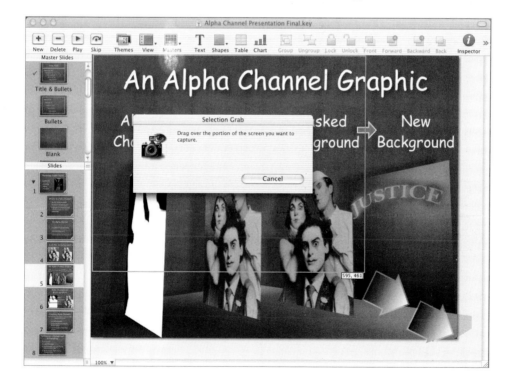

Figure 11.2

Drag to select the area you want to capture.

USE CONSISTENT LABELING FOR YOUR CAPTURES

When you send a set of slides to your service bureau, it's always a good idea to keep the filenames consistent and in the right order. Pick a filename (such as The Big Show) and then make sure to stick with it. Also, for 10 or more slides, make sure to add a zero in front of the first nine numbers (The Big Show 01, The Big Show 02, and so on), so your slides will maintain the correct order when you send them off the service bureau. (If you are unbelievably cruel enough to have more than 100 slides in your presentation, then make sure you add two zeros to your filename system: The Big Show 001 and so on.)

Once you have captured all your slides, you can simply send them to your service bureau online or record them to a CD-ROM. The only negative about capturing screens of your slides is that you convert them to bitmapped images. This means your captured slides are only at screen resolution and will not look good if you try to print larger versions (such as posters). Still, using Grab is a great way to get around the image degradation that occurs when you export to PowerPoint.

You can get the best of both worlds by importing your captured slides into PowerPoint. You can place each bitmapped screen inside PowerPoint, resave it a PowerPoint document, and then send it to Genigraphics or another service bureau for conversion to slides.

Figure 11.3

The finished slide image using the Selection mode of Grab

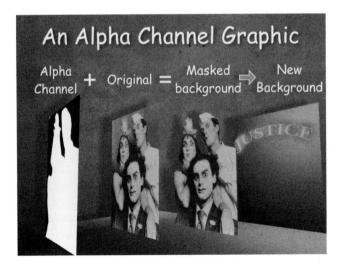

Improving Print Output

When you are writing a book about a new product or a new version of a product, one of the most frustrating things is needing to document areas that are "still under development." Yes, it's true—it is common practice these days for a software package to leave a few areas for cleanup in the next release of the product. Printing from Keynote is a good example of this problem. After its inability to handle media well, Keynote's limited print flexibility is the program's weakest feature. Yes, you do have some options in the Print Slides dialog box, but ultimately they are not implemented very well. With any luck, these will be improved in a future version of Keynote.

Print Formats

When you select File → Print Slides, the standard MacOS X print window comes up. If you delve a bit deeper, there are a few Keynote-specific print options you can set.

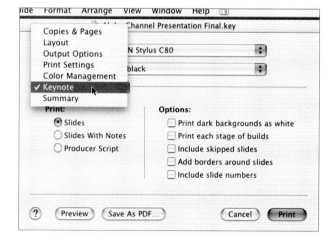

You have three formats that you can choose for print output:

Slides sounds just like it is—slides without anything else added.

Slides with Notes will add the notes you added in the Notes section of Keynote (see Figure 11.4). The only problem is that you can't change the font type, style, or size on the page.

Producer Script is a bit more functional in that it will print four slides per page (see Figure 11.5). It won't print your typed notes, but it will leave enough room on the side of each image to add your own notes.

Print Options

On the right side of the Keynote print window are five other options for fine-tuning print versions of your presentations.

Print Dark Backgrounds As White If you use a theme with a black background, such as Gradient or Blackboard, this option will turn off the background and make it white. Obviously, this will save on ink and probably make your presentation a bit more readable (see Figure 11.6).

However, you probably won't need this option with many of the themes, such as Parchment, Notebook, and so on. Still, keep in mind that even a lighter colored background can make text unreadable when it is printed in black and white.

Print Each Stage of Builds Unless you need to show every single build (such as in the storyboarding project in Chapter 7, "Video Storyboard: Building Slide Actions"), then you should leave this option unchecked. Otherwise, you'll print every single build in every slide, which will be incredibly tedious to the viewer.

Include Skipped Slides If you give a custom presentation where (in the interest of time) you need to skip various slides but you still want to give your client that information later on, check this option and all the slides you used the Keynote Skip command on will also print.

Add Borders Around Slides and Include Slide Numbers Both of these options are self-explanatory. The Add Borders option is good to use in conjunction with the Print Dark Backgrounds As White option, so your slide won't appear to be floating on the page.

Figure 11.4

The Slides with Notes option puts one slide with your notes on each page.

CUT: MCU ALLEY FRONT. KISMET strides quickly behind Anne, slightly out of focus over her shoulder. Now she's aware of something, and just as he is right over her shoulder...

Converting Keynote to Video

Besides an on-screen presentation, probably the second best way to show your Keynote presentation is using video. This will capture the cool transitions, other media files, and timing of your show. Macintosh systems today—particularly the laptop line—have direct video connections out or FireWire ports with which you can attach a digital video (DV) camera.

Before you transfer your Keynote presentation to tape, there are a few limitations inherent to video that you should keep in mind. You can correct many within your show if you know to look for them.

Video Limitations

You need to watch for three main "gotchas" when outputting Keynote to video: colors, size, and scan lines.

Colors

Ah, the freedoms we enjoy with computer monitors as compared to video monitors! While computer monitor technology gets better every year, the basic National Television Standards Committee (NTSC) video signal has barely changed since the first color broadcast of the Rose Parade on January 1, 1954. High-definition video is on the way, but television screens in consumer electronics stores around the country are still hobbled by the fact that they can only display thousands—not millions—of colors.

Computers use the Red-Green-Blue (RGB) color space, while video uses a different color space called YUV. In YUV, the Y stands for luminance (how bright the signal is), U means the red part of the signal (the Y signal without the luminance), and V stands for blue minus the Y. For the most part, each system can display similar colors.

Figure 11.5

The Producer Script option outputs four slides per printed page.

Figure 11.6

Your slides will be much more readable and waste less ink when you use the Print Dark Backgrounds As White option.

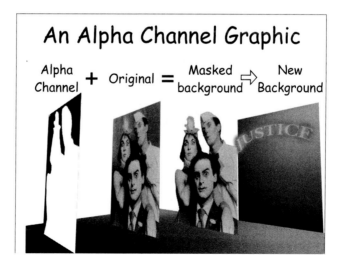

However, video's YUV video format is much more limited. For example, although computer monitors have no trouble displaying 100-percent white, red, or green, video monitors have problems with this. (See Figure 11.7.) All white is especially difficult for video to handle. The brightest white in the NTSC color space is actually only 80-percent bright.

To make sure you don't have any trouble with the bright whites in your show, make sure to set all-white text to 80-percent bright, which you can do using the Colors palette (see Figure 11.8).

The good news is that all the themes that Apple provided with Keynote use NTSC-compatible colors, so the main color schemes within each themes should work fine on the video screen. However, you will need to adjust the white text used in the Gradient and Blackboard themes from 100-percent white to a slightly gray 80-percent white. This ensures that you won't have any problems playing those on standard video systems.

Size

Keynote defaults to a computer monitor size of 800×600 pixels, but NTSC video (using the DV format) is only 720×420 pixels. Before exporting to video, you should adjust the size of your presentation to this size, which will also allow you to readjust your slide elements as needed.

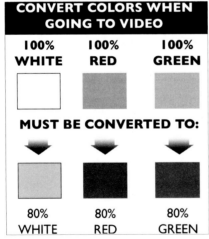

Figure 11.7

Before you use your Keynote presentation in video, you'll need to convert 100-percent white, red, and green colors so they are more acceptable for standard NTSC video.

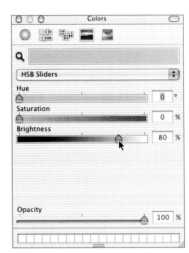

Figure 11.8

Use the Colors palette to set your white text and objects to a level that is compatible with video.

Next, you need to watch out for the video "safe" areas. As it turns out, you don't actually see the entire video image on most standard televisions; about 20 percent of the image is masked by the television case. To avoid having important television messages (is that an oxymoron?) or events covered, the Society of Motion Picture and Television Engineers (SMPTE) created a specification that defined two areas: title-safe and action-safe (see Figure 11.9).

About 10 percent from the edge of the image is the start of the area called *action-safe*. Inside this area, you can expect to see any action that occurs on the screen on most television sets.

The more important area is the rectangle 10 percent farther away from the edge, which is the area called *title-safe*. As long as you keep your text inside the title-safe area, you can be reasonably sure your audience will be able to see all of your text on just about any television set.

Scan Lines

Finally, don't use thin lines on your text and graphics. This is because—unlike computer monitors—televisions divide a single image or frame into two separate groups of lines, which are called *fields*. This again is another archaic holdover from the glory days of television, which thankfully computer monitor technology doesn't use. This process of breaking up and then displaying these scan lines super-fast is called *interlacing*.

Why is this a problem? Well, imagine a frame of film. A line running across this film would show up nicely. However, if you cut the frame into more than 500 pieces that you arranged in order on top of each other, you'd find that the single pixel line might show up in one field but not in the other. This causes on-screen flickering, which is annoying.

You can avoid this by making sure all artwork in your presentation does not use any objects that have single-pixel lines. The best thing to do if you are not sure is to hook up your laptop and view your slides on a video monitor or television set prior to exporting your show. This will show you whether you need to worry about flicker, as well as show any problems with image size or oversaturated colors.

Figure 11.9

Action-safe and title-safe areas in a video screen

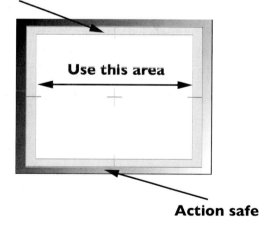

Television Safety Areas

Title safe

Use this area

Action safe

Once you've taken care of these elements, you are ready to transfer your presentation to video. As with many pieces of software, there are a variety of ways you can do this: laptop video, QuickTime DV conversion, and scan conversion. Which one you choose depends upon how much you are willing to spend and how much time you have available.

Laptop Video Output: Easy but Muddy Image

Every PowerBook and iBook these days is outfitted with a video output port, so you can connect your laptop directly to a VCR and make a recording. Most people don't appreciate what an amazing feat this is, but it is one of the great features of the Macintosh laptops. Just a few years ago it took a lot more hardware to get video output that didn't look nearly as good.

To record your presentation, all you need to do is connect a video cable from the video output port of your PowerBook or iBook and then hook that cable to the video input on your VCR (see Figure 11.10). It just doesn't get any easier than that.

However, there are some downsides to doing this. For example, the technology Apple uses to convert the Mac's signal to video uses a special type of image filtering called *convolution* to prepare the signal for display on a video monitor. Although in most cases this wipes out the irritation of flickering single-pixel lines, it also slightly blurs everything. Hence, what was sharp on your Mac screen will look slightly fuzzy when you get to video.

Figure 11.10

You can record Keynote presentations directly to video using your PowerBook's or iBook's video output.

QuickTime DV Conversion: Harder, Cleaner Image

The next method, where you convert Keynote to a DV movie, takes a bit more time but ultimately gives you a much better image because it keeps everything digital most of the way through the computer to video connection. To do this, you'll need the following:

- iMovie
- A FireWire cable
- A DV camcorder

The process is pretty simple, as shown in Figure 11.11.

First, you export your Keynote presentation as a QuickTime movie using the DV/DVC PRO-NTSC codec. To make sure you have this set up properly, you'll need to select Size → Custom in the QuickTime Export dialog box. Make sure you set the size of the presentation to 720×480 pixels, which is the standard size for DV video. Once you've done that, a new window will pop up for QuickTime settings. Click the Settings box, and you'll see a new dialog box that displays all the different codecs you can use. Make sure you set the codec to DV/DVC PRO-NTSC and the frame rate to 29.97, which is the correct frame rate for NTSC video (as shown in Figure 11.12).

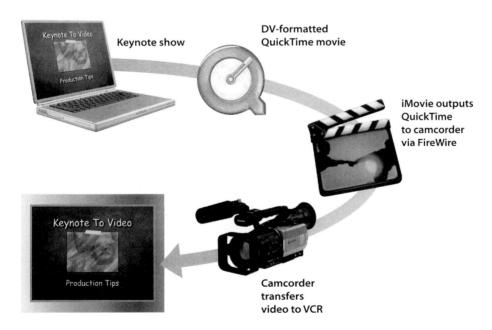

Figure 11.11

The Keynote to DV video conversion

TIPS FROM THE PROS: JESSE BUSBY
ON WORKING WITH SLIDE SERVICE BUREAUS

 Jesse Busby is the senior account manager for Genigraphics, a division of Power2 (www.genigraphics.com). For more than 25 years, Genigraphics has provided a way for users to convert their computer slide presentations to 35mm slides, prints, and transparencies. Jesse provides the following tips to first-time computer-to-slide customers:

Format your file size. Make sure your Keynote presentation is set at the size of your output, whether it is the size of a poster or formatted for 35mm slides. For example, the on-screen format that you see when you present slide shows from Keynote and Powerpoint is not at the correct aspect ration for 35mm slides. Instead, you need to readjust your Keynote or PowerPoint show to use a wide or landscape mode in the Page Setup dialog box so that it will properly map the aspect ratio of 35mm slides.

Send any custom fonts with your order. If you send your Keynote presentation in Portable Document Format (PDF) or PowerPoint format, make sure you have the right fonts to go with that presentation. Generally, this is only an issue when you import and use a custom font on your computer. Otherwise, the service bureau will have to substitute another font in your display.

Regroup files in PowerPoint. Anything that is imported into PowerPoint has to be regrouped before you send it to the printer so that it is embedded as a PowerPoint object. Otherwise, the object might not show up at all.

If you plan to print large, start with the right dots per inch (dpi). Any images that you import into Keynote with the idea of printing into posters, make sure that the dpi is set high. Keynote will only present the images on-screen at 72 dpi, but the image file will still retain its original resolution.

Once you've converted your show to a DV-formatted QuickTime movie, just bring that video file into iMovie. Inside iMovie, all you need to do is add your presentation to the timeline. You could even add some music at this point to spice up your show. When you are satisfied with everything, connect your camcorder to the Mac's FireWire port using a FireWire cable and then use iMovie's Print to Video command to send the DV movie of your presentation to the camcorder. Once it is recorded on your camcorder, you can either play your Keynote show back from the DV tape in your camera or make VHS copies from your camcorder to a VHS VCR.

Because you've sent the file digitally, you maintained a lot of resolution that might have otherwise been lost. However, keep in mind that if you make VHS copies of the DV tape, then you will be back to losing resolution.

Scan Conversion: Expensive, Best Quality

If you absolutely have to have the best-looking video possible and are willing to pay handsomely for this, then you can also have your Keynote show transferred to video using scan conversion hardware. Scan converters are expensive, specialized hardware developed specifically to convert computer and other nonstandard video sources to video at the highest resolution possible.

Most major postproduction facilities have a scan converter in-house or at least know where to find one. You set up a time to see them, bring your laptop in, and then drive the presentation while they record it to tape. The scan converter will actually take the image not from your video output port but from the external VGA monitor feed, so it works directly with the Mac's RGB signal while it is converting to video.

Your results will be impressive—as will your bill. You can expect to pay anywhere from $300 to more than $2,000 for this service, depending upon the tape format and length of your show.

Although all these extra steps to get your Keynote presentation onto different media may take extra time, in the long run it can make a major difference to your audience.

Figure 11.12

The correct settings for exporting Keynote to a DV format QuickTime movie

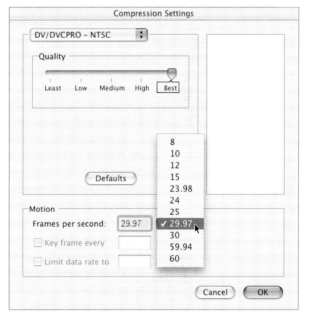

PART IV

Appendixes

The book's three appendixes offer additional information that will help you reduce your development time when creating presentations with Keynote. The appendixes list all of the keyboard and mouse shortcuts, describe the graphics that ship with Keynote, and show you where to find more information about the program and presentation technology.

Appendix A **Keyboard and Mouse Shortcuts**

Appendix B **The Keynote Graphics Inventory**

Appendix C **Additional Resources**

Keyboard and Mouse Shortcuts

This appendix will show you some keyboard and mouse shortcuts that will help you perform tasks quickly in Keynote. First, Table A.1 shows you general mouse shortcuts, including some of the options available to you when you use a two button mouse. The next set of tables lists the keyboard shortcuts in each section:

- Table A.2 lists the shortcuts you can use in the Slide Canvas

- Table A.3 describes shortcuts for editing text

- Table A.4 shows you shortcuts for playing a slide show

- Table A.5 gives you shortcuts for using the Slide Organizer

- Table A.6 lists shortcuts for editing chart data

- Finally, Table A.7 lists shortcuts for editing tables

To use the mouse shortcuts shown in Table A.1, you'll need to click the right button of a two-button mouse (an action called "right-click") or hold down the Ctrl key while clicking.

If you hold down the Ctrl+click or right-click the Slide Organizer, you'll have access to these commands:

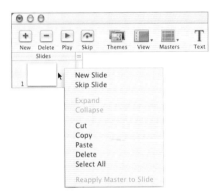

If you hold down the Ctrl+click or right-click the Slide Canvas, you'll have access to these commands:

If you hold down the Ctrl+click or right-click the Toolbar, you'll have access to these commands:

If you hold down the Ctrl+click or right-click a row in the Chart Editor, you'll have access to these commands:

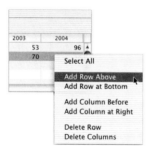

CTRL+CLICK OR RIGHT-CLICK ON...	TO ACCESS THESE COMMANDS...
Slide Organizer	New Slide, Skip Slide, Expand, Collapse, Cut, Copy, Paste, Delete, Select All
Slide Canvas	Bring Forward, Bring to Front, Send Backward, Send to Back, Align Objects, Distribute Objects, Zoom In, Zoom Out, Cut, Copy, Paste, Delete, Select All, Place, Reapply Master to Slide, Play Slideshow
Toolbar	Icon & Text, Icon Only, Text Only, Use Small Icons, Customize Toolbar

Table A.1

Mouse Shortcuts

ACTION	KEYBOARD SHORTCUT
Cycle through objects on the Slide Canvas	Tab
Cycle backward through objects the Slide Canvas	Shift+Tab
Move object by one pixel	Arrow keys
Move object by 10 pixels	Shift+arrow keys
Add (or remove) selected object to previously selected objects	Shift+click or ⌘+click
Add (or remove) selected range to previously selected objects	Shift+drag or ⌘+drag
Constrain movement of object	Shift+drag
Duplicate objects only	Option+drag
Disable alignment guides	⌘+drag
Rotate object	⌘+drag handle
Rotate object 45°	⌘+Shift+drag handle
Constrain aspect ratio when resizing object	Shift+drag handle
Resize object from center	Option+drag handle
Constrain aspect ratio when resizing object from center	Option+Shift+drag handle
Move to next slide	Page Down (scrolls page down)
Move to previous slide	Page Up (scrolls page up)
Move to first slide	Home
Move to last slide	End
Open shortcut menus for selection	Ctrl+click
Copy selected text or object	⌘+C
Paste selected text or object	⌘+V
Cut selected text or object	⌘+X

Table A.2

Getting Around the Slide Canvas

Table A.3	ACTION	KEYBOARD SHORTCUT
Editing Text	Move one character to the right	Right-arrow button
	Move one character to the right	Right-arrow button
	Move one character to the left	Left-arrow button
	Extend selection one character to the right	Shift+right-arrow button
	Extend selection one character to the left	Shift+left-arrow button
	Move to end of current word	Option+right-arrow button
	Move to beginning of current word	Option+left-arrow button
	Extend selection to end of current word	Shift+Option+right-arrow button
	Extend selection to beginning of current word	Shift+Option+left-arrow button
	Move to end of current line	⌘+right-arrow button
	Move to beginning of current line	⌘+left-arrow button
	Extend selection to end of current line	⌘+Shift+right-arrow button
	Extend selection to beginning of current line	⌘+Shift+left-arrow button
	Move to the line above	Up arrow
	Move to the line below	Down arrow
	Extend selection to the line above	Shift+Up arrow
	Extend selection to the line below	Shift+Down arrow
	Move to beginning of current paragraph	Option+Up arrow
	Move to end of current paragraph	Option+Down arrow
	Extend selection to beginning of current paragraph	Shift+Option+Up arrow
	Extend selection to end of current paragraph	Shift+Option+Down arrow
	Move to beginning of text	⌘+Up arrow
	Move to end of text	⌘+Down arrow
	Extend selection to beginning of text	⌘+Shift+Up arrow
	Extend selection to end of text	⌘+Shift+Down arrow
	Delete previous character or selection	Delete
	Delete the part of the word to the left of the insertion point	Option+Delete
	Scroll to top of the Slide Canvas	Page Up or Home
	Scroll to bottom of the Slide Canvas	Page Down or End
	Stop editing text and select the text box	⌘+Return
	Select text bullet and text	Click bullet
	Select bullet, text, and all sub-bullets and text and then move	Drag bullet

Table A.4	ACTION	KEYBOARD SHORTCUT
Playing a Slide Show	Play next slide	Space, click, right-arrow button, Down arrow, or Page Down
	Play previous slide	Left-arrow button, Up arrow, or Page Up
	End show	Escape, Q, or ⌘+. (period)
	Display black screen	B
	Display first slide	Home
	Display last slide	End

ACTION	KEYBOARD SHORTCUT	Table A.5
Create new slide at same level as last selected slide	Return or Enter	**Using the Slide Organizer**
Indent slides to the right	Tab	
Move indented slides to the left	Shift+Tab	
Extend selection to the selected slide	Shift+click	
Add the selected range to previously selected slides	Shift+drag	
Add (or remove) selected slide to previously selected slides	⌘+click or Shift+click	
Add (or remove) selected range to previously selected slides	⌘+drag	
Duplicate slide	Option+drag	
Select next slide	Down arrow	
Extend selection to the next slide	Shift+Down arrow	
Select last slide	⌘+Down arrow	
Extend selection to the last slide	⌘+Shift+Down arrow	
Select previous slide	Up arrow	
Extend selection to previous slide	Shift+Up arrow	
Select first slide	⌘+Up arrow	
Extend selection to first slide	⌘+Shift+Up arrow	
Delete selected slides	Delete	
Scroll to first slide without changing the selection	Home	
Scroll to last slide without changing the selection	End	
Scroll down a "page" of slides without changing the selection	Page Down	
Scroll up a "page" of slides without changing the selection	Page Up	

ACTION	KEYBOARD SHORTCUT	Table A.6
Complete a cell entry and move the selection down	Return	**Editing Chart Data**
Complete a cell entry and move the selection up	Shift+Return	
Complete a cell entry and move the selection to the right	Tab	
Complete a cell entry and move the selection to the left	Shift+Tab	
Delete the character to the left of the insertion point or delete the selection	Delete	
Move one character left, right, to the beginning of text, or to the end of text	Arrow keys (in text edit mode)	
Complete a cell entry and select the cell	Enter	
Move one cell in a given direction	Arrow keys (in cell selection mode)	
Move to the beginning of the row	Home	
Move to the last nonblank cell to the right in the current row	End	
Extend the selection by one cell	Shift+arrow keys	
Extend the selection to the beginning of the row	Shift+Home	
Extend the selection to the end of the row	Shift+End	

Table A.7

Getting Around Tables

ACTION	KEYBOARD SHORTCUT
Select all table cells, borders, or cell content, depending on initial selection	⌘+A
Copy contents of selected cells or whole table, if table is selected	⌘+C
Cut contents of selected cells or whole table, if table is selected	⌘+X
Paste the selection that was last copied	⌘+V
Delete selection (whole table, table border or border segment, or contents of selected cells)	Delete
Constrain the movement of the table and snap to guides	Shift+drag table
Duplicate table on move	Option+Shift+drag table
Switch contents of selected cell with contents of destination cell	Drag selected cell to another cell
Copy contents of selected cell into destination cell	Option+drag selected cell to another
Extend selection from selected cell to destination cell	Shift+click cell
Add/remove selected cell to/from selection	⌘+click selected or unselected cell
Stop editing text and select cell	⌘+Return or ⌘+click cell (in text edit mode)
Select text first, then multiple cells, depending on extent of drag	Click+drag cell (in text edit mode)
Select entire row or column border	Click border of selected table
Move row or column border, or border segment, to new position	Click+drag selected border or border segment of selected cell
Select/deselect border segment to select discontinuous border segments	Shift+click or ⌘+click segment of selected border
Add/remove row/column to selected edge of table	Option+drag outside border of table
Move selected table one pixel	Arrow keys
Move selected table 10 pixels	Shift+arrow keys
Select the next table cell to the left, right, up, or down	Arrow keys (in cell selection mode)
Extend cell selection by one cell	Shift+arrow keys (in cell selection mode)
Select text in next cell	Tab
Select text in previous cell	Shift+Tab
Insert a tab at insertion point in the selected cell	Control+Tab (in text edit mode)
Stop editing cell and select the table	⌘+Return (in cell selection mode)

The Keynote Graphics Inventory

Keynote comes loaded with stock pictures and graphics for you to use in your presentations. You can access all of these images by selecting File → Image Library. The images reside in four files: Flags.key, Objects.key, Pictures.key, and Symbols and Border.key.

Flags

The Flags.key file is pretty straightforward—it contains nine flags for you to use. These are high-resolution images, so you can scale these up pretty well to use in a backdrop or graphic image.

United States   United Kingdom   Canada

France   Germany   Italy

Japan   Russia   European Union

Objects

The Objects.key file contains various objects you can use in your presentations. These graphics all have alpha channels, so you can seamlessly add them into a background. The graphics include the traffic signs, money, and miscellaneous images shown in the following sections.

Traffic Sign Images

Miscellaneous Images

In the pictures of the black and white chess pieces and the dice, each piece is a separate image that you can use individually.

Money Images

Pictures

The 10 pictures included in `Pictures.key` are impressive; in fact, they're professionally shot. You can scale these high-resolution images up to twice their size, and they will still look good.

Symbols and Borders

The symbols and borders in `Symbols and Border.key` come in three colors: black, 50-percent gray, and white. You'll find a collection of asterisks, arrows, monetary symbols, and borders.

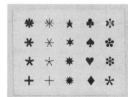

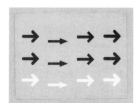

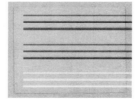

Additional Resources

With an evolving product such as Keynote, it is a good idea to have other resources that you can call on to get the latest information. This appendix includes a variety of sources for you, both specific to Keynote and generally related to media production.

Keynote Websites

The following websites relate to Keynote and appear in alphabetical order.

Apple's Keynote Page

www.apple.com/keynote/

Apple is a good starting spot for getting Keynote information, but you'll find more in-depth reviews, tips, and tutorials in third-party sites such as KeynoteUser.com and KeynoteHQ.

KeynoteHQ

`www.keynotehq.com`

KeynoteHQ is a community site, where users can exchange projects, tips, and news. Although not the prettiest site on the Web, KeynoteHQ is filled with Keynote information.

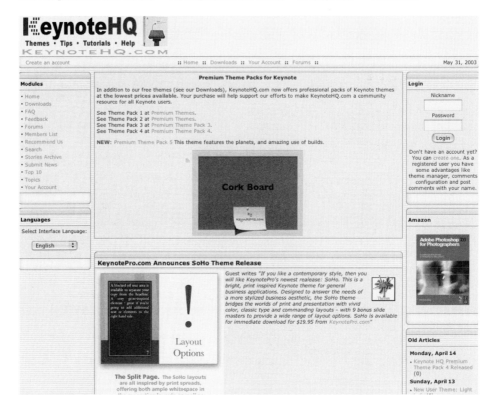

KeynoteUser.com

www.keynoteuser.com

This is a great site, filled with in-depth reviews and tutorials. You'll find exhaustive research on importing and exporting graphics, as well as other invaluable production tips.

The site also sells custom themes, which overall are quite good. However, even if you are not interested in the custom themes, you should definitely bookmark this site for future reference.

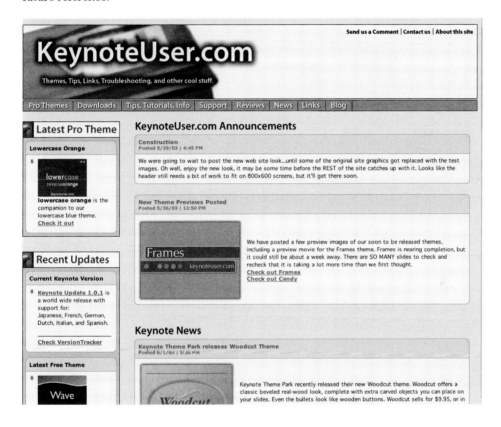

Keynote Theme Park

www.keynotethemepark.com

This is another good source for Keynote themes, many of which are reasonably priced.

Keynote Pro

www.keynotepro.com

This site offers a variety of keynote themes. Their Storyboarding theme is particularly impressive.

Atomic Learning

www.atomiclearning.com

Atomic Learning provides QuickTime movie tutorials on Keynote as well as other Mac software programs. This is a subscription site, so you'll need to pay to get in.

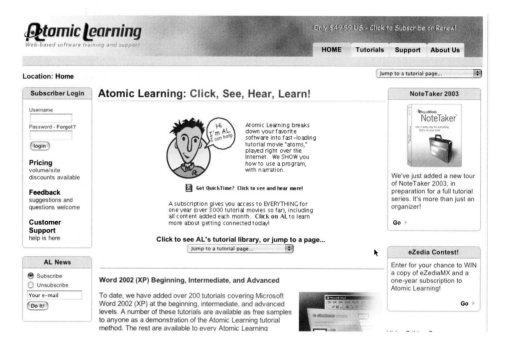

Jumsoft

www.jumsoft.com

Jumsoft is another Keynote theme vendor, with many different styles to choose from.

Keynote Gallery

www.keynotegallery.com

Keynote Gallery has some of the slickest Keynote themes around. They are not cheap, but can add a lot of pizzazz.

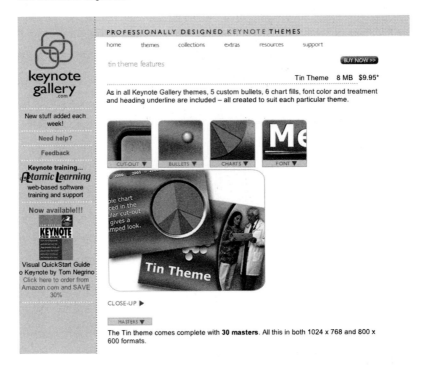

PowerPointArt.com

`www.powerpointart.com`

This site seems like it was originally designed as a site for PowerPoint users. However, you can use most of the custom backgrounds it offers in Keynote, either to build themes or to use as clip art.

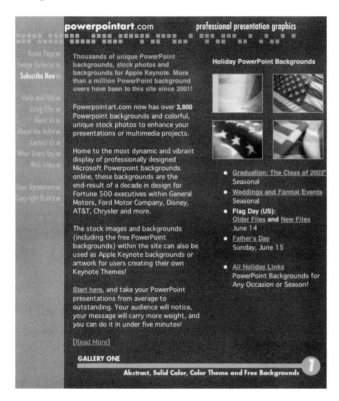

Mac-Specific Websites

The following websites are specific to Macs and appear in alphabetical order.

CNET

www.cnet.com

Sometimes CNET can be a bit intimidating with its dozens of departments and wide focus. However, Senior Editor Molly Wood does a great job at covering the latest and greatest Macintosh products for CNET.

Creative Mac

`www.creativemac.com`

This site, run by the nefarious David Nagel, is the best site on the Web for information on using a Mac in media production. Dave posts new tutorials and reviews every week, as well as updates the site with Mac-specific news daily. His editorials are outrageous but always on the mark.

MacInTouch

`www.macintouch.com`

Ric Ford started this site years ago, and it is a great source for information on anything technical. Ric's readers contribute dozens of posts on hardware and software programs—as well as some innovative solutions.

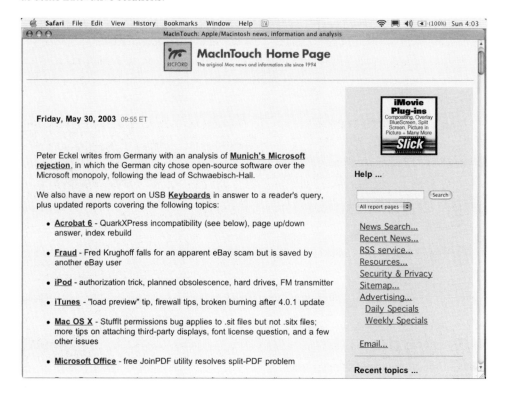

Presentations and Media Production

The following websites are general presentation and media production sites and appear in alphabetical order.

AV Video Multimedia Producer

www.avvideo.com

I'm a contributing editor for this magazine and proud of it. Every month AV Video Multimedia Producer has great articles on not just the technology but also on the business of media production. You can view it online, or if you are involved in media production, sign up for a free subscription.

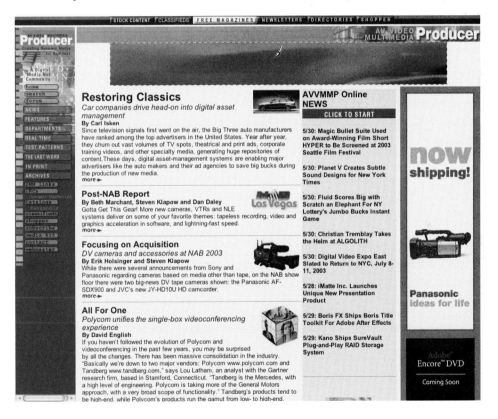

Digital Media Net

`www.digitalmedianet.com`

Several years ago I was one of the original founders of this industry hub. If you are involved in media production, there is something for you here. From animation to video editing, Digital Media Net has a specialized site for every aspect of media production with the latest news, reviews, and tutorials on your favorite digital media production tools.

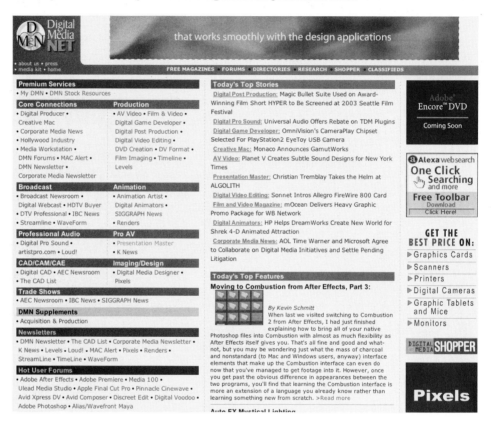

Digital Producer

www.digitalproducer.com

This is your news source for digital media production. The site spits out hundreds of news pieces for the press daily, but only a few of them really matter when you are doing digital media production.

Digital Video Editing

www.digitalvideoediting.com

Charlie White, an Emmy award–winning producer and editor, runs this site. His reviews of editing hardware and software are good and well researched. He has a bit of a PC bias, but you won't find a more knowledgeable authority on nonlinear editing systems.

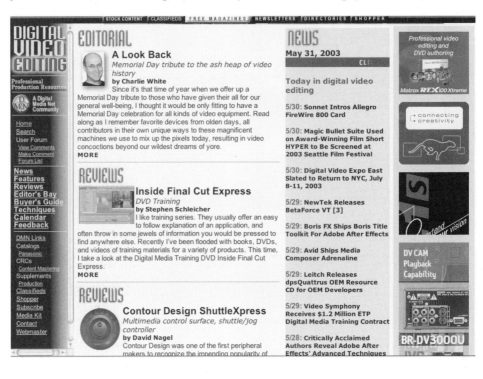

Presentation Master

www.presentationmaster.com

This is a site I started many years ago for Digital Media Net. It still has a lot of great information on presentation technology and production tips.

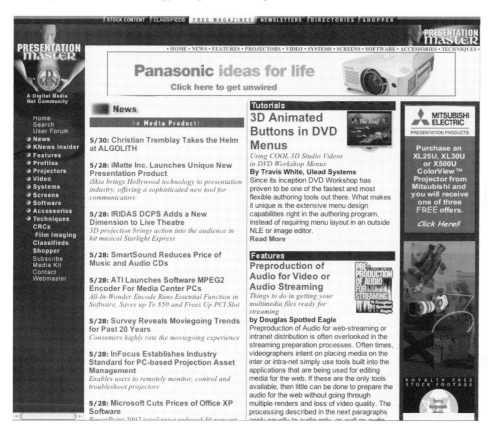

Index

Note to the Reader: Throughout this index **boldfaced** page numbers indicate primary discussions of a topic. *Italicized* page numbers indicate illustrations.

A

Aaland, Mikkel, 110
action-safe areas, 203, *203*
Add Borders Around Slides option, 200
Add to Favorites option, 41
AIFF (Audio Interchange File Format) files, 99–100
alignment, Text Inspector for, 39
alignment guides, 57, *58*
All Storyboard Images.key file, 129
Alley.jpg file, 107
Alley Side (door).psd file, 122
Alley Side (floor).psd file, 122–123
Alpha Channel Presentation Final.key file, 96
alpha channels, 15
    in PowerPoint, 159–161, *160–162*
    presentation about. *See* class lesson presentation
    for storyboards, 121–129, *122–127, 129*
AlphaChannelMask.psd file, 92
angles for drop shadows, 47
animatics, 114
ANSI lumens, 175–176
Apple Keynote Page, 223, *223*
Apple laptops, 182–184, *183–185*
Arrow keys for charts, 75
artist portfolios, 97
    building, 105–109, *106–109*
    converting files for, 101–103, *101–104*
    editing graphics for, 104
    importing files for, 98–100
    preparing for delivery, 109, 111
Atomic Learning site, 228, *228*

audience
    for artist portfolios, 110
    defining, 70–72
    for marketing presentations, 149
audio, 99–100
    adding, 147–148, *148*
    AV companies for, 191
    compressing, 151
    importing, 98
Audio Interchange File Format (AIFF) files, 99–100
AV companies, 188–191
AV Video Multimedia Producer site, 235, *235*
axes, 76, *76–77*

B

Back tool, 14
Backward tool, 19
baggage words, 42
bar charts, 79
Blackboard theme, 26, *26*
blur for drop shadows, 47
borders, 221, *221*
Build Inspector, 116
builds, 116
    camera focus in, 117–121, *118–121*
    working with, 121–129, *122–127, 129*
bullet points, 72–73
    san serif for, 39
    transitions for, 95, *96*
Bullet slider, 40
bullets
    graphics for, 48–49, *49*
    from PowerPoint, 164–165, *165*
    Text Inspector for, 40

Bullets & Numbering section, 40
Busby, Jesse, 206

C

camera focus, 117–121, *118–121*
cameras for storyboards, 128
captures, labeling, 198
categories of fonts, 16
Cathode Ray Tube (CRT) projectors, 179, *180*
chambers of commerce, 190
Character control, 40
Character palette, 16, *17*
Chart Colors.key file, 167
Chart Data Editor, 13, *13*, 20, 212
Chart Inspector, 75–80, *76–78*
Chart tool, 13, *13*
Chart Type button, 75
charts, 62, *62–63*, 73–75
    Chart Inspector for, 75–80, *76–78*
    entering info for, 62–63, *63*
    exploding pie wedges, 64, *64*
    fonts for, 74, *75*
    pie slice color, 63–65, *64*
    in PowerPoint, 167–168, *168–169*
    shortcuts for, 75, 215
    tables for, 64–65, *65*
    in themes, 135–136, *136*
    tips for, 79
class lesson presentation, 81
    details and notes in, 86–88, *87–88*
    graphics in, 88–92, *89–92*
    overall look, 83–86, *84–85*
    roughing out, 82
    slides for, 82–83, *84*

text for, 82–83, *84*, 91–92, *91–92*
theme for, 26, *26*
transitions in, 92–93, *93*, 95–96, *95–96*
Cleaner program, 103, *104*
cleaning up toolbar, 21
CNET site, 232, *232*
codecs (compressors/decompressors), 99–100
collaborators, 127
collections of fonts, 16
color
in design, 34
for drop shadows, 47
for pie slices, 63–65, *64*
in PowerPoint charts, 167–168, *168–169*
for text, 39, 43
in video, 201–202, *202*
color fill, 45
Colors palette, 16, *16*
column charts, 79
compatibility of Windows files, 170
complex transitions, 142–143, *143*
component comparisons, charts for, 79
compressing audio, 151
compressors/decompressors (codecs), 99–100
contrast ratio in projectors, 176–177, *176*
contrasting colors, 34
converting
QuickTime DV, 205–207, *205*, *207*
unsupported files, 101–103, *101–104*
video, 140–141, 201–207, *202–205*, *207*
Windows PC files, 164
convolution filtering, 204
copying to Slide Canvas, 6, *7*
corkboard image, theme for, 27, *27*
correlation comparisons, charts for, 79

costs
with AV companies, 190
in renting equipment, 174
Crayon Line theme, 29–30, *30*
creation tools, 11–13, *12–13*
Creative Mac site, 233, *233*
cropped PowerPoint graphics, 165–167, *166*
CRT (Cathode Ray Tube) projectors, 179, *180*
custom fonts, 206
Custom image section, 41
custom themes, 133–134
charts in, 135–136, *136*
saving, 137
starting, 134–135, *135*
text for, 136–137, *137*
custom toolbars, 16–21, *17–18*
Customize Toolbar tool, 20–21
Customize Toolbar window, 17
Cut transitions, 117

D

data point labels, 76
DeBabelizer program, 102–103, *103*
defining audiences and distributions, 70–72
Delete Slide button, 8–9
Demon Encounter.key file, 114–115, *115–116*, 117, 125
demos, 94, **111**
depth for 2D elements, 116
design basics, **34**
details in class lesson presentation, 86–88, *87–88*
digital cameras, 128
Digital Cinema projectors, 180–181, *180–181*
Digital Light Processing (DLP) projectors, 178–181, *179–181*
Digital Media Net site, 236, *236*
Digital Media Remote controller, 173, *173*
digital micromirror devices (DMDs), 178
digital portfolios, 97
building, 105–109, *106–109*

converting files for, 101–103, *101–104*
editing graphics for, 104
importing files for, 98–100
preparing for delivery, 109, 111
Digital Producer site, 237, *237*
digital video (DV), 140–141, 205–207, *205*, *207*
Digital Video Editing site, 238, *238*
disclosure triangles, 5
Display on Secondary monitor option, 186
Dissolve transitions
in PowerPoint, 163
for storyboards, 117
distributions, defining, 70–72
DLP (Digital Light Processing) projectors, 178–181, *179–181*
DMDs (digital micromirror devices), 178
documentaries. *See* Theater Simple
documents, location of, 168
dot charts, 79
DP 50 projector, 180, *181*
dpi (dots per inch), 206
dragging
to Slide Canvas, 6, *6*
text, 35
dramatic effects, text for, 43
drop shadows, 26
Graphic Inspector for, 47, *47*
in PowerPoint, 161–162, *162*
for text, 43
dual displays, 185–186, *187*
DV (digital video), 140–141, 205–207, *205*, *207*
DV-Bridge product, 141
DV/DVC PRO-NTSC codec, 205
DVCPro 25 codec, 99
DVI input in projectors, 181

E

e-mail encoding in Windows, 170
Edit Collections option, 41
Edit Data option, 75
Edit Size option, 41

editing
    graphics, 104, 138–140, *139–140*
    shortcuts for, 214–215
education. *See* class lesson
    presentation
emphasis
    in design, 34
    in storyboards, 128
    text for, 43
End key for charts, 75
entertainment in marketing
    presentations, 149
equipment
    from AV companies, 189–191
    renting, 174–175
exploding pie wedges, 64, *64*
Export tool, 19
exporting
    to PowerPoint, 159–163,
        159–162, 206
    Theater Simple presentation,
        148, 150–151, *150*
Extract plug-in, 139, *139*
Extras menu, 41, 43

F

families of fonts, 16
fans in DLP projectors, 179
fields, 203
filenames in Windows, 170
files
    converting. *See* converting
    exporting
        to PowerPoint, 159–163,
            159–162, 206
        Theater Simple presentation,
            148, 150–151, *150*
    importing. *See* importing
    location of, 168–169
    from Windows PCs, 164, 170
filler, graphics as, 34
fills, 44–46, *46*
Find tool, 20
FireWire cable, 206
flags, 217, *217*
Flags.key file, 217
Flash files, 100

Flexible Space tool, 21
flicker, 203
Flip Horizontally tool, 20
Flip Vertically tool, 20
Font window vs. Text Inspector, 61
fonts
    for charts, 74, *75*
    custom, 206
    selecting, 38–39
    in Windows, 170
Fonts palette, 16, *16*, 41–43, *41*
Ford, Ric, 234
formats, print, 199–200, *199–201*
formatting chart types, 135–136,
    136
Formatting Palette, 157, *157*
Forward tool, 19
frequency comparisons, charts for,
    79
Front tool, 14
full-screen QuickTime movies, 145
Fun theme, 32, *32*

G

G-90 CRT projector, 179, *180*
G4 PowerBooks, 179, 182
    12″, 183, *183*
    15″, 184, *184*
    17″, 184, *184*
generic text, importing, 164
Genigraphics wizard, 195
Get Fonts option, 43
Gettysburg Address slides, 53
ghosting, 178
GIF (Graphics Interchange Format)
    format, 100
global controls, 8–11, *8–11*
Grab utility for 35mm slides,
    195–198, *196–198*
Gradient theme, 25–26, *26*
gradients
    for charts, 78
    for fills, 45
graphic element transitions, 96
Graphic Inspector, 44, *45*
    for fill, 44–45, *46*
    for opacity, 48, *48*

    for shadows, 47, *47*
    for stroke, 46
graphic novels, 114
graphics, 43–44
    alignment guides for, 57, *58*
    for bullets, 48–49, *49*
    in class lesson presentation,
        88–92, *89–92*
    cropped PowerPoint, 165–167,
        166
    editing, 104, 138–140, *139–140*
    as filler, 34
    flags, 217, *217*
    formatting, in PowerPoint vs.
        Keynote, 157, *157*
    Graphic Inspector for. *See*
        Graphic Inspector
    importing, 49
    miscellaneous images, 219, *219*
    money images, *220*
    objects, 218, *218*
    pictures, 220, *220–221*
    for presentations, 58–62, *59–62*
    scanning for, 138
    for storyboards, 114, 121–129,
        122–127, 129
    symbols and borders, 221, *221*
Graphics Interchange Format (GIF)
    format, 100
Group tool, 14
grouping slides, 5, *5*

H

headlines, serif, 39
heat in DLP projectors, 179
Help tool, 20
Hewitt, Paul G., 94
hidden costs with AV companies,
    190
high-contrast screens in Windows,
    170
Holland, Llysa, 132
Holsinger, Erik
    on AV companies, 190
    on multimedia marketing, 149
Home key for charts, 75
horizontal scan frequencies, 181

I

iBook, 182–183, *183*
Icon Only option, 21
IMA codec, 151
Image bullet section, 41
image fills, 46
Image Library
    location of, 168
    for presentations, 58–62, *59–62*
images. *See* graphics
iMovie
    for audio, 147–148, *148*
    for QuickTime DV conversions, 205–206
importing
    files, 98–100
    graphics, 49
    PDF text, 35
    from PowerPoint, 163–168, *165–169*
Include Skipped Slides option, 200
Include Slide Numbers option, 200
indenting slides, 5, *5*, 56, *56*
Inspector palette, 15, *15*
Interactive Slideshow option, 146
interface, 4, *4*
    PowerPoint vs. Keynote, *156–158*, 157
    Slide Canvas, 6–7, *6–7*
    Slide Organizer, 5, *5*
    toolbar. *See* toolbar
interlacing, 203
item comparisons, charts for, 79

J

Jeff Beckstrom Portfolio.mov file, 109
Jobs, Steve, 174
JPEG (Joint Photographic Experts Group) format, 100
Jumsoft site, 229, *229*
JusticeAlphaInfog.psd file, 89, 91
JusticeNoBack.tif file, 89, 92
JusticeOriginal.psd file, 89

K

Katz, Steven D., 128
kerning, 40

Kerrypark02.psd file, 109
Kerrypark03.psd file, 108
keyboard shortcuts
    for charts, 75, 215
    for Slide Canvas, 7, 212
    for Slide Organizer, 215
    for slide shows, 214
    for tables, 216
    for text, 214
Keynote Gallery site, 230, *230*
Keynote Pro site, 227, *227*
Keynote Theme Park site, 226, *226*
Keynote Transitions, 93
KeynoteHQ site, 224, *224*
KeynoteUser.com site, 225, *225*
Keyspan Presentation Remote controller, 173, *173*

L

labeling for captures, 198
laptops
    for road presentations, 182–184, *183–185*
    video with, 204, *204*
large media file formats, 98–100
layering graphics, 104
layout control, PowerPoint vs. Keynote, 158–159
LCD (Liquid Crystal Display) projectors, 178, *178*
leading, 40
learning. *See* class lesson presentation
Leather Book theme, 32, *32*
legends for charts, 75
lessons. *See* class lesson presentation
Letterpress theme, 27–28, *28*
Limit Data Rate To option, 150
line charts, 79
Linen Book theme, 31, *31*
lines per screen, 42
linking objects, 14
Liquid Crystal Display (LCD) projectors, 178, *178*
Litzky, Andrew, 132
Lock tool, 19
lumens, 175–176

M

Mac Office X for file conversions, 164
MacinTouch site, 234, *234*
main points
    in design, 34
    establishing, 72
maintenance advantages in renting equipment, 175
marketing, multimedia, 149
Master and Margarita Keynote.mov file, 133
master slides, 10, 59–60, *60*
    for text, 35–36
    viewing, 24
Masters button, 11, *11*
media control, PowerPoint vs. Keynote, 157
media production, websites for, 235–239, *235–239*
mice
    rotating with, 45
    shortcuts, 211–213
    two-button, 22
mixing typefaces, 39
money images, *220*
monitors, 185–186, *187*
Morzenti, Marie C., 34
Move transitions, 117
moving images, importing, 98
moving tabs, 40
MP3 format, 101
MPEG-4 codec, 100
    for exporting, 150, *150*
    for QuickTime movies, 145
multimedia marketing, 149
multiple themes, 33

N

Nagel, David, 233
National Television Standards Committee (NTSC) video signals, 201–202
native resolution, 177
New Slide button, 8–9, *9*
news source site, 237, *237*
noise in DLP projectors, 179
nonstop slide shows, 111

Norvig, Peter, 53
Notebook theme, 30–31, *31*
notes, 10, 86–88, *87–88*
NTSC (National Television
 Standards Committee) video
 signals, 201–202
numbering
 builds, 124
 Text Inspector for, 40

O

object controls, 13–15
object palettes, 15–16, *15–16*
objects, graphic, 218, *218*
Objects.key file, 58, 65, 218
offset for drop shadows, 47
one-on-one shows, 109
opacity
 for drop shadows, 47
 Graphic Inspector for, 48, *48*
Open Image Library tool, 20, 49
opposite colors for text, 43
Optima typeface, 31
organization
 for artist portfolios, 110
 of projects, 52–53, *52*
Organizer view, 10
orientation of charts, 78
Original Size option, 45, *46*
OS X presentation peripherals,
 173–174, *173*
Outline view, 10, 55, *55–56*

P

Parchment theme, 28, *29*
pasting
 to Slide Canvas, 6, *7*
 text, 35
PDF (Portable Document Format)
 files, 99
 converting to, 101, *101*
 importing, 35
percentages, charts for, 79
peripherals for road presentations,
 173–174, *173*
Photoshop
 for editing graphics, 138–140,
 139–140

for file conversions, 102
Photoshop Elements, 102, *102*
phrases on storyboards, 114
PICT files, 99
pictures, 220, *220–221*
Pictures.key file, 61, 220
pie charts, 79
 exploding wedges in, 64, *64*
 slice color in, 63–65, *64*
Piná, C. David, 38, 42–43
planning for AV companies, 188–189
Play button, 9
playing slide shows, shortcuts for,
 214
Plot Row vs. Column option, 75
points
 bullet, 72–73
 in design, 34
 establishing, 72
Portable Document Format (PDF)
 files, 99
 converting to, 101, *101*
 importing, 35
portfolios, 97
 building, 105–109, *106–109*
 converting files for, 101–103,
 101–104
 editing graphics for, 104
 importing files for, 98–100
 preparing for delivery, 109, 111
Poser 4 program, 115
PowerBooks, 179, 182
 12″, 183, *183*
 15″, 184, *184*
 17″, 184, *184*
PowerPoint
 for 35mm slides, 194–195
 exporting to, 159–163, *159–162*,
 206
 importing from, 163–168,
 165–169
 vs. Keynote, 155–156
 graphic formatting, 157, *157*
 interface differences,
 156–158, 157
 layout control, 158–159
 media control, 157
PowerPoint in Keynote
 Examples.key file, 167–168
PowerPointArt.com site, 231, *231*

.ppt files, importing, 164
preproduction, 114
presentation.apxl file, 169
Presentation Master site, 239, *239*
Presentation Tips, 4, *4*
presentations, 51
 charts for, 62–65, *62–65*
 class lesson. *See* class lesson
 presentation
 design basics, 34
 Image Library graphics for,
 58–62, *59–62*
 organizing projects, 52–53, *52*
 portfolios. *See* portfolios
 road. *See* road presentations
 sales, 69
 charts for, 73–80, *73–78*
 extravaganza for, 70–73
 text in, 55–57, *55–57*
 themes for, 53–54, *54*
 transitions for, 65–66, *66*
 updating, 71
 websites for, 235–239, *235–239*
previsualization, 114
Print Dark Backgrounds As White
 option, 200, *201*
Print Each Stage of Builds option,
 200
print output, 199–200, *199–201*
Producer Script format, 199
production schedules, 149
projectors, 174–175
 placement of, 186–188, *188*
 selecting, 181–182
 specifications for, 175–177, *176*
 types of, 177–181, *178–181*
 video, 186
projects, organizing, 52–53, *52*
Pushpin theme, 27, *27*

Q

questions, presentations based on,
 94
QuickTime format, 100
 converting to, 102
 DV, 205–207, *205, 207*
 movies, 99
 tutorials, website for, 228, *228*
 video, 145

R

rack focus, 119–120, *121*
Red-Green-Blue (RGB) color space, 201
rehearsing, 94
remote presentations. *See* road presentations
removing toolbar icons, 17
renting AV equipment, 174–175
resizing
    elements, 116
    graphics, 104
resolution
    in projectors, 177
    in scanning, 138
resources, website
    Keynote, 223–231, *223–231*
    Mac-specific, 232–234, *232–234*
    presentations and media production, 235–239, *235–239*
restoring default toolbar, 17, *18*
Return key for charts, 75
RGB (Red-Green-Blue) color space, 201
Rizzo, John, 170
road presentations, **171**
    laptops for, 182–184, *183–185*
    perils of, 172, *172*
    peripherals for, 173–174, *173*
    projectors for, 174–182, *176*, *178–181*
    system setup for, 185–191, *185–188*
Roadrunner Repurpose file, 54
rotating
    graphics, 104
    with mice, 45
rulers, 40

S

S-Video signals, 186
safe areas, 203, *203*
sales presentation, 69
    charts for, 73–80, *73–78*
    extravaganza for, 70–73
sample presentation, 4

san serif fonts, 38–39
Sandstone theme, 29, *30*
saving custom themes, 137
scalability advantages in renting equipment, 175
Scale to Fill option, 45, *46*
Scale to Fit option, 45, *46*
scan conversions for QuickTime DV, 207
scan lines, 203
scanning, **138**
schedules
    for artist portfolios, 110
    for marketing presentations, 149
school. *See* class lesson presentation
screening, Graphic Inspector for, 48, *48*
Seattle Sales Show Images.key file, 72
selecting themes, 53–54, *54*
Self-Playing Movie option, 146
Separator tool, 21
series for charts, 76
serif fonts, 38–39
shadows, 26
    Graphic Inspector for, 47, *47*
    in PowerPoint, 161–162, *162*
    for text, 43
Shapes button, 12
Shapes menu, 43
Shift+Return key for charts, 75
Shift+Tab key for charts, 75
shortcuts, 211–213
    for charts, 75, 215
    for Slide Canvas, 7, 212
    for Slide Organizer, 215
    for slide shows, 214
    for tables, 216
    for text, 214
shouting with type, 42
Show Characters option, 43
Show Legend button, 75
Show Master Slides view, 10
Show Notes Separately option, 186
Show Notes view, 10
Show Preview option, 41
simplicity in design, 34

size
    elements, 116
    fonts, 16
    graphics, 104
    output, 206
    text, 43
    video, 202–203, *203*
Skip tool, 17–19
Slide Canvas, *4*, 6–7, *6–7*, 211–213
Slide Inspector, 93
Slide Only view, 10
Slide Organizer, *4–5*, 5, 211, 213, 215
slides
    for class lesson presentation, 82–83, *84*
    shortcuts for, 214
    transitions for, 65–66, *66*
Slides format, 199
Slides with Notes format, 199, *200*
small media file formats, 100
sound, 99–100
    adding, 147–148, *148*
    AV companies for, 191
    compressing, 151
    importing, 98
Space tool, 21
spacer tools, 21, *21*
spacing text, 40
spiral notebook theme, 30, *31*
status bar, 4
still images, importing, 98
Storyboard Images.key file, 117
storyboards, 113–114
    builds for, 116–129, *117–127*, *129*
    creating, 114–116, *115–116*
    transitions for, 117, 121
    website for, 227, *227*
Stretch option, 45, *46*
stroke, Graphic Inspector for, 46
student questions, presentations based on, 94
supporting points in design, 34
SVGA format, 177
symbols, 221, *221*
Symbols and Border.key file, 221

T

Tab key for charts, 75
Table Inspector, 65
Table tool, 12, *12*
tables
    for charts, 64–65, *65*
    shortcuts for, 216
tabs, 15, 40
Tag Image File Format (TIFF) files,
    98–99, 170
teaching. *See* class lesson
    presentation
technology in renting equipment,
    174
television signals, 201–202
text, 35–37, *36–37*
    alignment guides for, 57, *58*
    for class lesson presentation,
        82–83, *84*, 91–92, *91–92*
    for custom themes, 136–137,
        137
    Fonts palette for, 41–43, *41*
    in presentations, 55–57, *55–57*
    shortcuts for, 214
    Text Inspector for. *See* Text
        Inspector
    typography, 38–39, 42–43
Text & Icon option, 21
Text button, 11
Text Inspector, 37, *37*
    for bullets and numbering, 40
    for color and alignment, 39
    vs. Font window, 61
    for spacing, 40
Text Only option, 21
The Master and Margarita
    Sampler.key file, 141
Theater Simple, 131–133
    audio for, 147–148, *148*
    exporting, 148, 150–151, *150*
    image editing in, 138–140,
        139–140
    project setup for, 133, *133*
    scanning for, 138
    themes for, 133–137, *135–137*
    transitions for, 141–145,
        144–145

video for, 140–141, 145–147,
    146–147
Theme button, 9–10
themes, 4, 24
    Blackboard, 26, *26*
    Crayon Line, 29–30, *30*
    custom, 133–134
        charts in, 135–136, *136*
        saving, 137
        starting, 134–135, *135*
        text for, 136–137, *137*
    displaying, 9–10, *9*
    Fun, 32, *32*
    Gradient, 25–26, *26*
    Leather Book, 32, *32*
    Letterpress, 27–28, *28*
    Linen Book, 31, *31*
    location of, 168
    multiple, 33
    Notebook, 30–31, *31*
    Parchment, 28, *29*
    Pushpin, 27, *27*
    Sandstone, 29, *30*
    selecting, 53–54, *54*
    websites for, 226, *226*, 229–230,
        229–230
    White, 25
third-party conversion programs,
    102–103, *103–104*
35mm slides, 194
    Grab for, 195–198, *196–198*
    PowerPoint for, 194–195
3D transitions, 93
throw distance, 186
thumbnails, Slide Organizer for, 5, *5*
TIFF (Tag Image File Format) files,
    98–99, 170
Tile option, 45, *46*
time series, 79
Timed Screen, 196, *196*
title elements, transitions for,
    141–142
title-safe areas, 203, *203*
titles for charts, 79
to-do lists for storyboards, 128
toolbar, 4, 8, *8*
    creation tools, 11–13, *12–13*

customizing, 16–21, *17–18*
global controls, 8–11, *8–11*
object controls, 13–15
object palettes, 15–16, *15–16*
PowerPoint vs. Keynote, 157
shortcuts for, 212–213
traffic sign images, 218
transitions, 141
    bullet point, 95, *96*
    in class lesson presentation,
        92–93, *93*, 95–96, *95–96*
    complex, 142–143, *143*
    graphic element, 96
    in PowerPoint, 162–163
    for slides, 65–66, *66*
    in stages, 144–145, *145*
    for storyboards, 117, 121
    for title elements, 141–142
traveling presentations. *See* road
    presentations
Tutorial Storyboard Images.key file,
    118, 123
two-button mice, 22
2D elements, depth for, 116
2D transitions, 93
type size in themes, 30
typefaces, 16
typography, 38–39, 42–43. *See
    also* text

U

Ungroup tool, 14
Unlock tool, 19
unsupported files, converting,
    101–103, *101–104*
updating presentations, 71
User Samples, location of, 168

V

VGA input, 181
video
    adding, 145–147, *146–147*
    converting, 140–141, 201–207,
        202–205, 207
    with laptops, 204, *204*
    limitations of, 201–204, *202–204*

video projectors, 186
Views tool, 10, *11*
Vue d'Esprit 4 program, 115

W

Web-based demos, 111
websites
    Keynote, 223–231, *223–231*

Mac-specific, 232–234, *232–234*
presentations and media
    production, 235–239,
    235–239
weight of letters, 42
White, Charlie, 238
White theme, 25
Windows, file compatibility with, 170
Wipe transitions, 117

X

XGA format, 177

Y

YUV color space, 201–202

Z

Zelazny, Gene, 72, 79

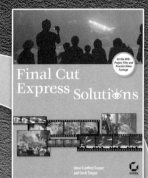

ABOUT SYBEX

Sybex has been part of the personal computer revolution from the very beginning. We were founded in 1976 by Dr. Rodnay Zaks, an early innovator of the microprocessor era and the company's president to this day. Dr. Zaks was involved in the ARPAnet and developed the first published industrial application of a microcomputer system: an urban traffic control system.

While lecturing on a variety of technical topics in the mid-1970s, Dr. Zaks realized there wasn't much available in the way of accessible documentation for engineers, programmers, and businesses. Starting with books based on his own lectures, he launched Sybex simultaneously in his adopted home of Berkeley, California, and in his original home of Paris, France.

Over the years, Sybex has been an innovator in many fields of computer publishing, documenting the first word processors in the early 1980s and the rise of the Internet in the early 1990s. In the late 1980s, Sybex began publishing our first desktop publishing and graphics books. As early adopters ourselves, we began desktop publishing our books in-house at the same time.

Now, in our third decade, we publish dozens of books each year on topics related to graphics, web design, digital photography, and digital video. We also continue to explore new technologies and over the last few years have been among the first to publish on topics like Maya and Photoshop Elements.

With each book, our goal remains the same: to provide clear, readable, skill-building information, written by the best authors in the field—experts who know their topics as well as they know their audience.